# DISCOVERING
## AMERICA

# DISCOVERING
## AMERICA

### travels in the land of guns, god, and corporate gurus

## JAMES LAXER

*The New Press*
*New York*

Originally published in Canada as *Stalking the Elephant: My Discovery of America* by Viking, 2000
Published in the United States by The New Press, New York, 2001
Distributed by W. W. Norton & Company, Inc., New York

LIBRARY OF CONGRESS CATALOGING-IN-PUBLICATION DATA

Laxer, James.
Discovering America : travels in the land of guns,
God, and corporate gurus / James Laxer.
    p.    cm.
Rev. ed. of: Stalking the elephant. 2000.
Includes bibliographical references and index.
ISBN 1-56584-710-5 (hc.)
1. United States—Description and travel.
2. United States—Social conditions—1980–
3. United States—Politics and government—1993–2001.
4. Laxer, James—Journeys—United States.
I. Laxer, James. Stalking the elephant.    II.  Title.
E169.04.L396   2001
973.929—dc21        2001031494

The New Press was established in 1990 as a not-for-profit alternative to the large,
commercial publishing houses currently dominating the book publishing industry.
The New Press operates in the public interest rather than for private gain,
and is committed to publishing, in innovative ways, works of educational, cultural,
and community value that are often deemed insufficiently profitable.

The New Press, 450 West 41st Street, 6th floor, New York, NY 10036
www.thenewpress.com

Printed in the United States of America

2   4   6   8   10   9   7   5   3   1

*To my children, Michael, Kate, Emily, and Jonathan,*
*and their cousins, Damon, Maggie, Christopher, Will,*
*Dan, Nick, Emma, and Erika.*

# contents

# INTRODUCTION

I REMEMBER BEING VERY IMPRESSED when my teacher told our Toronto grade-school class that we were privileged because we lived in the most powerful empire in the history of the world, which happened also to be the greatest force for good on this wicked planet. Naturally she was talking about the British empire. Our teacher, who was of indeterminate age, was dressed in the mandatory garb of female teachers in the mid-twentieth century, a loose-fitting dress that covered her from her neck to her ankles. I assumed that she had known Queen Victoria personally. She had strong views about the United States, "the rebellious thirteen colonies," as she insisted on calling the country. She warned us that a republic was bound to become a tyranny in the end and that the only sure way to sustain liberty was with a constitutional monarchy. Of course I had no idea that I was being fed a dollop of Rudyard Kipling along with a few offerings from Tocqueville and Gibbon. And how was I to know that the United States, not Britain, was already the greatest power on earth? My fascination with America was born in her classroom.

I had the great good fortune to be living in France in 1989–90 when the pro-Soviet regimes collapsed in one eastern European country after another. Since I was writing a book about Europe at the time, for a few exhilarating months I drove my car from Provence to the scene of one revolution after another. One day, a couple of weeks after the opening of the Berlin Wall, I was tearing along an East German autobahn listening to a local radio station playing Neil Diamond's song

"America." "Everywhere around the world, they're comin' to America." Wherever I went in eastern Europe, Soviet symbols were crashing to the ground, and American music and television were taking over the airwaves. At the headquarters of the Civic Forum in Prague in the heart of Wenceslas Square, on the day Václav Havel was installed as president of Czechoslovakia, stalwarts of the new regime rapturously embraced me because I was almost an American. "America," they kept saying as they put their arms around me.

When the Soviet Union perished in the aftermath of the collapse of its eastern European empire, the United States was left as the world's only superpower.

It is a rare moment in history when a single power bestrides the world like a colossus. America does it today, as Rome did in its part of the world two thousand years ago. The British did it in the decades following the battle of Waterloo. But there has never been a global power like America, armed not only with weapons that can destroy every person on the planet, but also with a culture that has penetrated the hearts and minds of foreigners more deeply than any culture ever has.

The global sphere of the United States at the beginning of the third millennium is vast indeed. Assessing its extent is no simple matter, since it is not a formal empire we are talking about. The Stars and Stripes flies over the territory of the United States and that of a few protectorates. But America's global sphere is enormous. It encompasses the whole of the Western Hemisphere, with the exception of Cuba. While prosperous western Europe exercises considerable sovereignty, and countries like France pursue their own global policies, which are often at odds with those of Washington, the United States remains the final arbiter of the European order. Europeans often resent this fact of life, but they never fail to recognize it, as crises in Bosnia, Kosovo, and elsewhere amply illustrate. American power extends far into the lands of the former Soviet empire. Even Russia itself, with its nuclear arsenal, and its undoubted continued status as a great power, lives on transfusions of cash from America and American-dominated international bodies. American military, economic, and diplomatic might is the key to maintaining the uneasy balance of power in Asia among rival regional powers—India and Pakistan, China and Japan. Australia and New Zealand are firmly within the wider sphere of the American world. American power is considerable in Africa, although its sway there is noteworthy as much for neglect as for intervention.

In principle, of course, the huge section of the world over which the United States exercises a determining influence is not an empire. The conventional wisdom of the American political elite is that the American republic was born in defiance of empire, its proudest boast that it has always eschewed empire. The American people would second the denial. In the American mind, empires are old-fashioned affairs like the empire over which Queen Victoria presided. And they are authoritarian behemoths, like the late Soviet empire. But what in theory is not an empire in substance turns out to be the most far-flung and advanced of all the empires in history. What makes the American global sphere an empire is not found in the formal ties of a multitude of nations to America, but in the substance of the systematic, enduring power that the United States exercises over them.

Pierre Trudeau avoided the debate about terminology when, as prime minister of Canada, he came up with a way of telling Washington's National Press Club in 1969 that America is indeed an empire, though he applied a more tactful formulation: "Living next door to you is in some ways like sleeping with an elephant. No matter how friendly or even tempered is the beast, if I can call it that, one is affected by every twitch and grunt."

Americans ended the twentieth century in a much more

optimistic frame of mind about their future than they displayed only a decade or two before. During the 1980s and early 1990s, it was fashionable to be pessimistic about the United States. What was called "declinism" was in vogue. The idea was that the United States, with its internal conflicts and its profit-driven corporations that thought only in the short term, was losing out to the new capitalism of Japan and Germany. And in the 1980s, the Cold War was still raging.

But things were changing, in America's favor. First, and of paramount importance, came the unanticipated collapse of the Soviet empire and the U.S.S.R. itself. Only two or three years before the opening of the Berlin Wall, analysts of a conservative bent were depicting the Cold War as a twilight struggle between two bitterly antagonistic systems. No one was ready for the Soviet Union to fall on its face and expire. The responses to that epochal development were many and far-reaching. American triumphalism made its appearance as early as the autumn of 1989 in the exciting months that led up to the opening of the Berlin Wall on November 9. Surprised, shocked by their victory in the Cold War, Americans were absorbing the conclusion that their system had won, that the twilight struggle had ended and the United States had been left standing.

Two other vast developments had to reach fruition for the American mood to grow unmistakably cocky and self-confident: Japan's deep economic and governmental crisis, and the new technological revolution. In the 1980s, analysts were still talking about the miracles that had been wrought by Japan, whose per capita national income had surpassed that of the United States by mid-decade. But Japan stumbled. It did not fall and expire as the Soviet Union had, but a collapse in real estate prices pulled down Japanese banks and the stock market. And with the crash, down went the mystique of the marvelous planning apparatus, as government cronyism was placed under a harsh spotlight, and suddenly the geniuses at

MITI didn't look so brilliant anymore. Then came the related development, the shimmering rise of the new American cyber capitalism and the unfolding of the longest economic expansion in the history of the United States. It was the age of Bill Gates, the era of the New Paradigm.

Technology has always been close to the American heart. Figuring out better ways to produce remains a divine mission in America. The United States is often depicted as a country based on an Idea. That Idea—of individuals living in freedom with a limited government—is tightly connected to the notion of progress. Free men, the American Idea promises, can confidently expect to live in ever-greater material plenty. No aristocracy or command economy or state bureaucracy can ever outperform free Americans when it comes to developing new techniques to improve production—that is the clarion call of America.

The new technology has transformed the landscape of corporate America, and it has ushered in a revolution among the young that is reminiscent of the impact of the rise of cars and rock and roll on teenagers in the 1950s. The corporate pecking order has been overturned with the rise of giants like Microsoft and the relative decline of long-established industrial corporations. By the end of the 1990s, Internet services were accounting for several hundred billion dollars' worth of the American Gross Domestic Product and had directly created at least a million new jobs. In the year 2000, however, the hard lesson was learned that the "new economy" was not immune to severe downturns, as tech stocks plunged, with the NASDAQ losing half its value in eight months. Despite the tech-sector crunch, the new technological frontier reinforced the can-do sense Americans had been losing. They've got back the feeling that they really are number one—economically, technologically, militarily, culturally—and that they really do lead the world in the ways that count.

The United States has an immense and unparalleled impact

on every person on the planet. The U.S.A. is the most powerful human creation of all time. I don't mean to be mysterious in calling it a creation. Of course, it is a country and a
nation. But it is a human venture, which projects unprecedented power around the world. America can even be seen as
a self-conscious historical conspiracy to hive off a portion of
humanity from the rest and make it invulnerable to threats of
domination by others, while it, in turn, exercises authority
over the entire human race.

America is the self-proclaimed leader of the world, the only
global superpower. It is the center of the world's first truly
global culture, the key player in the global economy, and the
overwhelmingly dominant military power on earth. Culture,
the economy, and the military form the three legs of the stool
on which American power sits. Benjamin Franklin once said
that each man has two countries, his own and France, in recog-
nition of the supreme position of France in matters of culture,
the intellect, and politics in the eighteenth century. Today, each
person on earth has two cultures, his or her own and that of
the United States. America has made the world bicultural at
the popular level, something never before achieved by any
dominant power.

"We are the world," sang American superstars in the 1980s
when they put their hearts and voices to work to raise money
to aid the starving in Africa. The song rose to the top of the
charts. It did not feel out of place for American entertainers
to claim that they sang for the world, that indeed they were
the world. The appropriation of "the world" as the platform
from which they appealed seemed only right, so great was the
cause for which they had come to perform. Canadian singers
were similarly moved to lend their voices to the same cause.
Their song, "Tears Are Not Enough," was well received. They
appropriated a universal platform of moral concern, but they
did not, could not, claim to speak for the world. It would have

been out of place, absurd. It would have been no less absurd had the singers been French, German, Chinese, or Brazilian. Only Americans would have the audacity to proclaim that they were the world.

The Super Bowl, the annual late-January showdown between the champions of the National Football Conference and the American Football Conference, is the most Roman of American pageants. It is a battle of titans, and it is not difficult to imagine it being fought in the Colosseum in ancient Rome. The Super Bowl involves only teams from the United States, and yet the word *world* is used repeatedly during the annual Super Bowl telecast. (The baseball World Series is another matter. The series was established a hundred years ago by a newspaper, *The New York World,* so technically the winners of the series are not claiming to be world champions. But broadcasters invariably call the winners world champions, thus ascribing a global significance to a championship where all the teams are based in the United States and Canada.)

There are, of course, genuine world championships in sport. The World Cup of Football (soccer), for example, involves the top teams that have survived a process of elimination involving teams from every major region of the world. There are also plenty of national or regional athletic pageants labeled clearly as such—the Commonwealth Games, for example, or the European Championship or the Canada Games. If it tells us much about the global pecking order that only the Americans would dare to seize the word *world* to signify a championship limited to the United States, it is even more revealing that Americans feel the need to do it. What would be wrong with calling the winners of the Super Bowl "American national champions"?

In 1989, when the Soviet empire in eastern Europe was crumbling and the Soviet Union itself was on the verge of disintegration, the argument that American power was needed so that the West could prevail in the Cold War suddenly lost its force. The old rationale for the United States in Europe was simple—the American military was in western Europe, particularly in West Germany, to deter a Soviet military attack. The Communist threat provided the cement that held the America-led "free world" together. But with the stunning collapse of the Soviet empire in eastern Europe, American strategic thinkers had to come up with a new rationale for a continued American presence in Europe, indeed in the rest of the world.

In the rush that ensued to find new arguments for a continued principal global role for their country, some Americans sounded, to use an old-fashioned word, distinctly imperialist. In a 1990 column, here is how *The New York Times* correspondent William Safire justified keeping the United States the leading world power: "Some nation is going to be No. 1; better it should be us, with our tradition of raising standards of living and of not starting wars . . . if we win, nobody loses."[1] A decade later, Madeleine Albright, Bill Clinton's secretary of state, had her own way of putting it. She developed a fondness for calling the United States "the indispensable nation." "Our greatest export," proclaimed George W. Bush in June 1999, as he kicked off his campaign in New Hampshire for the Republican presidential nomination, "is freedom." Here, in various formulations, was nineteenth-century-style Manifest Destiny refitted in positive language to serve in the post-Cold War era.

Perhaps it is a good thing that one single nation, a child of the Enlightenment, committed to individual liberty and limited government, now dominates the world. A plausible argument can be made that the world needs a leader, an exemplar and rule setter, backed up by vast economic and military might, to keep an otherwise anarchic international order from plunging into chaos. Could it be that America's rise to its unchallenged global position is a triumph for all that is best in the Western quest for material progress and human rights? On the other hand, Western political philosophy has included plenty of warnings about the perils of a single power accumulating unchecked, excessive dominance. Even if the power that has become dominant has a tradition of respecting the rights of others, who is to guarantee that this tradition will not attenuate as the need declines to pay attention to the views of others?

While the United States dominates the world, it is to an astonishing degree a nation *for itself*. It jealously guards its sovereignty and has no intention of sharing it with anyone. In no part of the American political spectrum, from left to right, will you find anyone who favors America making arrangements through which it actually shares sovereignty with other nations. In Europe, the order of the day is the voluntary pooling of sovereignty among nations on an unprecedented scale. America is not going down that road—not with its neighbors, and not with the world's other leading countries.

Undeniably, it is special to be American today. *"Civis romanus sum"*—I am a Roman citizen—was the boast of those among the ancients who were privileged to be citizens of that great empire. The special cachet of being Roman then, American today, definitely does things to a person's head. What has all this meant to the individual American? How have the people I know and have encountered in my travels in America been affected by the superpowerdom of their country? Does their membership in the great American conglomerate, brotherhood, collective, or whatever, make them different from me, different from the 95 percent of humanity that is non-American? There are 270 million Americans, enough to be a human universe all by themselves.

A decade after the great debate about whether the world reached the "End of History" with the collapse of Communism, the Americans I know do live in what I would call a post-historical space. They act as though the social and economic environment in which they live is a part of nature, just as we would accept the solar system and the earth's place in it as natural givens. They live their private lives as though the assumptions underlying their social order will never change, are not open to their influence. Could it be that the weight of the American enterprise is so great that it crushes the very individuals who make up its mass, their cherished individualism notwithstanding? If Descartes were alive in America today, he might proclaim: I consume, therefore, I am.

As is understandable at this moment in history, Americans are deeply, even obsessively, engrossed in themselves. They are absorbed in their economic prowess, culture, society, and politics, understanding their achievements as unique. They are not much inclined to compare their society with those elsewhere on the planet. Indeed, Americans are mostly interested in others only inasmuch as those others represent problems or opportunities for the United States.

Over the past several decades, America's attention has been turned for periods of time to external "problems" like Vietnam, OPEC, the Japanese economic challenge, the collapse of the Soviet empire, Saddam Hussein, Somalia, the breakup of Yugoslavia, and the looming threat of China. As each of these challenges has arisen, American media, politicians, and thinkers have focused on the new threat to determine how it will affect the United States and what the United States ought to do about it. This kind of response gives rise to a style of thinking: even while Americans consider what is going on elsewhere, they rarely depart from their central obsession with America itself.

Lord Acton's wise dictum that "absolute power corrupts absolutely" is not a bad starting point when you are dealing with the only superpower on earth. For centuries, the British found the prospect of Europe coming under the sway of a single power highly threatening. Furiously and famously, they plotted and schemed for a balance of power in Europe that would prevent the outcome they feared—domination by a single power.

Now the whole world faces domination by a single power. And the old British concern, that those who don't need to respect the power of others inevitably exercise their power in arbitrary ways, becomes a vital warning.

One of the benefits of being an English-speaking Canadian is that you can slip quietly across the border into the United States and take in the scene in complete anonymity. I have written *Discovering America* as a traveler from another land, open to adventures that shed light on the present and future course of the country. For the past few years, journeys in America have been my obsession. I have taken several kinds of journeys to write this book. Physical journeys—trips to events, to talk to people, to visit regions—have dominated my life. I have driven tens of thousands of miles in recent years in most of the states in the continental United States. My goal has been to explore America firsthand, to meet people, to get a feel for how the questions that roil American society are evolving. I have made intellectual journeys as well, analyzing American society through its books, newspapers, television, the Internet, and at times talk radio.

What I have encountered is a land of extremes. America's wealthiest man—at the zenith of his wealth before the recent plunge in the value of tech stocks—had capital assets equal to the capital assets of the one hundred million poorest Americans. In the United States the right to say whatever you like is defended more vociferously than anywhere else on earth. Yet there is little fundamental debate about the future direction of American society and almost no debate about America's role in the world. Americans celebrate individual ambition and achievement as the source of their country's success, while at the same time they lock up more than two million people in their jails—by far the highest incarceration rate in any developed country. America has a health care system where the affluent can get two CAT scans in ten minutes, as I learned in one of my adventures, while 40 million people have no health insurance. Americans elect the world's most powerful political leader, but only half of them even bother to vote.

To explore the American colossus at the height of its power is a rare privilege, even for a non-American like me, who is not particularly enamored of empires.

part ★ one

# *LETHAL* GAMES

# 1

# ON THE TRAIL OF THE
# MICHIGAN MILITIA

I AM DRIVING THROUGH FLINT, Michigan, en route to East
Lansing, where President Bill Clinton is to speak to the graduating class at Michigan State University. Two weeks have passed
since the bombing of the federal building in Oklahoma City
on April 16, 1995, the worst act of domestic terrorism in
American history. The bombing killed 168 people, including
children in a day-care center, and injured hundreds more.

On this trip, I aim to meet with the founders of the Michigan
Militia, a shadowy paramilitary organization that has suddenly
come into the public spotlight because Timothy McVeigh, who
has been charged in the Oklahoma City bombing, lived for a
time in Michigan and attended meetings of the Michigan Militia.
I have the phone number of Norm Olson, founder of the militia. I have already put some calls through to the number, and
I've spoken to Olson's son about a possible meeting. It's still
up in the air.

There is increasing drama surrounding Clinton's address to
the graduating class. Yesterday, two founders of the Michigan
Militia, Norm Olson and Ray Southwell, issued a press release

telling the president to stay out of Michigan, warning that at Michigan State he risked being the victim of "an attack by the CIA," which would then be blamed on the Michigan Militia. Sounding such conspiratorial alarms, based on no evidence, is vintage militia behavior.

I arrive in East Lansing with absolutely no idea how I'm going to get in to hear Clinton, trusting that luck will be on my side. The center of town is crowded with university students in graduation regalia, wearing gowns and caps, accompanied by their proud relatives. I figure they will lead me to Clinton, so I park the car and join their informal procession. Soon we have left the commercial streets and are crossing the campus with its lush green lawns, tall trees, and attractive classic academic buildings. It is the kind of American college campus scene that looks perfect for a Norman Rockwell painting. We cross a bridge that takes us over a broad stream. Not far ahead looms the football stadium. Obviously the president will speak there. The next thing I know, someone asks me if I have a ticket to attend the president's speech. I say no and am handed a ticket and a program. I'm in luck.

I climb high in the stands and find a seat in the sun that will take the chill off this windy spring day. The stadium is quickly filling with the students in graduate garb taking seats at one end of the field, while their families occupy the seats above. Around the top of the stadium at regular intervals are a dozen armed secret service agents, dark figures bristling with communications gear. After the forty thousand people are assembled, the dignitaries troop out onto the stage. They're all decked out in academic robes, even Clinton.

The first sitting president to address the graduation here since Theodore Roosevelt in the early years of the twentieth century, Clinton receives a huge ovation. The president knows how to speak to a gigantic crowd. His voice fills the stadium and he sounds strong, but he still seems to be speaking to each person in the huge assembly as an individual. This is no mean feat. I've seen few speakers who can do it.

The people here are expecting Clinton to talk about the militias and they are not disappointed. He declares that the members of U.S. paramilitary militias "have no right to take the law into their own hands." Those among them who claim such rights for themselves "are un-American." This is Clinton's fiercest attack yet on the militias, a clear reply to the challenge thrown to him by the Michigan Militia when its leaders warned him to stay out of the state.

The president delivers a civics lesson to the graduating class and their families and friends. He tells the overwhelmingly white and affluent crowd that "without the rule of law there is no freedom." He attacks the contention of the militias that the threat to freedom in America "comes from government." "You have broader rights here than you would have in any other country in the entire world," Clinton declares. While it is right and responsible to question government, he says, it is quite another thing to break the law and to launch assaults against officers of the law. "You don't have the right to resort to violence when you don't get your way." Since the bombing of the federal building in Oklahoma City, Clinton has been honing this message, not only to isolate the militias but to counter the antigovernment crusade of his main opponents, the Newt Gingrich Republicans. Michigan State is a good place to test a muscular version of his new line. Given class and racial voting patterns in the United States, it is a good bet that two-thirds of this audience didn't vote for him.

Clinton's speech catches fire when he contrasts the furtive figures in the militias with the respectable citizens in his audience. To an enormous ovation, he proclaims that "this is the real Michigan in this stadium today."

For the first time in his presidency, thanks to the Oklahoma bombing and the threat from extremists who claim the right to maintain private armies, Clinton has a chance to define the meaning of contemporary Americanism. His approval rating with the general public has risen as he has attacked those who preach hatred against the federal government and its employees. After the speech, Clinton climbs down from the stage and mingles with the graduates. He takes a long time, going from person to person, listening and talking.

I am thinking about my own upcoming encounter with the object of the president's attack, the militia, whose heartland lies about 250 miles north of Lansing. But first, it's time to eat. I find a cheery place that specializes in Buffalo chicken wings in the center of town, where graduates and their families are in full celebratory mode. These are the hottest wings I've ever eaten, including the ones they serve in the Anchor Bar in Buffalo. Even a pitcher of very cold beer doesn't take the heat out of them.

During the drive from Lansing to northern Michigan, the countryside changes and so too does the human landscape. Michigan, as you go north, shifts from classic Midwest plain to a hilly terrain of rock and pine.

Up here the cars are shabbier than farther south, and they are close to 100 percent American made. I begin to feel a little uneasy in my American-assembled Toyota Camry. It comes home to me that I am traveling to the viper's nest of American ultra-loyalists in a Japanese car. Is this wise? I tell myself that Japanese cars are so rare up here that the folks in this neck of Michigan probably wouldn't recognize one if they saw it. I am aware that in Michigan, where everybody knows what American cars look like, this is not a very solid line of reasoning.

My companion on the road north is talk radio, the medium that is the mother's milk of the paramilitary militias. Tens of millions of Americans listen to talk radio every day. Rush Limbaugh alone has an audience of 20 million. Limbaugh entertains and inflames his listeners with well-honed rants against

Clinton, the federal government, environmentalists, feminists, and the other usual suspects. But Limbaugh is tame when compared with other talk-radio voices and particularly against the standard set by local one-station ranters. I flip from station to station, listening to the folk wisdom of these backwoods Michigan right-wingers. Their stock-in-trade is conspiracy. The Michigan of gun enthusiasts, hunters, and, indeed, militia supporters is there to be heard, hour after hour.

The week after the Oklahoma City bombing WMKT, a radio station in Charlevoix, a small town in northern Michigan, suspended the nationally aired program of James (Bo) Gritz, a retired lieutenant colonel in the U.S. Army's Special Forces, who had compared the bombing to a work of art. In response to the decision to drop Gritz in this heartland of the Michigan Militia, the radio station's phone lines lit up for hours, as callers demanded the show be reinstated—which it was after a two-day hiatus.

President Clinton may have seized the high ground in the debate following the bombing, but there is no denying that there is another Michigan out there, indeed another America— overwhelmingly white, male, and very conservative—that pays attention to what the men in the militias have to say.

In the advanced, industrialized world, the American militias are unique. In western Europe, skinheads and neo-Nazis attach themselves loosely to far-right political parties like the National Front in France or the Austrian Freedom Party. But it is only in the United States that a homegrown movement of paramilitary forces, outfitted with ample weaponry, operates as a permanent shadowy opposition to the national government.

The bombing of the Oklahoma City federal building was far from an isolated event. For the past fifteen years, the United States has been subjected to a continuing wave of terrorist acts carried out by right-wing extremists. These acts include the murder of abortion doctors and the bombing of abortion clinics; the murder of employees of local, state, and federal governments by zealots who deny the legitimacy of these levels of government; racist murders carried out by neo-Nazis in the U.S. armed forces; the derailing of an Amtrak train by the "sons of the Gestapo"; and shoot-outs between well-armed extremists, who claim the right to secede from U.S. jurisdiction, and agencies of the U.S. government.

Indeed, the Oklahoma City bombing, which occurred on the second anniversary of the fiery conflagration that consumed David Koresh and his followers at Waco, Texas, was designed as a reprisal for the assault against Koresh's Branch Davidians by agents of the federal government. Earlier shoot-outs between far-right outlaws and the police have been treated as patriotic acts of defiance against the state by extremists in the militias and other far-right movements. In 1983 Gordon Kahl, a member of the far-right Posse Comitatus, refused to pay taxes or obey the conditions for his parole from prison. He was involved in a gunfight in which two deputy U.S. marshals were killed. A few months later, Kahl was hunted down by police in his hideaway in the Ozark Mountains. After he shot a county sheriff, Kahl was shot dead and his body was burned as his cabin went up in flames. His funeral was attended by hundreds of far-right extremists, who saw him as a hero in the patriotic struggle. The accidental killing of the wife and son of the far-right fugitive Randy Weaver at Ruby Ridge, Idaho, by FBI agents in 1992 has similarly been elevated by extremists to the level of an epic struggle against the federal government.

Those who stockpile weapons to engage in combat against armed U.S. federal authorities do not operate in a vacuum that seals them off from the American political spectrum. They are connected to the mainstream right in myriad ways and have become one of the mass bases of the Republican Party. At annual meetings of the Council on National Policy, a right-wing organization that does not allow the press to attend its meetings, Republican leaders such as Pat Robertson, the founder of the Christian Coalition, and congressional heavyweights like Dick Armey and Tom DeLay, have rubbed shoulders with far-right radicals like Larry Pratt, the leader of Gun Owners of America, a body even more extreme than the NRA. In 1996 Pratt was exposed as having ties to the paramilitary right and white supremacists.

Republican members of the House of Representatives and the Senate have pandered to far-right sensibilities by holding hearings on Waco and Ruby Ridge, while never conducting a thorough investigation of the militia movement. While in Congress, Vice President Dick Cheney played to this constituency when he voted against all gun-control legislation, including a proposed ban on what are commonly called cop-killer bullets.

I spend the night in the northern town of Grayling, Michigan. The town's adjoining military base was soon to be named in media reports as a possible terrorist target by some men with ties to the Michigan Militia. From my motel room, I call the number I have for Norm Olson. I tell the guy who answers the phone that I'm going to be in Olson's neck of the woods tomorrow and that I'd like to drop in and interview him. The response—I think from Olson's son again—is to call in the morning and we'll see.

I am on the road early the next morning, heading north on the interstate. My destination is the tiny hamlet of Alanson, located just below the point where Lake Michigan and Lake Huron meet. About twenty miles from Alanson, I am overtaken and passed by five shiny black Chryslers roaring down the highway in tandem and doing about ninety miles an hour. What is this—the FBI? I wonder. Are they heading for the same place I am?

When I pull off the interstate, I stop to check a detailed map
I bought of this region of northern Michigan. Every hamlet
and crossroads is marked on it. I work out exactly where
Olson's house is and I head there. I figure I should take a look
at the house before I telephone. Maybe I still have those shiny
black Chryslers in the back of my mind. The ranch-style house
with a shed at the side is right next to a crossroads in open
country. It looks reassuringly quiet. Anyway, it's not in the
middle of a forest. I drive to a gas station about a mile away
and I call the house. It's the same voice on the line and he tells
me to come right over. As I pull up in the driveway, I notice
that the curtains are pulled tight in all the windows. On the
shed beside the house, which doubles as a retail gun shop,
there is a sign on the door that reads "Closed Until Further
Notice." I knock on the front door, which has a sign on it that
reads "The Lord is in this House," and a tall man wearing olive
fatigues and boots and a military cap emblazoned with the
slogan "Enough Is Enough" answers and welcomes me inside.
It is Norm Olson, the preacher and gun dealer who founded
the Michigan Militia. Olson, in his late forties, is tall and fit-
looking. He has big hands and big ears.

He guides me to the round kitchen table and offers me
coffee. I accept and pour whitener and sugar into the black
pool in the cup. Just then a slight blond man, younger-
looking than Olson, enters the room. He is nattily dressed in
a fashionable dark suit. He forms an odd contrast with big
Olson in his fatigues. I am introduced to Ray Southwell, a real
estate agent and a cofounder of the Michigan Militia. Sitting
in the living room next door is a middle-aged woman I pre-
sume is Olson's wife. The living room is furnished with plaid
beige-and-brown sixties-style armchairs.

Olson is the man in charge here. He asks me what I want to
know. What did you think of Clinton's all-out attack on the
militias at Michigan State yesterday? I ask. This question gets

Olson charged up. He describes the president as a puppet whose strings are being pulled by evil figures in "a field of power" surrounding him. The picture that emerges is of a shadowy supercabal that is actually running the United States. While Clinton is corrupt and unimportant, others wield the real authority, Olson explains, among them foreign bankers. He claims that some figures from the CIA have been hired on to serve the evil people who are actually in power. Olson is a good storyteller and his story reminds me of *The Thirty-nine Steps* by John Buchan, a tale in which the hero is up against a sinister enemy called the Black Stone.

As befits the leader of a secretive band of men, Olson has mastered the art of monologues, which range from the sentimental to the ruthless, from historical ramblings to warnings of civil war. He starts one of his monologues softly, speaking scarcely above a whisper. The pace quickens and the voice rises until, at the climax, the effect is harsh, physical. And while he tells you a story, he looks you right in the eye. I refused the urge to drop my glance.

It was Olson who had the political imagination to capitalize on the deep alienation of his cronies and men like them. Along with twenty-seven others, Olson founded the Michigan Militia in April 1994. Since then, the militia's state-wide membership has mushroomed to twelve thousand, and similar militias have been formed in many other states. Perhaps sensing my rising unease at his description of the militias, he adds that the Michigan Militia is "nondenominational, nonpolitical, and nonracial."

"Why the guns and the camouflage?" Olson asks rhetorically. "Because we wanted to get people's attention. We could have gone out with placards in three-piece suits and no one would have noticed."

The high point of the conversation is about the bombing at Oklahoma City. Olson is in a rage on the subject. He insists that Timothy McVeigh, the former soldier, would never have

killed women and children, and therefore couldn't be responsible for what happened in Oklahoma. It is a conceit of the
members of the private armies that call themselves militias
that comrades-in-arms are the only ones who can provide the
United States with moral leadership in its hour of peril. By
definition, that moral leadership could never be capable of
threatening women, children, hearth, and home.

Olson, his voice rising in anger, rejects the very idea that
a soldier "trained to fight other soldiers" could be guilty of
the bombing. McVeigh attended a couple of meetings of the
Michigan Militia. I figure this is one reason Olson is so quick
to leap to his defense. (In June 1997 a jury found McVeigh
guilty, and he was sentenced to death.)

A few days ago, Olson had resigned as commander-in-chief
of the Michigan Militia because of the fallout from his widely
publicized insistence that an international conspiracy was
responsible for the Oklahoma City bombing. But he remains
the charismatic inspiration behind this militia.

Olson insists that the Michigan Militia is the direct descen-
dant of the militias of the American Revolution. He reminds
me that when the British army ordered the colonial militia
to put down their weapons at Lexington Common in 1775,
the colonials refused. "No one knows who fired the first shot,
the shot heard round the world," he says, and quips, "maybe
it was the CIA." Then he makes his point: "We hope a second
shot will not be necessary." This allusion to the potential for
a civil war in the United States is the central myth that sus-
tains the militias.

In a country where conspiratorial and violent bands of men,
such as the Ku Klux Klan, have often sprung up in the South,
the militias have a Northern feel about them. These are white
men, some of them Vietnam War veterans, who feel pushed
aside in the strange new world of information technology and
cultural heterogeneity.

In their attacks on NAFTA, the GATT and its successor the

World Trade Organization, the G-7, the Trilateral Commission, and the White House, the militias have exhibited an undeniable populist flair. At their core, though, despite their rhetoric about being the defenders of the U.S. Constitution, they are deeply anti-democratic. Their faith is in their military training and weapons, in leaders like Olson and in an interpretation of American history that, they insist, gives them the right to use force, if necessary, to resist an alien government. The militias are a marginal force, certainly. But the terrifying simplicity of their vision is a feature of an American societal psychosis, which is anything but marginal. How sinister, and yet absurd, to encounter men in an advanced democratic country whose only conceivable purpose for assembling weapons and undertaking military training is to use force, if necessary, against their own government.

If we are being fed lies about the bombing at Oklahoma City, I ask, then what does Olson think really happened? Forcefully waving his large hands for dramatic effect, Olson launches into an explanation. American spy agencies were responsible for the gas attack on the Tokyo subway. Then, in a disinformation campaign, the Japanese government blamed the attack on a Japanese cult. Meanwhile, Japanese agents prepared and carried out the deadly bombing at Oklahoma City. Then Olson spins the dark and murky tale of a Japanese takeover of high-tech communications at the White House in 1993–94, which he claims has completely compromised U.S. intelligence. In what sounds like a plot from *Mission Impossible,* Olson tries to convince me that the White House has been outfitted with Japanese-made computers and that the Japanese state has used this as a way inside the inner workings of the executive branch. He finishes the rant by handing me an audio-tape labeled in ink "Who Really Bombed OKC?" and tells me that I will find it very instructive.

We are suddenly interrupted by three bangs that sound as

if they are coming from below. Olson explains that his son is down in the basement where there is a communications center and that whenever he receives an important message, he signals with the three bangs.

As I get up to leave, Olson points to a piece of braid that he is wearing on his fatigues. What's it for? I ask. It's of Somalian design, he replies. He tells me he is wearing it to draw attention to the terrible hunger being endured by the Somalian people. Tears well up in Olson's eyes. This, to put it mildly, is not what I had expected from the founder of the Michigan Militia.

I was not unhappy to leave that dwelling. I drove more than a hundred miles from Olson's house, and the government spooks I'm sure were staking it out, before stopping for gas off the interstate.

Later, back in Toronto, I listened to the tape Olson gave me. It is a recording of a talk-radio show that had aired in Salt Lake City, Utah. Martin Davis, the host of Supertalk 1320 on KCNR radio, interviews California-based Debra Von Trapp, who elaborates on the conspiracy I've already heard from Olson about the "real" explanation for the Oklahoma City bombing.

Debra Von Trapp describes herself in the interview as a Republican who was hired as a computer expert by the Democrats to install the computer software used for the celebrations for the inauguration of Bill Clinton in January 1993. In addition, Von Trapp's firm, based in Irvine, California, was hired to install software in the White House as well as other key buildings in Washington, D.C. In the lengthy, convoluted interview, Von Trapp relates the story I'd heard from Olson and then adds some bits he didn't tell me. She embellishes the tale I'd already been told about disaffected U.S. intelligence operatives working for the Japanese embassy in Washington, with the claim that transponders were planted in hardware and software going into the nerve centers of the U.S. government. This allowed the Japanese embassy, Von Trapp insists, to listen to every word and intercept every computer key stroke at the Clinton inaugural, and later in the Clinton White House. To the bit I'd heard from Olson about the U.S. government discovering all this much later and retaliating with the Tokyo subway attack she adds a startling claim. According to Von Trapp, she was tipped off by Washington operatives, who appear to have been working both for the Japanese government and American intelligence, that the "Japanese were going to take out a federal building." Twenty-four hours later, the federal building in Oklahoma City was blown up. At this point, Von Trapp says, Attorney General Janet Reno and the FBI were desperate to find someone whom they could blame for the explosion. Timothy McVeigh, she continues, ended up being the fall guy. She insists that McVeigh was "in the wrong place at the wrong time" and "had nothing to do" with the bombing. Von Trapp concludes that because McVeigh was involved with the militias, he was an ideal choice for Reno and the FBI. If the American people were convinced of his guilt, it would allow the authorities to blame the bombing "on militia groups across the country." Now the militias, she says, are to be targeted and the constitutional rights of militia members are going to be infringed.

It's easy to see why Norm Olson preferred the Von Trapp theory to the allegation that Timothy McVeigh was the architect of the most monstrous act of domestic terrorism in U.S. history. And it seemed that in the strange world of talk radio a lot of other people were prepared to pay serious heed to this theory. As I pondered the tales I'd heard in Olson's kitchen and on the Von Trapp tape, I wondered just what Americans were supposed to think about all this. Everyone knew that the government in Washington lied about some things, some of the time. How were people to disentangle genuine lies and disinformation from crackpot conspiracy theories of the Olson and Von Trapp variety?

Marshall McLuhan contrasted television, which he saw as a cool medium, with radio, a hot medium he thought was tailor-made for ranters. I'm sure the tape I heard on the Oklahoma City bombing would have confirmed his view that medium and message had found their perfect match.

# 2

# SMITH & WESSON
## AND ME

Y OU'LL FIND GUN MAGAZINES on the racks of any newsstand or bookstore. There are dozens of such magazines, catering to sportsmen, hunters, gun lovers, and to those who believe that the freedom to bear arms is a fundamental American right. Some of the magazines appeal to men who dream of the life of the mercenary, the soldier of fortune who signs up to go on dangerous missions to distant continents. Other magazines dwell on the craftsmanship that goes into manufacturing the guns and on how to use them. Whatever their particular slant, the magazines are all agreed that Americans should be allowed to enjoy their guns with minimal government interference. These magazines are the voice of the American gun culture. I decided the best way to get a close look at this culture was to be a part of it, if only for a few days.

Smith & Wesson has been manufacturing firearms since Horace Smith and Daniel B. Wesson formed a partnership in 1852 to produce a lever-action pistol whose critical feature was that it had a tubular magazine capable of firing an entirely self-contained cartridge. The partners began their operation in Norwich, Connecticut, but following financial ups and downs and corporate reorganization, in 1856 they began the production of a new revolver in Springfield, Massachusetts.

Today the name Smith & Wesson is as American as apple pie. The company still makes guns in Springfield and has run a firearms academy there since 1968. When I was leafing through a Smith & Wesson magazine, *Handguns '99,* I learned about the academy and the courses it offers the public. The one that caught my eye was called "Dynamics of Personal Protection." It was for beginners, unlike exotic and advanced courses with titles like "Defensive Handgun Tactics and Techniques" or "Concealed Handgun Carry." A blurb informed me that I would learn not only how to handle a firearm safely in my home and how to carry a handgun in populated areas without endangering others but also how to reload my gun under stress and how to engage multiple attackers with my weapon.

There was no question that I did not know about these things. I had not fired a gun since the age of fifteen when I directed bullets down the range in the basement of our school with an ancient rifle during cadet training.

To register for the two-day course, I had to satisfy Smith & Wesson that I was not a convicted criminal. The easy way to do that was to send them my handgun permit number. As a Canadian with no permit, let alone a handgun, I had to go the second route. To get a police clearance showing that I had no criminal record, I went to a private agency in Toronto and was fingerprinted for a fee of $25. I mailed the prints and a certified check for $28 to the Royal Canadian Mounted Police in Ottawa. The first time the Mounties lost the check, but on the second try, with a money order, I had more luck. In the mail, I received my prints with a reassuring statement that these prints could not be associated with any known crime. I was in the clear.

The firearms academy sent me a list of items I would require for use in the course. I was much relieved that Smith & Wesson would lend me a gun and provide me with ammo. For these extra items they charged me nothing on top of the fee for the course, which was us$300. I chose a .38 revolver, on the grounds that I had heard of it, and it didn't look too big in the glossy pictures, so I hoped the recoil wouldn't be too vicious. I was instructed to bring hearing and eye protection—the kind worn by people working with jackhammers. I would also need a holster and a small high-powered flashlight, the kind favored by survivalists who think the world is about to end and that they might be attacked by their suddenly crazed neighbors.

I arrived for the start of the course shortly after eight on a warm Wednesday morning in November. Something was rumbling in my stomach from my dinner the night before, but I ignored it and rang the doorbell. Doors that separate one section of the attractive, recently renovated firearms academy from another are tightly locked. Imagine what would happen if the wrong kind of people broke in here and laid their hands on the arsenal inside. Two guys in their mid-thirties, both enrolled in my course, as it turned out, were inside the first locked-up segment of the building. They looked a bit like Mutt and Jeff, one tall and bald with a bit of a paunch, the other short and mousy with a meek little mustache. The tall guy was a Canadian from southern Ontario. When I told him I was also a Canadian, he muttered, "It tells you something about the state of firearms training in Canada." The other guy was from Poughkeepsie, New York, a town on the Hudson River about ninety miles north of New York City. He was quiet, but he seemed intensely focused on the excitement to come.

Someone came down the hall on the other side of a big locked door and opened it for us. We filed through and headed the short distance to our classroom, where eight or nine men were already sitting behind the tables. All of them were white, and they ranged in age from their thirties to their fifties. Two heavy-set fellows in the front row had snowy white hair and bulldog faces. They sprawled in their seats. No one blinked as we walked in. This was not a cheery crowd. During the next ten minutes, as I fished through the documents the academy had placed in front of each seat on the tables and checked out the comple-mentary Smith & Wesson coffee mug and baseball cap, several more people filed in, including a young blond woman in tight blue jeans.

At eight-thirty on the dot, our course director arrived. Brent Purucker served on the Michigan State Police for many years, where he was a member of a crack SWAT team sent in when violent criminals were holed up, sometimes holding hostages. He is fit and looks young, although he must be in his late for-ties. His carefully cropped beard and his glasses give him a thoughtful, even intellectual, appearance. But this is a guy with powerful muscles on his forearms. He is compact and he moves like a cat. Brent, who told us right off the bat that he hasn't got much use for his own last name, talks easily and attractively. He explains that in this session, he will talk to us about when it is appropriate to use deadly force and how to carry a firearm safely and keep one in your home or office.

From the first word, Brent makes it clear that he regrets the intrusion of laws that complicate the lives of gun owners and limit their rights. The states on the Atlantic and Pacific coasts are not too friendly to gun owners, while those in the middle of the country are much more pro-gun, he explains. He just assumes that everyone in the room is pro-gun. Heads nod as he talks about the woes of the gun owner in present-day America.

Next, Brent leads the discussion into deep philosophical waters. When are we justified in taking a human life? Brent asks. He answers his own question: we must never take a human life solely for the protection of property. I feel as though we are back on solid ground with that. But not for long, as it turns out. Brent repeats an adage that if you shoot someone at your front door, make sure they fall inside and not out. We seem to be sliding back to the issue of appearances, and away from hard and fast ethical rules about when it is proper to kill. We are being taught how to spin our actions, not whether they are morally justified.

When Brent uses his computer to project onto the screen the current rules in Massachusetts law about when it is considered self-defense to kill someone, the students in the class groan their disapproval. The rules are pretty strict. You have to face a very clear threat of death or bodily dismemberment to use lethal force in Massachusetts. Not very gun friendly. Brent soothes his audience by reciting another adage: "I'd rather be judged by twelve than carried by six."

He settles on a piece of strategic advice that fits in somewhere between morality and mere tactics. Don't ever aim your gun at something you're not prepared to shoot. "And whatever you shoot, you own," he declares. He repeats this slogan several times as a kind of mantra. Now we're on solid ground.

Not far into the session, Brent asks how many of us have brought our own guns. About eight of the fourteen students put up their hands. Where are your guns? he inquires further. Each of us has brought a so-called range bag containing our gear. The guns are not loaded? asks Brent a little warily. No, everyone replies. We were told in no uncertain terms in the literature we received from Smith & Wesson that we were not to arrive at the academy with a loaded gun.

Brent eases away from the moral question about when it is proper to kill to the tactical question of how best to carry a concealed handgun. He gives the gun fanciers in the room some cautionary advice. Don't ever take your gun to a bar, he says. If you keep it in the glove compartment of your vehicle, don't put your registration in the same place. That's because if you're pulled over by a cop and he asks for your registration, there could be trouble when you open the compartment and the officer sees your gun. In the same vein, Brent cautions that if a policeman asks you to get out of your car when you're "carrying," you've got to follow a very specific protocol. You must tell him you've got a weapon on your person and indicate where it is located. But never, ever gesture toward the part of your body where you're packing.

Should you tell your friends you carry? Brent advises not. If you tell them you're packing a gun, they may ask to see it. And then, well, one thing leads to another. It's just not a good idea. This gets us into a related subject. Should those of us who are taking a course like this tell our friends about it? A buzz goes through the room. The general sentiment is that it is not wise to divulge this kind of information. The young woman, from a suburb of New York City, joins the fray for the first time. She would not want her friends to know she is taking the course, she says. The only person she told about it was her husband. Gun carrying and training, it appears, are rather cultish, and you don't want to share the mysteries or potency with others.

Brent adds another powerful Don't to his advice about not carrying a gun into a bar. Don't leave your gun right beside your bed so you can reach it without getting up. To illustrate the risk of reaching for your gun before you've shaken the cobwebs out of your head, he tells the story of one man who woke up in the night and thought he saw an intruder standing at the foot of his bed. The half-asleep man reached for his gun and fired, hitting himself in the penis and one leg. On another unhappy occasion, a gun-owning woman who had asthma reached for her nasal aspirator in the middle of the night but inadvertently picked up her gun, pulled the trigger, and blew much of her head off.

Since this course was advertised as teaching how to defend ourselves, Brent reviews some alternatives to guns. In most states, he laments, you can't carry those little open-out batons that are so good for whacking people at close range. The best bet as an alternative to a gun is pepper spray, he advises, telling us he often carries it himself. I'm wondering why anyone would feel the need for pepper spray in a town like Springfield, which is not exactly a crime capital. The downside to pepper spray, he says, is that it only shuts down your opponent's vision. It leaves him wide open to flail away at you with his limbs.

Brent asks if any of us feel as though we are being followed. The question didn't ring any bells with me, but it caused quite a stir in the room. A number of people came to life and nodded, including one of the two old vets in front of me and the young woman. Brent advises where to go if you're being followed in your car. He used to advise people to head for a public area, but his daughter recently was in a car being pursued by someone and when she arrived at a McDonald's, no one there was prepared to call the police to help out. "I've lost my faith in people," Brent laments. His reconsidered advice is to drive to a police station, a firehouse, or the emergency door at a hospital and lean on your horn because "they'll help you— that's what they're there for." In his opinion, most people spend their lives wandering around in a daze, not watching what's going on around them. You've got to be alert, he stresses, especially if you "carry." For instance, he never stops his car right behind another vehicle at a stoplight. He leaves himself room to pull out and wheel around in case a gunfight breaks out.

One thing we're doing in this course, Brent says, is getting prepared in case we find ourselves in a gunfight. He gives us a few dramatic statistics. The average gunfight is only three to six seconds in duration, but a lot goes on in that short time frame. The second fact is that on average, when a police officer is involved in a gunfight, he is only two arms' lengths away from his opponent. Despite the close proximity, a cop usually hits his target with only 20 percent of his shots. What hap-

pens to the other 80 percent? Brent asks rhetorically. Members
of the class nod knowingly, apparently sharing the view that
policemen can't shoot straight.

After a short break from the classroom part of our training, we head down the hall to the range where we are to receive
initial instruction on the care and firing of our guns. We put
our range bags against the wall, and those with their own guns
treat them with reverence. They strap on their holsters and
slide their guns in. While I often think Freud was out to lunch
in his conjectures, the occasion did seem to be laden with
phallic ritualism.

Those of us who are borrowing guns line up at a little window where our weapons are handed out. I show Brent the holster I purchased at an army surplus store. He looks at it
disdainfully and says, "Why don't you give it to your dog?" He
hands me a .38 revolver in a holster, which I strap on, along
with a little case for speed loaders to reload the ammunition
swiftly. Everything they say is true. I feel instantly powerful
and better endowed.

Next, we head out on the firing range, which is like an airplane hangar. Brent gets us to stand in a line facing him. He
gazes steadily at us with his gun in his holster and tells us he
wants to be sure none of our guns is loaded. Satisfied, he pulls
out his gun, a pistol, or as he calls it "a bottom feeder," meaning that you reload it by shoving magazines full of cartridges
into it. He demonstrates how to prepare various models of
pistols to fire, going through the same ritual with revolvers,
like my .38. Then he teaches us how to hold the pistol or
revolver in a two-handed stance with our non-firing hand
supporting our firing hand so that the recoil will be controlled
when we fire.

Behind Brent on the firing range is a row of targets, flat affairs
shaped like the upper half of a human being, including the torso
and head. In the center of the torso is a yellow circle. Brent

turns to the targets and tells us he does not want us to try to hit dead center with every shot. "That's not how you take some-one down. You've got to fire all around this area." That way you take out the blood and the insides. Earlier he'd told us that a higher proportion of people with knife wounds die from them than is the case for those wounded by guns. The trouble with a gunshot wound is that it is a neat, small hole, and the bullet can even cauterize the wound as it travels along. He made a gun-shot wound seem rather surgical. It dawns on me that the course is designed specifically to teach us how to kill people. Naturally, we will be acting in self-defense when the time comes, but the purpose of this whole exercise is sitting a little heavily on me.

When you shoot a deer, I hear Brent say, it can run up to 250 feet after it has been hit in the chest. Deer haven't seen Hollywood movies, so they don't know that they're supposed to fall over when they're hit. To bring a deer down, you've got to hit it over and over in this critical chest area to destroy the internal organs.

I began to feel a little light in the head and to sense darkness at the edge of my peripheral vision. Never having fainted, I nevertheless recognize the symptoms, so I bend over a little in the hope that more blood will flow to my head. I don't want to draw attention to myself by sitting down on the floor.

"If you've ever seen an autopsy of a person who's been shot, it's very much like the look of a deer that's been hit," Brent continues. "There's blood all over the place and the insides are coming out."

I straighten up, telling myself that lunchtime is approaching. The next thing I know, I'm lying on my back with my knees propped up. There's something soft behind my neck and I'm looking up into a sea of faces. Later, a witness at the scene related that I went down like a tree. When they turned me over on my back, I was out cold for about two minutes and there was blood trickling out of the corner of my mouth. My eyes had rolled up in my head, I was told. Before I knew it, the ambulance arrived and I was lifted onto a stretcher and wheeled outside and hoisted into the ambulance. I was a little weak but I wasn't feeling any pain and my mind was clear.

A couple of guys are in the ambulance with me and they keep asking, in a very kind tone, how I'm doing. They take my blood pressure and stab my finger for a little blood to do a preliminary blood analysis. They ask me which hospital I want to go to, giving me two options. I choose Mercy Hospital in Springfield, the smaller of the two, where they tell me the service is likely to be a little quicker.

At the hospital, I am wheeled straight through the emergency waiting room and into a room where they hook me up to monitors and stick an IV needle in my hand. Someone asks if I have medical insurance, so I hand over my university insurance card and they take it away, bringing it back a few minutes later. A nurse then attaches a whole bunch of cold tabs all over my body so that they can do an electrocardiogram. Another nurse arrives and gently withdraws four vials of blood. Above my head, I can see my heartbeat jumping along on a screen and above that my blood pressure numbers flowing along. Not very much time passes before they start to lose interest in the machines and the numbers. They've discovered the truth—a healthy guy who fainted. Nothing more.

The doctor who's dealing with me has chosen emergency room work as his specialty. He's from the West Indies and once studied at Queen's University in Kingston, Ontario, where I did my own graduate work. He's a gentle man and I feel good in his care. He gets me ready for the six stitches I will need to close the cut under my right eye. He freezes me. The stitches go in easily.

They want to give you a CAT scan, he tells me. Wow, these Americans sure love their high-tech gear, I think. I'm steered down the hall in a wheelchair and into a domed room with a great machine that looks like a huge sculpture rendered out of metal and plastic. They lie me down on my back to be fed backward into the orifice of the sculpture. From an adjoining room, someone pushes buttons that move me backward and under the eye of the monster. Twice they do this.

After a few minutes, a doctor comes out of the adjoining room to ask what happened to me. I tell him I passed out during a firearms training course at Smith & Wesson. "What are you—a white supremacist?" he asks in a tone of gentle irony. This is an instant pal, I sense, so I tell him and the others in the room that I am a Canadian writing a book about the United States and that this is one of my many journeys, one that has apparently gone astray. They all seem to think this is good fun and we fall into a discussion about Canadian medicare. Does the Canadian system really work? Is everyone covered? Are there long waiting periods for service? What do people think?

Back to business. The doctor informs me that they have found a small, likely benign, cyst in my brain. They'd like to do another CAT scan, this time injecting dye into me to enhance the contrast. I sign a consent form—apparently there's a tiny chance the injection of the dye could kill me. Once more I'm sent into the opening. A few minutes later, they ascertain that it's a little cyst, benign, perhaps there since birth. Nothing to worry about.

I leave the hospital in a taxi to return to the Smith & Wesson Academy. The automatic card I was given at the beginning of the course works on the main door, and inside I am quickly joined by a young employee of the academy. He takes me upstairs to the office of the director. I am introduced to Gilbert A. Duvernay, who is seated behind his desk, a gun in his holster. Odd office attire, I cannot help thinking. Mr. Duvernay, who has sand-colored hair and a flourishing mustache, rises to greet me. He would have made a fine knight of the realm in the Middle Ages. He says I would be welcomed back to the academy anytime, should I wish to take the course again. A genteel attitude, I think, toward one so recently stricken on the field.

Downstairs, I return to the firing range, where through a window I can see my fellow students blasting away at the targets. Spent cartridges are popping out of pistols, and there is an unholy mess of empty magazines all over the floor. At a lull in the shooting, I am directed inside, where Brent comes up and shakes my hand warmly. He's actually a sweet guy. Some of the students crowd around to look at me. I suppose they feel the satisfaction of having prevailed on the very ground where one of their fellow students fell. That's certainly how I would look at it if I were in their place.

Two weeks later, Smith & Wesson refunds my course fee. A few weeks after that, I get the bill for my medical treatment: $2,500.

# THE HIGH-RISK LIFE OF
# THE MARLBORO MAN

THE MARLBORO MAN IS RUGGED, handsome, and fit, the very picture of American virility. His favorite terrain is the mountains—remote, challenging, forbidding.

The Marlboro man smokes and is usually seen with horses. But during his decades-long career, he has shown a capacity for other manly pursuits. He is the kind of man who is right at home with pickup trucks and firearms. Cigarettes, automobiles, and firearms—three products that are legal and potentially lethal—have been particularly important to the definition of male culture in America. Mobility and a very particular sense of individual freedom, however transitory or illusory, are the ideals of American manhood. Far more American males have died for the cause of tobacco, cars, and guns, however, than in all the wars in U.S. history.

Each of these products has left its deep imprint on the United States. The lure of profits from the sale of tobacco launched Virginia, the most influential of the Thirteen Colonies. The plantations of the lordly tobacco magnates were the most important early sites for the use of slaves in America.

In the United States, power grew out of the barrel of a gun from day one. Guns determined who had control and who did not in a slave-owning society, in wars with the Native Americans and in the settlement of the continent by migrants from the East. Today, every eighteen months, guns take the lives of as many Americans as died in the Vietnam War, making the United States by far the most violent of advanced societies. So important have guns been to America that the right to bear arms is written into the U.S. Constitution, although not as straightforwardly as many people think.

The automobile, more than any other mass product, was the key both to the rise of the American economy to global industrial supremacy and to the differentiation of American urban life from life in other countries.

Widespread pleasure in the lethal but legal says a great deal about a civilization. Hollywood films, which both reflect and encourage specific behaviors, typically portray American maleness with the presence of at least one of these products. Remember Fred MacMurray in the film noir classic *Double Indemnity,* with his cigarettes, his car, and, in the end, his gun; many of Humphrey Bogart's roles; or the rebel James Dean? A thousand other examples could be given. Cool, restless, and deadly—those are the qualities that cigarettes, cars, and guns have inspired in American men.

Although the number of Americans who die annually as a consequence of smoking-related illnesses cannot be reported exactly because it is based on interpretations of other data, it is estimated to be in the range of 400,000 a year. (In one year, that is almost as many deaths from tobacco as all the deaths of Americans in wars over the course of the entire twentieth century.) Smoking, it is clear, is by far the most lethal chosen activity of Americans. By contrast, a little more than 14,000 people died from drug-induced causes in the United States in 1995, and approximately 20,000 perished from alcohol-induced causes.[1] While tobacco is the grim reaper's most efficacious accomplice in America, autos and firearms are not exactly negligible death dealers. In 1995 approximately 43,000 people died in the United States as a consequence of motor vehicle accidents. The same year, nearly 36,000 people died in the U.S. as a result of the use of firearms.[2] Of course, what distinguishes these deaths from those resulting from tobacco is that deaths caused by guns and autos are often inflicted on those not wielding guns or driving vehicles.

Over the past four centuries, the gun has been central to political power. Without the muskets and cannon of the sixteenth and seventeenth centuries, primitive though they were, Europeans could not have conquered the indigenous inhabitants of the New World. The Spanish, French, and English all established their empires out of the barrel of a gun. The inhabitants of the Thirteen Colonies may have been in search of freedom when they left the Old World for the New, but they were on a voyage of oppression as well.

To us, the crude weapons of the colonists look barely more threatening than medieval swords and shields, but to indigenous peoples these were weapons of terror that they were incapable of resisting. Eventually the Native Americans acquired firearms from the invading hordes, who had a seemingly endless supply.

As guns pushed out the natives, they were also essential to slavery. The guns and sailing ships of early modern Europeans were adequate to undertake the African slave trade. And once the slaves were in the Spanish empire to the south or in the southern tier of the Thirteen Colonies, guns kept them there.

For a quarter of a millennium, until the slaves were freed, and for a century after that, while their descendants were held down by segregation, guns gave slave owners and white supremacists their margin of dominance. Resistance by slaves against their condition took many forms, from avoiding work to efforts to escape alone or in groups, sometimes into towns, where slaves tried to pass as free people, or into the wilderness, where they might set up small communities of their own. Resistance also took physical forms, including attacks against their masters and on occasion murder. In Maryland in the eighteenth century, there were reports of women slaves poisoning their masters.

Slave revolts were the ultimate, and most feared, form of resistance and they were more numerous in America than is popularly thought. Most histories of the United States don't bother to mention them. The first major revolt in the Thirteen Colonies broke out in New York in 1712, when about twenty-five black slaves and two Indians set alight a building and killed nine whites who had arrived on the scene. After these rebels were captured, twenty-one were executed, some having been tortured for hours before their deaths. One was burned over a slow fire for many hours. In South Carolina in 1739, about twenty slaves rebelled and were joined by eighty others. Before they were crushed, they fought a pitched battle against the militia, during which about fifty slaves and twenty-five whites died. What was probably the largest slave revolt in American history occurred near New Orleans in 1811. Between four and five hundred slaves assembled after a struggle at a plantation. Armed with primitive weapons, they marched from plantation to plantation gathering recruits. When they were met by U.S. army and militia units, sixty-six of the rebels were killed at once. Sixteen more were later tried and executed. In 1822, an audacious conspiracy led by Denmark Vesey, a free black, planned the burning of Charleston, South Carolina, to be followed by a general slave uprising throughout the region. The conspiracy was thwarted and thirty-five blacks, including Vesey, were executed.[3] Fear of such rebellions existed in slave-owning regions of the United States, particularly in regions where black slaves constituted the majority or a very large minority of the population, until abolition after the Civil War.

Thomas Jefferson once said that though slavery was evil, it was much like grasping a snake by the throat: you didn't want to hold on to it, but you dared not let it go. At Monticello, in Virginia, the magnificent mountaintop mansion that he designed for himself and his family is a graphic illustration of the hierarchy of a slave-owning society. Jefferson occupied the top floors of the aboveground portion, the section of the mansion that is most renowned. Here is his dining room with the lazy susan and the dumb waiter he designed, as well as his elegant invention to hoist wine bottles from the cellars below.

When I visited Monticello, I anticipated only the famous aboveground rooms, so I was struck by the way Jefferson had planned the mansion so that kitchens, wine cellars, and other work areas were underground, connected to the central dwelling by a kind of subterranean mall. In a number of these rooms, the most favored of Jefferson's two hundred slaves had their quarters. The rest lived in rustic dwellings, which no longer exist, on the side of the mountain. Some of the slaves were skilled craftsmen. This strange community produced furniture, nails, and bread, among other things. Jefferson's estate, like those of the Virginia tobacco quasi-aristocracy, was largely self-sufficient. Their operations substituted for the activities of towns, of which there were precious few in early Virginia.

The slave-owning communities were held together by force, as Jefferson understood so well. During his lifetime, this renowned father of American liberalism and individual rights, the author of the Declaration of Independence, freed only two of his slaves. And like many other slave owners, he had a sexual relationship with one of his slaves. Essential to the cohesion and survival of this community, in which some were free while others were not, was the authority vested in firearms.

Robert E. Lee was working for the United States in the days before the launch of the Confederacy, when he presided over the execution of John Brown, the abolitionist who was hanged in 1859 after his violent effort to provoke a slave revolt at Harper's Ferry, Virginia, where he and a small band of followers attempted to seize a federal army arsenal to provide weapons for the slaves. No wonder Brown is detested to this day by American conservatives, who have always insisted that he was insane. His raid was an extreme political provocation—putting guns in the hands of slaves threatened to overturn the social order. The building in Harper's Ferry where Brown and his comrades made their last stand remains a shrine to freedom among African Americans.

When I visited Harper's Ferry, I saw what a perfect setting the place was for the great American drama. The town is located in a deep rocky gorge close to the confluence of the Potomac and Shenandoah Rivers. Eighty miles from Washington, D.C., Harper's Ferry is a natural strategic point in any North-South conflict, as it proved to be in the war that broke out two years after Brown's ill-fated raid. At that time, the town was on the Virginia frontier, across the river from Maryland and only a few miles from Pennsylvania. Today Harper's Ferry is in West Virginia, the state that was torn out of old Virginia in 1863, in the middle of the Civil War.

The Second Amendment to the U.S. Constitution, which guarantees "the right of the people" to bear arms, shapes the contemporary battle in America on the contentious issue of guns and gun control. The amendment, one of the ten that constitute the Bill of Rights, was fashioned in 1791 shortly after the Constitution came into force. It expressed the consciousness of those who had won independence in the protracted war with Great Britain. Among their convictions was the belief that standing armies menaced freedom and that an arms-bearing citizenry organized into a "well regulated militia" guaranteed liberty.

Members of the powerful gun lobby in contemporary America interpret the Second Amendment to mean that individual American citizens have an untrammeled right to own and keep guns. For editors and commentators in gun-promotion magazines, this amendment is the holy grail. They fulminate against any restrictions on gun ownership.

Chuck Klein, a writer in the May 1999 issue of *Guns and Ammo* magazine, in an article titled "Second Amendment: Fight for Your Firearms Freedom!," claimed the Second Amendment "expressly forbade infringing the right to keep and bear arms." That's a very slippery way of putting it. I've noticed that firearms magazines don't often reproduce the actual wording of the Second Amendment, which reads: "A well regulated militia, being necessary to the security of a free State, the right of the people to keep and bear arms shall not be infringed."[4] The amendment, as can plainly be seen, is about the operation of a militia, which is to be "well regulated"; the right to "keep and bear arms" is a means to that end. Note that this right is conferred on "the people," that is to say, on Americans collectively. There is nothing in the amendment about individual Americans, outside the context of the militia, having the right to bear arms without restriction. Despite the actual wording, which is quite different from what gun lobbyists would have people think, most Americans with whom I have discussed the Second Amendment simply believe it guarantees the right of individual Americans to own and keep guns. In this, they are accepting the National Rifle Association's (NRA) version of the Constitution.

Gun advocates have an interpretation of history from ancient to contemporary times whose moral is that an armed citizenry is a free citizenry. Writing in *Gun World* magazine in May 1999, David Kopel laments that "the depressing historical ignorance of most Americans" is a major reason the Second Amendment is under so much attack from those who want to expand the power of the state. He tells the story of the Roman republic, a virtuous historical model to the Founders of the American republic, because in Rome before Julius Caesar the citizens were armed and therefore were able to resist tyranny. What allowed Caesar, "the murderer of the Roman republic," to overthrow this exemplary system was his creation of a standing army. Kopel draws the moral that "as the Roman standing army secured the vast Roman Empire against barbarian incursions, the people of the Empire, having lost their martial valor, lost their capacity for self-government." Then came the inevitable— the "degenerate Roman people" were overrun by the barbarians, the latter made up of German tribesmen who were armed and manly and who restored a spirit of freedom as they destroyed decrepit Rome.

Kopel draws the lesson for contemporary Americans: "The ownership of firearms by modern Americans is important not just for practical reasons (such as protecting homes from criminal invaders) but for moral ones. A homeowner who never has to use his gun for self-defense still possesses something his unarmed next-door neighbor does not: he has made the decision that he, personally, will take responsibility for defending his family. The armed homeowner's self-reliance has powerful moral consequences, as does the disarmed neighbor's decision that his family's safety will depend exclusively on the government, and not on himself."

The fierce battle over guns and gun control is not some arcane controversy over the meaning of an eighteenth-century text. It is a struggle between different elements of contemporary American society. The gun lobby, whose most powerful organization is the NRA, speaks for a highly defined constituency, overwhelmingly made up of white male gun owners and their sympathizers, who hue to a sharply right-wing political outlook. The lobby defends the right of citizens to own and carry semiautomatic weapons and armor-piercing bullets. It opposes the extension to gun shows of the Brady Bill, which requires a three-day background check on gun purchasers before they get possession of their weapons. And it opposes any background-check requirement for the sale of weapons by gun collectors who are not gun dealers.

The NRA's movie-star president, Charlton Heston, lends his status as a famous personality to the pro-gun position. After all, not every lobby has a guy who starred as Moses on the big screen as its spokesperson. He buys into the gun lobby's in-your-face right-wing ideology and has been criticized for displaying an exclusionary outlook where gays and ethnic minorities are concerned.

In a speech to the Free Congress Foundation in December 1997, Heston declared, "I find my blood pressure rising when Clinton's cultural shock troops participate in homosexual-rights fund-raisers but boycott gun-rights fund-raisers—and then claim it's time to place homosexual men in tents with boy scouts and suggest that sperm-donor babies born into lesbian relationships are somehow better served." In the same speech, on the subject of white pride, he said, "The Constitution was handed down to us by a bunch of those wise old, dead, white guys who invented this country. It's true—they were white guys. So were most of the guys who died in Lincoln's name, opposing slavery in the 1860s. So, why should I be ashamed of white guys? Why is Hispanic pride or black pride a good thing, while white pride conjures up shaved heads and white hoods?"[5] Heston is the celebrity spokesman for a lobby whose less famous exponents adhere to a culture that is narrow, macho, sexist, homophobic, and virulently anti-liberal.

In this neck of the American political woods, right-wing Republican politicians are the standard bearers. One is Bob Barr, a member of the House of Representatives and a House manager in the impeachment trial of President Bill Clinton. In the spring of 1999, after the mass shooting at Columbine High School in Littleton, Colorado, Barr was a point man in the gun lobby's effort to prevent the outrage of the American people from being translated into new gun-control legislation. In television appearances, he made the case for freedom for gun buyers, insisting that the three-day waiting period for the purchase of a gun should not apply to gun shows because it could adversely affect the shows, which usually last only two days.

You get an idea about Barr's politics from the fact that in June 1998 he turned up as a speaker at a meeting of the Council of Conservative Citizens in Charleston, South Carolina. The council is a white supremacist group that is opposed to marriage between people of different races and that wants to ban nonwhite immigration to America. Some of its members favor the deportation of all non-European Americans to Third World countries. The council was expelled from the Conservative Political Action Conference, because as David Keene, the head of CPAC, told *The Washington Post,* "They are racists."

When Alan Dershowitz of Harvard Law School drew Bob Barr's address to wider public attention, Barr said that when he spoke to the group he had no idea they were white supremacists. This disclaimer was flatly contradicted by the council's chief executive, who said the congressman had been given copies of the group's magazine, which made its racist views quite apparent. Barr also sat through a panel discussion during which the group's racist ideas were plainly displayed, before he himself spoke.[6] An even more high-profile Republican who spoke to the Council of Conservative Citizens is Senate Majority Leader Trent Lott. When he came into the spotlight for speaking to the group, he claimed he had "no firsthand knowledge" of the council. This did not prevent him, however, from delivering the keynote address to the group's 1992 conclave in Greenwood, Mississippi. On that occasion Lott declared that the members of the council "stand for the right principles and the right philosophy."

The number of homicides in the United States, including those perpetrated by assailants with guns, has been declining in recent years. But what has put the gun manufacturers and gun lobbyists on the defensive has been a series of spectacular school shootings in which students turned firearms on their fellow students and their teachers. Media frenzies have accompanied the shootings, particularly the massacre at Columbine High School, which was timed to occur on April 20, 1999, the anniversary of Adolf Hitler's birth. In that slaughter, two students killed twelve fellow students and a teacher before turning their guns on themselves.

One reason the shootings cut so deeply in America is that the perpetrators of the rash of school massacres were white males who lived in rural areas and in the suburbs. If black kids in Cleveland or Detroit or Hispanic kids in L.A. had shot up inner-city schools, the whole thing could have been put down to racial or ethnic problems. White America could have looked on smugly. The problem was that these shootings were in the parts of America where there were few minorities and where white Americans had fled to escape the dangers of the cities. One woman interviewed in prosperous Littleton, a suburb of Denver, wailed plaintively, "How could this happen in a neighborhood like this where people drive such wonderful cars?"

The leading media impulse was to put teenage America on the couch to try to diagnose its ills. Those ills apparently included having watched thousands of hours of violent television, having listened to antisocial rap music, and having played vicious video games simulating highly realistic killings. And there was the mysterious world of the Internet, far from fully understood by most adults, who thought it imbued kids with neo-Nazi ideas and tutored them on how to make bombs and kill their classmates. Some cultural analysts saw the shootings as postmodern outbursts, centerless narratives, in a setting in which technology had created the potential for everyone to act out parts in a drama with the real and virtual spheres hopelessly entangled. The Republican response to the shootings was to blame Hollywood and parents and to insist that if you put the Ten Commandments on the walls of schools it would help appreciably. Meanwhile, Republicans like Bob Barr and Trent Lott wriggled and twisted in all manner of contortions to avoid any serious legislative extension of gun control.

What the gun manufacturers and gun lobbies feared most was that they were entering a period during which the action would shift from legislatures to the courts. Class-action suits, of the kind that were threatening the tobacco industry, have become the new menace they face. Gun advocates have been quick to see the parallel and to position themselves alongside embattled tobacco manufacturers. Chuck Klein, in his *Guns and Ammo* article, makes the connection:

> "They," the politically correct, our government, anti-(fill-in-the-blank) groups and the news media, are setting us up just like "they" did to the tobacco makers. . . . What "they" did was, using government funding, establish pseudo health organizations such as the Centers for Disease Control to declare and publish tainted findings that cigarettes are not only harmful to the health of Americans, but as such, the health burden to treat these unhealthy citizens costs the government money. . . .
>
> Armed with false health reports, "they," using taxpayer money, instigated civil lawsuits to force an out-of-court settlement. The tobacco companies, as large and rich as they are, soon realized they were no match for the endless funding of the government. The result was exactly what the government and the lucky (read: greedy) lawyers who handled the cases wanted: money—lots and lots of money. The certainty that there is no constitutional basis for this rape of a legitimate industry is totally ignored by "they."

Already, the federally funded Centers for Disease Control

has come out with position papers saying that guns are a health risk. Some cities, using the same tobacco-style logic of having the expense of medically treating gunshot victims with public money, have already filed suits against gunmakers. Only this time, in addition to money, "they" seek an outright ban on guns. Because we have slid so far down the slippery slope, "they" just might be able to get away with it.

In 1998, New Orleans became the first city in the United States to file a lawsuit against gun manufacturers, in order to seek compensation for the huge public health costs generated by firearms violence. Since then, a couple of dozen similar lawsuits have been launched. Under pressure as a consequence of the threat of lawsuits, and sensing that public opinion was turning against the firearms makers, in March 2000 Smith & Wesson, the largest manufacturer of guns in the United States, agreed to a "code of conduct" that included a commitment to provide safety locks on its new handguns within sixty days and to make them child resistant within a year. The deal, reached with federal, state, and local government officials, also committed Smith & Wesson to distribute its guns only through authorized dealers that accepted conditions for their own conduct. If a disproportionate number of crimes were committed by people using weapons purchased from a dealer, that dealer's right to distribute Smith & Wesson products would be terminated. In return for its commitments, all three levels of government agreed to dismiss pending lawsuits against the company and undertook not to bring new suits against the company.[7]

I have already noted that almost 36,000 people were killed by guns in the United States in 1995. What I didn't mention was that half of the gun-inflicted deaths in America are suicides. The dirty little secret of the gun culture in the United States is that over time the bulk of the mayhem is shifting from murders to suicides. And a very large proportion of those who commit suicide are white males over the age of fifty-five.

Deaths caused by firearms are divided into three categories: suicides, homicides, and accidents. In 1995, 18,503 people in the United States used guns to commit suicide.[8] The same year, 13,798 people in the United States were murdered by firearms.[9] That left a total of 3,656 people who were killed by guns in accidents in the United States in 1995.

In keeping with the trope of the Marlboro man, it is accurate to say that being shot to death, either by someone else or by one's own hand, is overwhelmingly a "guy thing" in the United States. In 1995, 13.9 people per hundred thousand died in the United States as a consequence of injuries suffered from the use of firearms. But men were six times as likely to suffer death from firearms as women.[10] In 1995, while 3.5 white women per hundred thousand and 6.8 black women per hundred thousand died from firearms injuries, the corresponding rates for white men and black men were dramatically higher, 19.3 and 55.6 respectively.[11]

By themselves, these figures do not reveal the full dimensions of the shocking story. There are two peaks in the figures, which tell us a great deal about guns and American society. The first peak, the higher of the two, is the number of young black males who are the homicide victims of killers using firearms. One hundred and twenty-one black males per hundred thousand, aged fifteen to twenty-four, were killed by guns in 1995.[12] To appreciate the significance of this number, picture a small city of one hundred thousand people—say, Stamford, Connecticut. How alarming would it be if 121 people were murdered with guns in Stamford in the course of one year?

The other peak, also shocking but the subject of much less public discussion, is the number of white males over fifty-five who use firearms to commit suicide. From the age of fifteen on, the use of guns to commit suicide is higher for white males than for black males. The higher rate among white males becomes particularly pronounced in later life. Although white women are more likely to shoot themselves than black women, both white and black women are much less likely to use firearms to commit suicide than are men of either race. Among white men between fifty-five and sixty-four, the rate of suicide using firearms is 16.6 per hundred thousand per year, compared with rates of 7.5 for black men, and 2.6 for white women of the same age. (There is no precise figure for black women, which is lower still.)[13] After age sixty-four, the tendency of white males to shoot themselves continues to increase sharply to 23.9 per hundred thousand per year for those from their mid-sixties to their mid-seventies, then to 38.2 for those in their mid-seventies to mid-eighties, and incredibly to 49.5 for those over eighty-five. The rate for black men peaks at 13.9 for those who are between seventy-five and eighty-four, while for women of both races the rate remains very low in the later years. A white man of eighty is nineteen times as likely to shoot himself as a white woman of the same age.[14] For both genders, and for both whites and blacks, the use of firearms is the leading method of committing suicide.

The leading theory about why ageing white males are so much more likely to shoot themselves than are other Americans is that they often suffer from ego depletion. Late in life, white males are especially prone to experiencing a shrinkage of self-worth. Traditionally, white males have held the largest proportion of economic and political power in America. As they age, a significant number of them come face-to-face with the demon of doubt about whether they have been successful in the ways those of their race and gender define success.

If shooting yourself is a guy thing in America, it is also a regional thing. There are very wide regional variations in the suicide rate in the United States. While the overall suicide rate in the United States is 12.0 per hundred thousand per year, the suicide rate is 23.4 per hundred thousand per year in Nevada, the state with the highest suicide rate. The District of Columbia, which is 70 percent black in population, has the lowest suicide rate in the country, only 5.1 per hundred thousand a year. Among the states, New Jersey at 7.3 and New York and Rhode Island at 8.2 per hundred thousand per year have the lowest suicide rates.[16]

The Marlboro man was created, of course, to sell cigarettes, and it is that purpose that now most imperils him. Under immense pressure in the United States from smoking bans and class-action lawsuits, the tobacco industry has been shifting its focus back to what was its original raison d'être centuries ago, overseas markets. As I noted earlier, Virginia, the most important of the Thirteen Colonies, had tobacco as its chief economic support. The great market for colonial Virginia's tobacco was across the sea in Europe. Today, the U.S. tobacco giants are striving to win increased access to huge overseas markets while they are engaged in hand-to-hand combat to preserve their markets and solvency in the United States. The greatest overseas prize is the Chinese market. American tobacco companies have been engaged in negotiations with the state-run China National Tobacco Corporation in Beijing to widen their access to Chinese smokers. At present, smoking causes about 750,000 premature deaths each year in China. If trends continue, the number of premature deaths due to smoking in China could soar to three million a year by the middle of the century.

As tobacco giants play their high-stakes game in China, they are aggressively diving into other overseas markets, as well. A few years ago, the Marlboro man himself put in an appearance in downtown Kiev, the capital of Ukraine, when the gray streets were lit up with colorful billboards featuring craggy cowboy features and blazing sunsets. In Manila, capital of the Philippines, boys as young as ten dart in and out of traffic on the streets selling Marlboros and Lucky Strikes to motorists.[17]

The shift in the global market for cigarettes and global demographics is driving the cigarette companies offshore. Over the past decade, the total U.S. domestic market for cigarettes has grown by only 5 percent. Meanwhile, per capita consumption of cigarettes in Africa is up 33 percent and in Latin America 25 percent. Moreover, the age profile of Third World countries is sharply different from that of the United States and other advanced countries—in less-developed countries, the proportion of the population made up of teenagers and young adults is much higher. Targeting their young is the key growth strategy for the tobacco industry in the twenty-first century.

If current global smoking trends persist, almost one-tenth of the world's population will die from tobacco-related diseases in the next half century. That includes two hundred million of today's children and teenagers, almost 70 percent of them in the Third World. Such a toll would dwarf the combined number of all those killed worldwide in the wars of the twentieth century.

Between 1985 and 1995, the proportion of Americans who smoked declined from 30.1 percent to 24.7 percent. Of particular concern to tobacco companies and government authorities, although for diametrically opposed reasons, have been the smoking trends among young Americans. Most new smokers are hooked during the teen years and early adulthood. Tobacco companies want new clients for life, while governments want the downward smoking trend to continue. Between 1985 and 1994, the proportion of smokers, both male and female, declined in all age categories over twenty-five. Among young males aged eighteen to twenty-four, 28 percent smoked in 1985, after which the proportion dropped a little, then increased before it leveled off at 27.8 percent in 1995. In 1985 more young women than men smoked, 30.4

percent. By 1995 the proportion of young women who smoked declined to 21.8 percent.[18]

Among teenagers the truly worrying numbers are encountered. The federal Centers for Disease Control and Prevention reported that more than 1.2 million Americans under eighteen began smoking daily in 1996, up sharply from 708,000 in 1988. In 1996 seventy-seven of every thousand nonsmoking teenagers took up the habit. This was 50 percent higher than in 1988, when fifty-one of every thousand nonsmoking teenagers became smokers.[19] Critics of the tobacco industry sharply criticized R. J. Reynolds for the introduction of Joe Camel in its advertising in 1988, the year smoking rates among teenagers began to increase sharply. President Clinton was among those who asserted that Joe Camel was conceived to attract teenagers to smoking. In 1997, after a barrage of criticism concerning the character, R. J. Reynolds retired him.

Overall, more men than women smoke in America, 27 percent in 1995 compared with 22.6 percent.[20] As in the case of guns, American men have paid the supreme sacrifice in the cause of tobacco, in higher numbers than American women.

The battle over whether the tobacco companies have been deliberately targeting teens is only one front on which today's tobacco wars are being fought. The other great fight is over the liability tobacco companies will have to pay for damaging the health of smokers and the manner in which they will pay that liability. Left to face the wiles of class-action-suit attorneys, the tobacco companies have confronted the risk of liabilities so vast that they could literally sink them. The alternative has been for the companies to sign on to a deal with some or all state governments, with or without the federal government, agreeing to pay a sum of money in the hundreds of billions of dollars, which would then be used to settle claims against them.

Tobacco companies have vastly increased their lobbying

efforts in Washington to fight for the best possible political deal. Given George W. Bush's policy positions and the connections of some of his closest advisers to Big Tobacco, it is not surprising that tobacco lobbyists salivated at the prospect of his presidency. When he was governor of Texas, Bush was opposed to a federal lawsuit against the tobacco companies and was against an increase in tobacco taxes. He strongly backed tort reform that limits the right of consumers to sue producers of dangerous products, like tobacco. Karl Rove, a close friend of Bush and a key political adviser, was on the payroll of Philip Morris from 1991 to 1996 as a political intelligence operative.[21] Now Rove is senior adviser to the president in the Bush White House.

In the United States the Marlboro man, once the symbol of the outdoors and manly freedom, will likely end up living in a confined space whose exact proportions will be determined by the effectiveness of Big Tobacco's lobbying of politicians and the fallout in the courtrooms. Provided there is enough money to go around for everyone, a lethal product will continue to be a legal product.

One broiling summer day, when I was trying to drive from Michigan to Iowa, I ran into the unholy mess that is the I-80 south of Chicago. The I-80 spans the United States from Atlantic to Pacific.

The horror show began about ten miles east of the Illinois border in Gary and East Chicago, the industrial cities that sprawl from Chicago into Indiana. We crept forward at between five and ten miles an hour until we crossed into Illinois just south of Chicago. Here the interstate was being ripped up, rebuilt, reconnected, and rerouted. New bridges were under construction. We were shunted from lane to lane. It was as though we were tiny organisms passing through a heart bypass zone while the surgeons were operating. The whole nightmare took more than two hours—to drive about twenty-five miles—before we broke free and sailed toward the West.

The difficulty of trying to drive past Chicago in the summer is one of countless cases of the hardening of the arteries that surround America's great cities. Try motoring into Washington, D.C., New York, Boston, or Los Angeles anytime except between 2:00 A.M. and 5:00 A.M. and you will understand that driving into America's greatest cities has become 99 percent boredom and 1 percent scared-shitless panic.

America's metropolises are now surrounded by rings of multilane expressways, which bear some resemblance to the great stone walls Europeans built around their cities during the Middle Ages. Just as you had to penetrate a wall to enter fourteenth-century Avignon, you must penetrate the expressway wall to get inside any large American city in your automobile in the twenty-first century. The days of lighthearted travel on America's roads and of easy commutes from distant suburbs to work are now long in the past. The American auto system is strangling in its own excesses.

America's love affair with the car was the key to the creation of a new civilization over the past century. When we look back at the twentieth century, "the American Century," we may see it as the century of the automobile, which did so much to reshape American culture. Cars and trucks inspired the rebuilding of the entire human landscape in the United States. Henry Ford, a man with as much right as anyone to being regarded as the century's quintessential business titan, figured out how to manufacture cars more quickly and with a lower price than anyone else. He launched the affordable Model T in 1908. By 1912 there were seven thousand Ford dealers in America.[22] Bill Gates may yet own the twenty-first century, but Ford, more than any other individual, influenced America in the twentieth century.

In the nineteenth century, railways made possible linear

linkages between cities on a continental scale. The automobile produced a new urban configuration, with cities radiating outward over great areas. William Levitt created the first great suburb in 1947, when he began the construction of Levittown on Long Island, but it was the car that made Levitt's revolution possible. Cars bestowed a sense of individual freedom on Americans during a historical epoch when the country's population was rising rapidly, cities and their suburbs were mushrooming, and wealth was being concentrated in fewer and fewer hands.

Centuries from now, when the American empire has receded into history and future historians investigate it the way we do the histories of the Roman and British empires, they will certainly see the automobile as a defining feature. To us, the thought of Roman troops being dispatched down the Appian Way and then along the empire's excellent system of roads to a point on the frontier where they would do battle with some unruly tribe seems characteristically Roman and ever so distant from our own world. Eventually, America and its freeways may seem like that, characteristic of a civilization and yet impossibly remote from those future observers. We can imagine them talking of a time when people constructed strips of asphalt, painted lines down the middle of them, and drove vehicles with internal combustion engines up and down the two sides, with the vehicles colliding not uncommonly.

Thomas Jefferson was filled with foreboding that the urbanization and industrialization of America would foster a class system of the kind that existed in Europe. It would breed a rootless, propertyless proletariat that would have to be held down by an autocratic ruling class. The only escape he saw from this was the hope that yeoman farmers would multiply and extend their realm across the continent. Yeoman farmers were the only dependable mass base for democracy and an egalitarian society in Jefferson's eyes. What he feared and

America's few Marxists counted on was the rise of the cities and an industrial working class. To a very great extent, the car and the suburbs enabled American society to escape what looked like a grim fate in the early days of the burgeoning factories in the nineteenth century. The car created freedom of mobility unknown in all of human history. Ordinary individuals could climb into their own vehicles and set out with their friends and families across town or across the country. The horse and buggy was nothing compared with this. As highways were constructed, linking distant cities, Americans could chart their own course across the country when they liked, where they liked. In the 1950s the Eisenhower interstate highway system, financed and planned by the federal government ostensibly to ensure the movement of the military in the event of war, completed the construction of nationwide superhighways.

The dark side of the prodigious expansion of highways and the proliferation of motor vehicles has become increasingly apparent in recent decades. In 1995, 123 million cars prowled American roads, along with 70 million trucks. The number of trucks, including Jeeps, vans, and sport utility vehicles, doubled in only fifteen years, while the number of cars increased by just under 20 percent during that period.[23] Not many decades into the twenty-first century, the number of vehicles is likely to pass the number of people in the United States.

That the car was a killer was apparent from its earliest days, of course, but the late nineteenth and early twentieth centuries were marked by countless train wrecks, with thousands killed annually. Great fires in major American cities occurred then— Chicago burned, as did San Francisco and others—occasioning considerable loss of life. Against that backdrop, the auto appeared relatively innocent. At the dawn of the new millennium, however, the auto's reputation is stained, not merely because of the number of people who die in road accidents but also because of the environmental damage wreaked by it and because of the transportation gridlock it has created.

Despite what would appear to be the handwriting on the wall for big gas-guzzling cars in the twenty-first century, Detroit's automakers kicked off the new millennium with offerings that seemed designed to provoke nostalgia for the great days of America's love affair with the auto. In January 2001, at the garish North American International Auto Show in Detroit with five thousand journalists on hand from around the world, the models that were on display pointed toward an emphasis on style and power, with fuel-saving and environmental concerns taking a backseat. Ford announced the rebirth of the Thunderbird four years after it was last produced. With styling touches evoking images of the fifties and sixties, the new Thunderbird is to be a foot longer than its original 1955 predecessor and to weigh nearly nine hundred pounds more. With its powerful engine, eggcrate grille, and an optional removable hardtop with a porthole window, the new 'Bird is clearly aimed at baby boomers.

Another Ford nostalgia offering at the auto show was the new Forty-Nine, a vehicle inspired by the company's popular sedans built from 1949 to 1951. Whether the new Forty-Nine will actually be produced depends on whether the concept that has been unveiled takes off with the public. The powerful new sedan is a deep, shiny black, with round headlamps and twenty-inch chrome wheels. Ford president and chief executive officer Jac Nasser talked of the bygone days when American autos were owned by real auto enthusiasts: "They were passionate about their automobiles," he said. "And sometimes, they were passionate in their automobiles . . . or so they tell me."[24]

GM, at the auto show, unveiled powerful new concept vehicles that seemed aimed at the youth market. The offerings included a Buick Bengal sport roadster that company spokesmen claimed was inspired by golfer Tiger Woods. It is a two-seater that can be easily converted into a four-seater. It boasts a six-speed automatic transmission. "I could see it appealing to Woods. He could buy one. He could have one from us," said GM president and chief executive officer Rick Wagoner, in reference to the popular golfer who does Buick commercials.[25]

The new concept vehicles were being rolled out at a time when auto sales were plunging in the United States and auto companies were announcing production slowdowns and layoffs. As for the automakers themselves, they seemed much more determined to hang on to what had worked in the past than to prepare for a changed world in the future.

The Marlboro man has cut a wide swath through American culture and politics, though lately he's been dragged into the fight of his life, with cigarette manufacturers up against exceptionally costly class-action lawsuits and gun manufacturers face-to-face with a similar fate. While automakers certainly do not confront the prospect of being driven out of business by class-action suits, they have endured them in the past and are likely to experience them in the future. The auto crisis of the twenty-first century, and it will be a global crisis, will be about environmental degradation and urban congestion.

The first and most successful of the modern world's revolutions was the American Revolution. America's revolutionary origin has imbued the country with a wild streak, personified by the Marlboro man, that remains in all its turbulence at the dawn of the new millennium. He has entered the twenty-first century looking a little tattered, but though the cultural tides may have shifted against him in some ways, he still has a lot of fight left in him.

# 4

# AMERICAN CARNIVAL

IT'S A BEAUTIFUL, UNSEASONABLY WARM Sunday in December in Orchard Park, New York, home of the Buffalo Bills. In the parking lots that circle the eighty-thousand-seat stadium, a party is under way. Hundreds of people are barbecuing sausages, steaks, and wieners. The sweet scent of cooking meat drifts in the soft air.

With several companions, I've just come to join the festivities as the Bills take on the L.A. Raiders. The overwhelmingly male white revelers, many of them dressed in red-blue-and-white Bills paraphernalia, are guzzling copious quantities of beer. Nerf footballs are soaring as grown men and boys fantasize about the upcoming game. There are few portable toilets here, and the lineups are long. The men have turned a small patch of scraggly woods at the edge of the parking lot into a giant urinal.

Hawkers sell an endless line of Bills memorabilia—caps, hats, shirts, mitts, and footwear complete with the stylized charging buffalo that is the team logo. Some are wearing Bills boxer shorts over their head-to-toe athletic outfits.

This is an old-time American crowd—men who've never got over being boys, wearing baseball caps and oversize sweaters— with a strong preference for big vintage American cars.

Close to kickoff time, people are packing up their barbecues and beginning to gravitate toward the stadium, which sits like a giant pod in the middle of the huge expanse of parking lots. We head to our entrance. The gates to the stadium are primitive affairs, holes in the wall that the crowd moves to like sand flowing through a funnel. As you get closer, people jostle to squeeze through the ever-narrowing space. Since I don't like small spaces, I take an interest in what is going on and see a problem ahead. Just inside the gate, officials are searching every single fan on the way in. I get it. They are on the lookout for beer and other alcoholic beverages. They sell beer inside and want to maintain their local monopoly. Gallons of beer are being brought into the stadium in the abdomens of patrons who have just completed their tailgate parties, but sneaking beer cans inside in a capacious Bill's sweater is frowned upon.

I get to the entrance and an official gives me the once-over, reaching his hand up the inside of my arms. It strikes me as odd in a country where individual freedom is such a watchword that this sort of invasive behavior is so easily tolerated. I have been to plenty of sporting events in Canada over a period of decades and nothing like this has ever happened to me. Later I see the large guy who went in ahead of me and who was cursorily examined reaching up inside his Bills shirt to pull out a couple of cans of beer.

My seat is behind the end zone about halfway up the stands. From my position, the stadium is an awesome spectacle. The playing field is a gaudy green carpet. Because the stadium is partially sunk into the ground, you only see how huge it is when you are inside. I look around to check out the demographics. I count faces and come up with the following tally: 98 percent of this crowd is white and 90 percent of it is male.

Beer gets things going. As soon as they settle into their seats or even before, they are chugging it down, suds from the outlets and from cans up their sleeves. Beer is not the only alcohol in the stadium. Out come the flasks, their bottoms pointed skyward as all manner of Scotch, rye, Southern Comfort, and homemade concoctions slip down expectant throats.

As I settle into my seat and explore the wider scene, I soon become aware of the fact that the fans sitting directly in front of me, for at least ten rows down toward the field, are even more homogeneous than the wider crowd. These are beefy white men, mostly in their thirties, with close-cropped haircuts. A lot of them are wearing white T-shirts with the slogan "Out on bail" emblazoned on the back in black lettering. I briefly entertain the idea that these are former jailbirds who've been brought to the stadium by their parole officers. And then I understand. They're all cops. That's why they look so much alike—clean-cut in a heavyset, muscular way. In a way, I'm a little disappointed. It's as if I'm sitting with my own security department. How much fun can that be? Then I see that some of them are guzzling from regulation cups sold at the stadium, but that others have smuggled in beer cans, and still others are imbibing the contents of flasks and gourds. Cops who don't mind bending the rules on their day off can't be all bad.

Cheered by the sunshine and warmth of this mid-December day, the crowd is in a good mood. For one thing, the home team, led by quarterback Doug Flutie, is winning easily against the hapless Raiders. The plucky little quarterback, who starred for years in the Canadian Football League but was first thought too small to make it in the NFL, is putting on a one-man show, completing passes and dodging tackles on the artificial turf.

From my seat well above the field, I have a bird's-eye view of the unfolding pageant, though the game is so far away that it is a little difficult to see the details of what is happening. I experience a momentary longing for a television close-up, which would somehow seem more real than this miniature before my eyes.

A little rain is beginning to fall on the festivities, or is it a golden haze of beer foam that is drifting down from above? Bits of paper float above my head, some of them landing on my lap. About twenty rows below me, someone releases a huge pinkish balloon shaped like a naked woman. It hovers above the fans for a while. The Jills, the cheerleaders for the Buffalo Bills, are doing a turn right in front of us at the edge of the field. They are outfitted in tights—I guess the mid-December date ruled out shorts. The cops on their afternoon off are paying more attention to the gyrations of the Jills than to the game at the moment. I hear crude suggestions about what they would do if some of the Jills would join them in the stands. A couple of small balloons in the shape of breasts hover just above us.

The cop in front of me is a state trooper from Corning, New York, a small town famed for its glassware, situated not far from the Pennsylvania border. He is an amiable guy and he explains that the policemen live for these outings to Bills games. Whenever the team scores a touchdown or a field goal, they all leap to their feet in a vicarious brand of macho. They probably wish they had Jills to cheer them on in their pursuits. I find myself doing "high fives" with the cops.

A small airplane is buzzing overhead, turning in circles above the stadium, pulling an advertising streamer behind. The streamer reads, "Buffalo Gun Center—Harlem Rd. 'Go Bills.' " Half an hour later the plane is back, this time with a streamer that reads, "I love U, Sue Miller. Will you marry me? Justin."

I turn around to look at the crowd and the stadium behind me. And there in big letters, a permanent part of the stadium, in a place of honor above me, is the name O. J. Simpson. Orenthal James Simpson was the greatest player ever to wear a Bills jersey. Even though he never led the Bills to the Super Bowl, for years O. J. *was* the Buffalo franchise. I have seen O. J. on those magical replays you see the night before the Super Bowl when great players are featured in NFL documentaries. There he is, running effortlessly, wonderfully, play after play.

Like millions of others in North America, I happened to be watching television on that June night in 1994 when O.J. was pursued by police in the famed "low-speed chase" along the L.A. freeway that ended at his mansion in Brentwood. The car chase has been an American staple for decades, of course, but there had never been one like this. This was a procession, with police cars respectfully following the celebrity fugitive, while helicopters with television cameras buzzed overhead and brought the melodrama live to millions of people around the world. Along the route followed by O.J., who was driven by a longtime friend, people gathered on bridges to wave and display banners. Cars, vans, and trucks pulled over to the side to allow the odd little motorcade to pass. O.J.'s journey was so captivating to broadcasters that the telecast of an NBA playoff game was sidelined so that the chase took up most of the screen and the game was relegated to a corner of it.

Homecoming for the fallen idol. After brief negotiations by cell phone, O.J. was allowed to walk into the mansion where he drank a glass of orange juice. The mansion was hard-won, the fruit of his sweat on the gridiron. O.J. had been a ball carrier, the job of the nimble and the courageous. From the gridiron, he had been catapulted to a media career—part journeyman actor, part pitchman. O.J. had made it with the wider white public, part of that acceptance concentrated on his possession of a young and beautiful white wife.

As millions of Americans took a passionate position, one way or the other, during the O.J. trial, for huge audiences in the rest of the world O.J. and his dream team became celebrities in a television drama that ran night after night, competing with American reruns like *Melrose Place*.

We are about halfway through the second quarter and the

mood is beginning to shift. A certain uneasiness gathers in the crowd. A lot of the beer has now been processed in intestinal systems and men are climbing to their feet and heading for the urinals. I get to one of the huge washrooms, pretty basic facilities, at halftime. Long lines of men, many of them with potbellies and pink faces and wearing Bills hats, stand in line in front of communal pee troughs. Some fans find this all too slow. On the other side of the washroom are large communal sinks with signs that read, "Do not urinate in sinks." Whether the signs give people the idea or not, I have no way of knowing. Fans are furiously peeing in all of the sinks. I forget about washing my hands.

Once I'm back in the stands for the second half, the mood is darker. Fights break out in corners of the stadium quite a long way from where I am sitting. To see them, you look for a cluster of fans standing up to form a perfect circle; at the center is the point of conflict. Sometimes you actually see the fight, sometimes you are blocked by all those on their feet trying to catch a glimpse. There is now much more energy being poured into fight watching than game watching.

Even the cops are beginning to look restive. One guy a few seats over in the row in front of me is wearing wraparound sunglasses. He has a protruding stomach and his pink face is blotchy. He grapples with a companion on his left, grabbing his arm and twisting it. It's in fun, but he's getting more aggressive minute by minute. The state trooper from Corning is still good-humored, but he's tipsy. He tells me the guy with the pink face and the big stomach always gets like this. "He doesn't know his own strength," he says jovially.

There's a stir in the row in front. One of the cops is lying across three or four seats and then his comrades pass him from seat to seat. All of a sudden they hurl him up and back and he falls onto the laps of a couple of men right beside me. The cop with the blotchy pink face looks meaner as he wrestles less playfully with the guy beside me. A while ago, I thought these cops were like Rotarians, clubby guys who feel best in each other's company. Quite a few drinks and a dull game later, they're starting to look like the "Out on bail" message on their shirts. Overhead, the drizzle of beer is getting thicker.

Enough. It's time to leave, my friends and I decide. We get up to go, and one of our party drops into the washroom on the way. A few minutes later he is back, holding his jaw. He explains that when he entered the washroom, security guards were confronting a man with a bloody face. The man with the bloody face took a roundhouse swing at no one in particular and hit my companion. The guards asked my friend if he wanted to press charges. "No thanks," he said. "I'm just going home to Toronto."

There is one more thing to do before we cross the border. Buffalo is the world capital in one narrow corner of the culinary universe. What Lyons is to French cuisine, Buffalo is to chicken wings. The restaurant that started the Buffalo wings craze was Frank and Teresa's Anchor Bar on Main Street, in the heart of the city's old downtown. Inner-city Buffalo is a sad place, its fine architectural monuments ironic, even cruel, reminders of the city's proud past.

When I was growing up, not many miles away in staid Toronto, Buffalo was vibrant, especially alluring to young people because of its night life and the fact that you could drink beer there at eighteen, while in Ontario you had to be twenty-one. But technology and the political economy shifted, and the fortunes of the two cities were switched. Toronto took off because it was the financial capital of Canada, located at the center of the country's major manufacturing region. A steady stream of immigration brought hundreds of thousands of new residents to the Queen City north of the border. In Buffalo, however, the trend was relentlessly down. Montreal won its revenge against the Erie Canal—Buffalo's waterway link to

New York City—with the completion of the St. Lawrence Seaway during the 1950s. Buffalo's commercial and political representatives fought tooth and nail against the Seaway without success. When the Seaway was complete, Buffalo lost the grain trade, which bypassed it in favor of Montreal. Although Buffalo's industrial production increased as a consequence of the Vietnam War during the 1960s, in the following decade disaster struck. First, there were massive layoffs at the steel plants, followed later by layoffs at auto-parts plants. With the core of the city's economy ravaged,[1] the white middle classes fled the downtown, leaving it derelict and abandoned. Even the ring of suburbs around the hollowed-out center failed to grow quickly enough to prevent population from declining in the metropolitan area as a whole. Over the past couple of decades, Buffalo has experienced one of the sharpest drops in population of any major metropolitan area in the United States. Between 1980 and 1996, the population slipped from 1.24 to 1.19 million. Of 273 metropolitan areas treated in a study by the Bureau of the Census, the Buffalo area was ranked 258th in population change.[2]

As we approach the Anchor Bar at four in the afternoon, the streets are deserted, which is typical of downtown Buffalo: you could fire a cannon anytime along Main Street without hitting a soul. You can park anywhere you like. We park in the lot at the Anchor Bar, where there are at least a few vehicles huddled together.

The dingy dining area at Frank and Teresa's serves a range of items, including some hearty salads, but chicken wings are the draw. Wings are graded according to their firepower—mild, medium, hot, and suicide. In my pilgrimages here, I have never tried suicide. I used to think I could handle hot, but now I have settled for medium. Before I eat wings, I always munch two Rolaids. I think this is advisable for anyone over twenty-five.

These days chicken is associated with low-fat diets. But Frank and Teresa invented Buffalo wings long before anyone had ever heard of fat grams. When they are at their best, and they usually are, Anchor Bar wings are delivered to your table piping hot, saturated with cholestoral-generating oil and coated with the orangy-red sauce of your preference. A sour cream dip is provided to cut the ferocity of the wings.

With my companions, I eat my twenty medium wings, making a mental note that later I will have to scrub my skin with strong soap to remove the stain.

# *CHOICE* AND *ITS FOES*

D R. SUZANNE POPPEMA is an ebullient, vivacious woman who loves to travel to the world's beautiful places. Ten years ago, she journeyed with her husband, John Cramer, and their two sons to a little mountain town in the south of France. There they spent six months exploring the wonderful countryside, making friends, eating good food, and drinking the best wines. It was time off for Suzanne and John, both graduates of Harvard Medical School.

Suzanne and her family do not have to travel far to find enchanting surroundings. They live in a picture-book setting in Everett, Washington, about twenty miles north of Seattle. Their luxurious house, surrounded by high gates and guarded by a huge dog, appropriately named Bear, looks out over Puget Sound and the Olympic Mountains on the far side. This is an American Shangri-la, where Suzanne loves to barbecue salmon and sit out on the enormous deck watching the sun set.

What makes Suzanne very different from her affluent neighbors is that she is an abortion doctor and as such has put herself on the front line of an American cultural and social

war. You can find her name on the notorious Web site known
as the Nuremberg File, which lists the names of America's
abortion doctors and targets them for death. Those who are
alive and well are listed in black, those who have been wounded
are marked in gray, and those who have been killed have a line
drawn through their names. The Nuremberg site lists Suzanne
T. Poppema and her fellow practitioners as "baby butchers."
Above their names is a graphic that simulates dripping blood.

Originally, the Nuremberg site was mounted by the
American Coalition of Life Advocates and other pro-life
groups. Abortion providers, not unreasonably, regarded the
Web site as a provocation to commit murder. In the winter
of 1999, a federal jury in Oregon ordered those responsible
for the site to pay damages of approximately $107 million to
four abortion doctors, Planned Parenthood, and others. The
jury decided that those mounting the site had violated federal racketeering laws and the 1994 Freedom of Access to
Clinic Entrances Act, which makes it illegal to incite violence
against abortion providers and their patients.[1] Since the court
ruling, the Web site has been kept on the Internet by other
extreme anti-abortion groups.

Suzanne Poppema was born and raised in a Catholic family
in rural New Hampshire. Her mother, a native of Quebec City,
met her father when he was stationed with the U.S. military
there during the Second World War. Suzanne, who spent many
of her summers in Quebec City with her mother's relatives,
is fluently bilingual. She attributes her rejection of what she
was taught in the Catholic school she attended as a child to a
natural assertiveness that developed into a concern for justice
and then into an enduring feminism. With humor she notes
that she was an especially headstrong toddler who almost scared
her relatives out of their wits. Her assertiveness led her into
constant battles in the Catholic rural school she attended. As
an adult, she fought what she describes as the "war machine"

during the Vietnam conflict and developed an unshakable conviction that women must have control over their bodies. She has little use for men who think they have a right to involve government in making decisions for women about whether to terminate unwanted pregnancies. To her, this is unvarnished patriarchy. How long would men put up with a government committee made up of women determining what was going to happen to their bodies?

Suzanne had an abortion when she was a young woman. She says she had no emotional connection to the young man with whom she had become pregnant, and didn't want a relationship. The thought of becoming a single mother terrified her, and she was afraid that plans for her career would crash to the ground if she had the baby. She now draws on her own experience to help women deal with their feelings after they have an abortion.

Social struggles are often called wars to give them an extra sense of drama, but in the abortion conflict, there are bombings, murders, woundings, and death threats, all happening within a civil society ostensibly at peace. During the 1990s, seven abortion providers were murdered in the United States, two of them in 1998. Over the course of the decade fifteen abortion clinics were bombed, dozens subjected to acts of arson, and hundreds were the victims of vandalism. In many cases, hostile opponents invaded clinics. Abortion providers were the victims of hundreds of acts of assault and battery against their persons and they have frequently had their lives threatened. In numerous cases, their enemies stalked abortion providers.[2] The life of an abortion doctor makes being a cop look safe.

On a July morning, I drive to the clinic in suburban Seattle that is owned and operated by Suzanne. The unprepossessing building is surrounded by a parking lot. Down the hall and to the left, I find the office. I buzz at the door as instructed and introduce myself. I can see two women at a desk on the other side of the bulletproof glass. They click the button to open the door, and I push it and enter. The clinic's director greets me. She is in her early thirties and has held the job at the clinic for about ten years. We pass through the waiting room, which is full of patients, some accompanied by their partners. These are mostly working-class women, about evenly divided between whites and women of color. The waiting room is not a happy place.

In the director's crowded office, we talk about the clinic and the battle of the pro-choice forces to counter the recent assaults that have been mounted by the anti-abortion side. One opponent of abortion shows up several days a week and stands outside this building. A court order bars him from entering or even standing on the privately owned parking lot outside. The protester makes a show of praying on the street as patients and the clinic's staff members pass him on their way in.

Once, a couple of years ago, he came right inside to speak to the patients. The director tells me that the patients and staff were terrified since they had no idea what to expect from him. It was this episode that led to the court's order that the protester was to stay out. Suzanne later informs me that when she drives to work and sees him standing outside, she is reassured if she can see his hands. As long as she is sure he is not armed, she is not too alarmed. But who knows what someone like this could do someday? After all, he is a fanatic, one who takes the trouble to show up here to protest day after day for months on end.

A few years ago, the clinic was plagued for a time with protesters carrying signs and marching on the street outside. One day a prominent anti-abortion activist managed to get inside the clinic, and he stayed in the waiting room for several hours without being noticed. Everyone assumed he was a relative or friend of one of the patients until one of the patients told a staff member that he was handing out anti-abortion literature. Called to the front desk and asked what he wanted, he insisted on "talk[ing] to Dr. Poppema about having her stop murdering babies." Finally, he left and hasn't been back.

Recently, about a dozen noisy protesters showed up in front of Suzanne's house, where they picketed for a few hours. About the same time, another group of fifteen to twenty demonstrators led by a man with a loud hailer waged a similar one-day protest in front of the clinic. For a while, Suzanne has been looking for a new location for her clinic, but repeatedly she runs into real estate companies who say they are not anti-choice but they just don't want the hassles that would go with having the clinic on their clients' premises.

Suzanne wears a bulletproof vest to work. Not so long ago the clinic was visited by security advisers who recommended that she drive to work each day by a different route and park in a different spot. Sometimes, she tells me, she has trouble remembering where she has parked when she leaves the clinic. The trouble with all this precaution is that she drives a silver Mercedes convertible, a car that sticks out a mile.

Suzanne's clinic averages sixty surgical abortions a week. Patients pay $400 for the procedure. In some cases, part of this fee is covered for people who qualify for Medicaid. For those who are permanently disabled, the fee is paid by Medicare. In addition to surgical abortions, the clinic is one of the few in the United States that is experimenting with medical abortions as part of a trial for RU 486, a drug that was developed in France. In France, about 44 percent of abortions are medical rather than surgical and the drug is used until the seventh week of pregnancy. In the U.S. trials, including Suzanne's clinic, the drug is provided until the ninth week. When a woman uses the so-called abortion pill, she first takes mifepristone, a drug that stops a fertilized egg from attaching itself to the lining of the uterus. Two days later, she takes miso-prostol, which triggers contractions of the uterus.

Suzanne tells me at lunch later that "medical abortion is the answer." She believes that within five years, the drug will have transformed the situation in the United States for those wanting abortions. And yet, ever since the U.S. Food and Drug Administration approved RU 486 in 1996, on a con-tingent basis, calling it a "safe and effective nonsurgical method of abortion," abortion opponents have fought to block its avail-ability in the United States.

Other obstacles prevent RU 486 from reaching the U.S. market. No manufacturer is willing to produce it, nor is the French pharmaceutical company that developed it willing to manufacture it in the United States, fearing that the anti-abortion movement will mount a boycott of its other prod-ucts. Suzanne and her colleagues are hopeful that another European manufacturer is prepared to step in.

The right-to-life movement is apprehensive that the wide-spread availability of RU 486 could spell doom for their political activities. Their campaigns are premised on the fact that abortions are conducted in clinics whose locations are known. If a woman can go to a doctor's office and simply get a prescription, which can then be filled by a phar-macy, the ability of right-to-lifers to hound their targets will vanish.

Another nonsurgical procedure that could dramatically alter the abortion picture in the United States is the so-called morning-after pill. In 1997 the FDA decided that certain birth-control pills, dispensed in high doses, could be safely used as emergency contraception following unprotected sex. In 1998 *The New England Journal of Medicine* published a study that con-cluded that more than half the unwanted pregnancies in the United States could be prevented if morning-after pills were made widely available. Beginning in December 1997, the state of Washington has permitted pharmacists to dispense the pills without a doctor's prescription.

The state also has a law on the books that translates the results of the landmark *Roe v. Wade* case, legalizing abortion for American women, into state law. Even in the event that the Supreme Court overturns *Roe v. Wade,* abortion would still be legal in the state of Washington.

Despite legal protection in states such as Washington and the promise of nonsurgical developments, abortion providers have been put on the defensive by the power and relentless aggressiveness of the anti-choice movement. The antis are well organized and tactically skilled. Although their ultimate objective is abolition, they block abortions every way they can. They have found a highly effective way to assault the position of the abortion providers through the seemingly less comprehensive issue of so-called partial-birth abortion. The term, which is not a medical one, describes abortion techniques that some people see as interruptions of live births occurring late in a pregnancy when a fetus might be viable. The antis deploy arguments against partial-birth abortion that actually apply to a wide range of abortion procedures currently in use.

At least five different abortion methods are employed at present in the United States. The first method is oral medication, such as RU 486, taken within the first seven to nine weeks to induce miscarriage. The second is extraction abortion: the amniotic fluid is drained from inside the uterus, and nonsuction instruments are employed to complete the procedure. The third method is suction aspiration (with manual or electrical suction) to empty the uterus. The fourth procedure is suction aspiration with instrument-assisted removal of fetal parts (commonly referred to as a dilation and evacuation). The fifth method is extraction: after the amniotic sac is emptied of fluid, the fetal brain is drained and the fetus is removed. This latter method is sometimes called an intact dilation and evacuation and is used for several reasons: to reduce the like-lihood of uterine trauma from extracting instruments; to avoid a C-section in women with fetuses unlikely to survive, such as those with fatal hydrocephaly, a severe abnormality that leaves the fetal head so grossly enlarged with fluid that it can-not pass through the cervix; and to save the life of a woman whose delivery becomes complicated by sudden tearing away of the placenta from the uterine wall, causing hemorrhage and maternal death unless the fetus can be removed quickly to allow access to the placenta to stop the bleeding. The second, third, fourth, and fifth procedures could be banned by laws that prohibit partial-birth abortion, depending on how these laws are drafted.

Focusing on what they call partial-birth abortions, the anti-abortionists have horrified the public with sensational photos and stories of beautiful almost-newborns being slaughtered. Armed with such potent imagery, they press for legislation at the state level, right across the country, that would ban some of the techniques described above. Other legislative objectives are to enforce a twenty-four-hour waiting period before any abortion can be performed and to require parental approval of abortions for young teenagers. In the spring of 1999, then Governor George W. Bush piloted a bill through the Texas legislature that requires notification of parents of young teenagers before they can have an abortion. Presumably Bush was hoping this measure would show the antis that his heart was with them in the great abortion debate, while not being too offensive to the pro-choice majority of voters on whom he would have to rely in his bid to be elected president of the United States.

But parental-approval laws can be pernicious, particularly in the cases of teenagers who have suffered abuse at home. And waiting periods hurt poor women who have to travel away from home for an abortion, forcing up their expenses. At present, 83 percent of the counties in the United States have no facilities for the provision of abortions.

In Missouri, in the summer of 1999, the two houses of the state legislature passed a bill that created a felony called "infanticide." Under the bill, anyone who caused "the death of a living infant . . . by an overt act performed when the infant is partially born or born" could be charged with a criminal offense equivalent to murder. When Missouri's Democratic Governor Mel Carnahan vetoed this sweeping bill, ostensibly aimed at outlawing partial-birth abortions, large majorities in the state House and Senate, both controlled by Democrats, voted to override the governor's veto. With his veto nullified, the governor warned, "This bill is far more extreme than its proponents claim." He insisted it outlawed any abortions undertaken later than six weeks into pregnancy, not just late-term partial-birth abortions. Because the bill allowed for no exception to protect the mother's health, Carnahan argued that it was unconstitutional.[3]

After Planned Parenthood, Missouri's largest provider of abortions, filed a lawsuit challenging the new state law, a federal judge issued an order temporarily blocking its enforcement. Only then did Planned Parenthood decide to resume abortions in Missouri, having previously taken the position that the new law was "so broadly and vaguely worded as to put plaintiffs at risk of criminal prosecution for virtually any abortion they perform, regardless of the stage of pregnancy."[4]

The partial-birth-abortion issue has forced abortion providers to spend a lot of time thinking about how they present their own position to the public. They have held retreats where media consultants are hired to advise them to concentrate on "staying on message." In media interviews, the abortion providers have often been required to explain horrific-sounding procedures. Instead, what they want to do is to drive home their essential message: American women should have a right to safe and available abortions in the event of unwanted pregnancies; and their right must not be thwarted or negated by a minority largely made up of religious fundamentalists whose broader agenda is the subjugation of women. Suzanne and her colleagues believe that what truly motivates the antis is a deep desire to return women to the traditional position they occupied prior to the steps toward emancipation taken during the twentieth century.

Humiliating, exposing, threatening, and scaring women is a big part of the modus operandi of the antis. Demonstrators can scare off women who are considering an abortion. Patients often say that they first drive by a clinic to see if they will be hassled if they go inside. Only when they see no problem outside do they go in. Some women say that they fear being recognized when they go to the clinic. Other women, including some patients, are more ambivalent about the right to abortion. Sometimes, even on the day they are having a procedure performed on them, they say they plan to go out and vote for a Republican candidate who is opposed to abortion. Abortions will never be banned, such women say. I've heard this often from pro-choice Republican women. They shrug when their party's stance on abortion is raised. Ironically, such Republican voters are relying on the Democrats and the courts to prevent the Republicans from actually doing what their program commits them to. Still, it must be disquieting to such women that pro-choice Republicans have little hope of winning the nominations of their party for president or for vice president.

Subjected to all the sound and fury of the debate, the American public is divided on what it thinks about abortion. A Gallup/CNN/USA Today poll conducted in November 1997 revealed that 27 percent of women and 24 percent of men think abortions should be legal under all circumstances, and that 16 percent of women and 15 percent of men believe they should be legal under most circumstances. On the other hand, 38 percent of women and 42 percent of men think abortions should be legal in only a few circumstances. Just 18 percent of women and 16 percent of men believe abortions should be illegal in all circumstances. If public opinion polls make it clear that only a small minority of Americans would go all the way with the right-to-life movement to ban abortions, they also reveal a close correlation between beliefs on abortion and the educational and income levels of Americans.

Highly educated and higher-income Americans are more inclined to approve of abortion than those less well educated and with lower incomes. An ABC News/*Washington Post* poll conducted in June 1996 showed that 67 percent of respondents with post-graduate degrees believed abortions should be legal either in all cases or in most cases, while only 40 percent of those with less than a high school education shared those beliefs. Although only 8 percent of those with post-graduate degrees would make abortions illegal in all cases, 29 percent of those with less than a high school education would ban abortions. All along the educational scale between these two extremes is a consistent increase in support for the right to abortions as educational levels increase.

The opinions of Americans on abortion show a similar, if not as simple, pattern when the incomes of respondents are considered. Seventy-six percent of those in the highest income bracket—above $75,000 annually—favor making abortions legal in all or in most cases. Only 4 percent of these high-income earners would make abortions illegal in all cases. At the bottom end of the income scale—those earning less than $12,000 a year—only 39 percent of poll respondents favored making abortions legal in all or most cases, while 22 percent would ban abortions in all cases and 34 percent would make them illegal in most cases. For poll respondents located between the two income extremes, approval of abortions increased in a fairly straight line as incomes increased.

The political implications of these attitudes on abortion are potentially explosive. In the United States, most high-income earners vote Republican. Polls show that these people have a markedly liberal outlook on the question of abortion, and yet most of them support a political party committed to drastically limiting abortions in the short term and abolishing them outright through a constitutional amendment to protect the lives of the unborn in the long run. For years high-income Republicans, who make major financial contributions to political campaigns, have grumbled about their party's commitment to banning abortions. These "country club" Republicans have a very different outlook from the stalwarts of the Christian right, who are often much lower on the income scale.

At times when the abortion debate has been on the back burner and it appeared unlikely that established abortion rights were about to be sharply abridged, these contradictions in the views of supporters of the Republican Party could be papered over. George W. Bush began his drive for the White House as a moderate pro-lifer who was able to reassure wealthy pro-choice Republicans that he would not really do anything that would effectively curtail abortion rights in America. He sent a signal to such supporters when he said that in making appointments to the Supreme Court, he would select men and women who were qualified but would not make opposition to the court's position on *Roe v. Wade* a litmus test, as the strident pro-lifers do. But in his fight for the Republican nomination against Senator John McCain, Bush was pushed sharply to the right. To defeat McCain in South Carolina, Bush tied himself closely to Pat Robertson and the Christian Coalition. The pro-life movement came out strongly in support of Bush against McCain. On the Web pages of pro-life groups, McCain was savaged as completely untrustworthy, while Bush was lauded as a stalwart of the anti-abortion cause. That left the Texas governor occupying a solidly anti-abortion position, which made him potentially vulnerable to attacks from the Democrats that as president he would lead an assault against a woman's right to choose. Abortion rights were a much more salient issue in the 2000 presidential election than in previous presidential elections.

As president-elect, George W. Bush chose former Missouri senator John Ashcroft, an opponent of the right to abortions even in cases of rape and incest, as his attorney general. One of Ashcroft's first official acts was to withdraw U.S. funding to international organizations that provided abortion counseling. Taken together, these were unmistakable signals to anti-abortion militants that Bush had not forgotten their support.

A nurse practitioner I meet at the clinic is infectiously enthusiastic about what the clinic is doing to help women deal with the real problems in their lives. She decries the shame that has been engendered by the antis over the past decade. She announces to me, quite abruptly and happily, that she has had two abortions herself. She thinks the abortion movement needs to get back to its more straightforward attitudes of a couple of decades ago. It needs to be less defensive.

The nurse practitioner, who is disarmingly direct about her belief that abortions are to be preferred to delivering unwanted children into the world, gets my mind back to what ought to be central in the whole debate, the reasons women decide to have abortions. A survey of American women who had abortions in 1987 found that 68 percent felt they were not able to afford a baby at the time of their pregnancy. Twenty-one percent put this at the top of the list as the most important reason for their abortion. Fifty-one percent said they were having problems with their relationship and that they wanted to avoid ending up as single parents. For 11 percent of the women, this was the most important reason. Other significant reasons for choosing abortion included a woman's not wanting others to know she has had sex or was pregnant; younger women asserting that they were not mature enough or too young to have a child; women deciding they have had all the children they want, or that their other children had all grown up; and women who reported that a husband or partner wanted them to have an abortion.[5] The reasons women choose to have abortions are exactly what you would expect: practical reasons that have to do with the central realities of their lives. The list of reasons is an eloquent counterpoint to the absolutist opposition to abortion that, on paper at least, is the Republican Party's stance.

At lunch, Suzanne, her director, and I are sitting outside at a pleasant eatery not far from the clinic. A few weeks earlier at a convention of abortion providers in Vancouver, Suzanne was elected president of the board of directors of the National Abortion Federation. She tells me that her goal during her term as president is to campaign to make abortions safe, legal, and available, when suddenly there is a loud bang—probably a car backfiring. Suzanne gasps and stiffens. I begin to see the terrible pressure she lives with constantly. Earlier when I asked her whether she is afraid of being attacked, she told me that she lives in denial. In 1996, when she wrote a book, *Why I Am an Abortion Doctor,* she didn't go on a media tour to publicize the book because, she says, that would have been like putting a bull's-eye on her chest.

Four months after my visit to Suzanne's clinic, Dr. Barnett Slepian, an obstetrician-gynecologist who performed abortions, was shot and killed in the kitchen of his home in suburban Buffalo by an assassin firing a rifle from a wooded area a hundred feet away. Prior to his murder in October 1998, Dr. Slepian had been the target of protests and threats over many years. In the way it was carried out, the slaying of Dr. Slepian bore a strong resemblance to four earlier attacks that wounded but did not kill abortion providers in New York State and in Canada.[6] The murder of Dr. Slepian was a stark reminder that when abortion providers like Suzanne contend that they face dire warnings and threats, they are speaking the plain truth.

A Web site mounted by the so-called Army of God, a Virginia-based anti-abortion organization, ran a chilling "Ode to Slepian" by someone identified as Rev. Donald Spitz. In part, it read:

> From the cold, the man watched baby killer Slepian inside his comfortable half million dollar house.
>
> The man who watched; a godly, righteous man; could no longer sit passively by while this evil beast enjoyed the fruits of his depraved blood trade. . . He rested his head against the tree which hid him from direct sight of the baby killer and his family and prayed, then he calmly pulled the trigger.
>
> Hallelujah to the LORD . . . The baby killer lay in his own filthy, stinking, unclean blood, his worthless life seeping out of this body, his soul preparing itself for the eternal fires of hell. . . .
>
> A true American hero slipped away into the darkness having had the honor to be chosen as an instrument in the hands of the LORD.

Above this prose is a photograph of Dr. Slepian; below it lies a picture of his tombstone.

The Army of God Web site displays another ghoulish document, the "Army of God Manual." This guide instructs readers on how to sabotage abortion providers in ways that extend from relatively minor to lethal. Readers learn how to screw up clinics by squirting Krazy Glue in door locks and cement into sewage systems, or by jamming phone lines or staging park-ins at clinic parking lots. The manual also tells how to blow up abortion clinics with readily available materials. Finally, it counsels readers on killing abortion providers and ends with this declaration: ". . . we, the remnant of God-fearing men and women of the United States of Amerika, do officially declare war on the entire child-killing industry . . . Our Most Dread Sovereign Lord God requires that whosoever sheds man's blood, by man shall his blood be shed. . . . Not out of hatred for you, but out of love for the persons you exterminate, we are forced to take arms against you. . . . Vengeance belongs to God only. However, execution is rarely gentle." Intended no doubt to provide protection against criminal prosecution, the following caveat accompanies the "Army of God Manual": "The Army of God Manual is reproduced here as an historical document of the anti-abortion movement. It is not to be construed as sanctioning any group or individual to perform any action."

The murder of Dr. Slepian and the wounding of other abortion providers are episodes in a conflict that continues to rage. There is absolutely no doubt that at one extreme of the right-to-life movement is a wing determined to get its way not through persuasion or democratic reform but through violence and intimidation. The key to their strategy is to wear down the abortion doctors, to make their lives such hell that they will quietly move to other medical practices. Without abortion doctors, the extremists calculate, there will be no abortions.

Suzanne believes in the work she is doing. She has no doubt that the medical service she provides helps give women control of their lives. But she is not going to do this difficult job, with its terrible strains, forever. A little longer, she tells me, and she will have done her part.

# DEATH AND GOD *IN TEXAS*

I'M ON MY WAY TO the scene of an execution. It is January 1998.

I'm driving to the execution instead of flying so I can see this huge slice of the center of America. My present journey takes me from the north to the Ohio Valley and across Kentucky and Tennessee. At Memphis, I will cross the Mississippi and head southwest through Arkansas, then on to Huntsville, Texas. Leaving the snow-covered farmlands of Ontario behind, I head south from Detroit. Once past the Detroit-Toledo industrial corridor, I have clear sailing along Interstate 75. A thin dusting of snow covers Ohio's flat fields.

Past executions, I admit, have haunted me, running through my mind after I have read descriptions of them. This goes back, I believe, to the electrocution of Julius and Ethel Rosenberg on June 19, 1953. I was eleven years old when they died in the electric chair, convicted of espionage. As I delivered papers on my afternoon route on the day after they died, I read how it took Ethel longer to die than her husband. At the time, I thought of the Rosenbergs, who had children of their own, and wondered in horror if my own left-wing parents could be threatened with a similar fate in Canada in those McCarthyite days.

Part of the hold executions have over you is their pornography. From a description written by Christopher Hitchens in the January 1998 issue of *Vanity Fair,* I can picture Samuel Lee McDonald, a forty-eight-year-old African American lying strapped to a gurney with a sheet covering him up to his chin. His head is turned toward his relatives, who are behind the glass in the witness room. The condemned is talking disjointedly, trying to comfort his family. At two minutes after midnight, he gags and arches his back. An injection of sodium Pentothal, administered remotely, has just hit him. In swift order, this is followed by a dose of pancuronium bromide, which stops his breathing, and a shot of potassium chloride, which immobilizes his heart. The convicted killer of an off-duty policeman is the twenty-seventh person executed in the lethal-injection chamber at the Potosi Correctional Center in Mineral Point, Missouri.

Compared with other ways of being put to death, this doesn't sound so bad. I think of Ted Bundy, the multiple murderer, being led meekly to sit in Florida's electric chair. When he died, witnesses saw a puff of smoke erupt from his ankle, where an electric line hooked him to the source of the voltage. Near the prison, gleeful revelers celebrated when they heard that Bundy had been "smoked." Some held a raucous tailgate party, like the ones staged before Buffalo Bills games outside the stadium in Orchard Park, New York. When their barbecuing was done, they ate Bundy Burgers.

I'm not going to Huntsville for cheap thrills. I figure that you learn a lot about a civilization from its executions. Few things tell us more about inclusion and exclusion in a society than the decisions it makes about whom to execute and whom to spare. Since the United States resumed executions in 1977, after a nine-year hiatus, all those put to death have been found guilty of murder. Executions for rape, once common in America, have ceased—between 1930 and 1967, 455 men, 405 of them black, were put to death for rape.[1]

Karla Faye Tucker was born into a poor, broken family in Houston. Her mother was a prostitute. Karla Faye was a doper by age eight and a prostitute by the time she was fourteen. As she admits, in 1984, strung out on a slew of drugs, Tucker and her boyfriend murdered a man and a woman with a three-foot pickax. The murder was the crazed climax of a robbery gone wrong. There is no evidence that the murders were pre-meditated. Karla Faye admits that each time she swung the pickax into her victims, she experienced a surge of sexual pleasure. Even hard-bitten Houston was horrified by the murders. Karla Faye's boyfriend, the one she was so eager to impress, later died in prison of liver disease. She alone is to face the executioner.

Today, she is articulate, telegenic, and, according to numerous accounts from within the prison system and outside, she has completely transformed her life. Preaching the Christian gospel from death row and ministering to the needs of others has made her, she claims, no longer a "part of the problem, but a part of the solution." She corresponds with people across the country, counseling them about their difficulties, drawing on the lessons from her own early life. In her lighter moments, she describes herself as "a really huggy, touchy-feely person" who would love to be a mother.[2] Fellow prisoners, prison guards, ministers, the brother of the woman she killed, and many others insist that on death row she has become a caring person with much to offer others mired in poverty, crime, and drugs. Detractors say that her case is drawing attention only because she is pretty and white. From capital punishment opponents, such as the members of Amnesty International, to Pat Robertson, the founder of the conservative Christian Coalition, an army of sympathizers is demanding that Tucker's sentence be commuted to life imprisonment.

Four days from now, on Tuesday, February 3, Karla Faye is scheduled to die in the lethal-injection chamber in Huntsville. Executions are routine events there, where thirty-seven men were put to death in 1997. That's about one every ten days. Since then, Texas has continued to crank out far more executions than any other U.S. state, which makes Huntsville the capital punishment capital of the Western world. What makes this execution momentous is that Karla Faye will be the first woman to be put to death in Texas since the Civil War. As the sands of time run out for Karla Faye, the man who will have to make the final decision as to whether she lives or dies will be George W. Bush, the governor of Texas.

I cannot help contrasting Karla Faye's diminishing hopes for life with O.J. Simpson's very different fate. When O.J. was charged with the vicious butchering of his wife and her friend in June 1994, the death penalty was never seriously contemplated. L.A. prosecutors were savvy from the start that it was impossible to seek the execution of O.J. Simpson. (As events showed, his celebrity, and their own incompetence, denied the prosecutors a conviction, even though they refrained from asking for the death penalty.) No such wealthy and celebrated person had ever been executed in the history of the republic. Beyond the daunting task of finding a jury whose members would countenance the death penalty for O.J., there was the wider question of how the public would react. Americans, most of whom, in all regions of the country, favor the death penalty, prefer that those executed in their name be anonymous monsters. Not celebrities.

As the winter sun sets, I am in southern Ohio, circling around Cincinnati, the city on the Ohio River whose fortune was tied to the river traffic that linked Cincinnati to the commerce of the whole Mississippi region during the nineteenth century. Cincinnati is firmly in the North, but its soul is at least partly Southern. There was much sympathy for the Confederate cause here in the early days of the Civil War.

Across the river, I am in Kentucky, the border state that was the birthplace of Abraham Lincoln. Although dramatic representations of Lincoln have often featured him as a baritone, he actually had a tenor voice and delivered the Gettysburg Address with a distinct Kentucky twang. From the hallowed address, Lincoln's oft-quoted phrase "that this nation, under God, shall have a new birth of freedom" has echoed through the American mind ever since. During the Eisenhower presidency, "under God" was added to the Pledge of Allegiance, a reassuring addition for religious conservatives. But Lincoln was expressing his belief in the promise of redemption. His troubled nation was to have "a new birth." Did that mean that sinfulness could be washed away through faith? If that was possible for a nation, what were the prospects for an individual like Karla Faye?

Down past Bowling Green, for a time the Confederate capital of Kentucky, and on to Nashville, where more Bibles are printed than in any other city in the world. Nashville boasts that it is "the buckle on the Bible Belt." I have entered the land of the personal God, the land where every opinion is conditioned by the presence of the living God. God is mentioned, without affectation, in just about every conversation here. Where I come from, God is a distant force. Here, he is a partisan, a booster for causes, and an ally in vexatious disputes. The argument about whether Karla Faye should live or die is cast as a debate about whether God is loving and forgiving or righteous and vengeful. Her defenders, her adversaries, and her would-be executioners are all God-fearing. What kind of God is this, so amenable to serving in causes so antithetical?

The endless Tennessee forest parallels the interstate to

Memphis. Memphis, where the idol of my teenage years is buried at Graceland, in the world's most singular secular shrine. Memphis, where Martin Luther King Jr. was gunned down in 1968, one augury of a time of troubles for American society and institutions that has not yet ended.

Crossing the Mississippi at Memphis, I motor into Arkansas, and I can see the skyline of the great city on the river receding in the rearview mirror. On the west side of the river is a huge billboard proclaiming that Arkansas is the birthplace of President Bill Clinton, whose face beams from the sign. Arkansas away from the great river is scrubby, with vast stretches of swamp along the way. Farms and dwellings dotting the landscape are even more derelict than in Tennessee. The interstate takes me straight into the heart of Little Rock, a city of wide streets that are mostly empty on a Saturday afternoon. On the west side of the downtown, in a pleasant hilly quarter of luxurious houses, is the governor's mansion. Against the fence, there is a plaque commemorating the rise of Bill Clinton from governor to president of the United States. It's not hard to understand why a clever boy with a verbal gift would want to escape from this place.

On the interstate west of Little Rock, I discover where everyone is. On either side of the highway for about twenty miles are parallel roads crowded with restaurants and commercial establishments of every size and description. Traffic along these roads is bumper to bumper.

It is still a long way across mostly flat tree-covered Arkansas before I reach Texarkana, a jumble of fast-food places and retail outlets that sprouts up on both sides of the interstate, right on the border with Texas. At last, Texas. It is a warm, windy night when I stop at a filling station a few miles west of Texarkana. Twelve hundred miles from Toronto and still a long way to Austin, the state capital. It is just past midnight and I have been on the road for two long days. I consider the fact that we are now in the early hours of Sunday. Karla Faye is scheduled to die the day after tomorrow.

After spending the night at a motel on the edge of a small town in eastern Texas, I push on toward Austin across the endless green, flat farmland. Dead armadillos, lying luridly on their backs, make up a large part of the roadkill here. Ruefully, considering I am en route to an execution, I note the anti-littering signs, which read, "Don't mess with Texas."

When I finally reach Austin on Sunday evening, I check into a ratty motel located practically right under Interstate 35. From there I drive downtown to find a bar where they serve food and, I hope, play the blues. Austin is one of the great centers of blues music in the United States. Through a side door and into a bar I find a lineup of people heading past tables with ticket collectors. It is a fund-raiser for the Democratic candidate for county judge. I am waved inside when I explain that I am a visiting Canadian wanting to hear some good music. About three-quarters of the crowd is black—a wide range of ages. The candidate, who is black too, speaks from a mike on the stage. He used to be the county commissioner. He makes a pretty moderate speech, stressing his record on issues like affordable housing. "If I don't win," he jests, "I'm going to have to count on a lot of you to feed me and look after me." The crowd laughs, and he leaves the stage.

At the bar, I talk with a black couple in their late thirties. He is well dressed, a long-time Democrat. In answer to the question whether race will be a factor in the election, he first says no, then pauses and corrects himself. "Race is always a factor. That's why it won't be so easy for him to win." He sympathizes with Karla Faye, thinks her death sentence should be commuted.

The music is great. An old blues singer sits on a chair, grinding out a string of tunes. More and more people dance. I eat a smoked turkey leg, which is ever so sweet and greasy, and beans.

Monday morning is cloudless. I am in Austin, where Karla Faye's fate will be determined. I hear on the radio that she has been flown at dawn from the women's prison in Gatesville to a death cell in Huntsville.

Austin is a small city in comparison with Dallas and Houston, a government town, with a well-endowed university. The neo-classical state Capitol is the imposing center of the city. The other dominant structure is architect Paul Cret's University of Texas tower, from which a gunman once killed and wounded a large number of passersby.

Governor George W. Bush parks his silver Chrysler in front of the Capitol where the only parking space is reserved for him. Down the hill from the Capitol is commercial Austin. Across the street, to the southwest, is the Governor's Mansion, a big comfortable house surrounded by a high wall. A wrought-iron sliding gate controls access to the driveway.

I am at the Capitol to find out how the state Board of Pardons and Paroles has ruled on the commutation petition submitted days before by Karla Faye's lawyers. I run into a television crew walking outside the main building. The on-air guy tells me that the board has turned Karla Faye down by a vote of sixteen against with two abstentions. Inside the ornate building in the media relations office, I get a photocopy of the decision.

I visit the Austin office of the *Fort Worth Star-Telegram,* where reporter Jay Booth is expecting me. He has been doing a lot of writing on the Tucker case. He is in his mid-thirties, a friendly, professional guy who speaks French and has done work for Radio-Canada and the French television networks. He thinks Bush will go ahead with the execution and that it's not likely to hurt him politically. The Bush backers in Texas are pro–death penalty. Booth says the governor would be far more afraid of commuting her sentence, which would mean she would get out of prison in a few years. This would really bother the Bush constituency. A free Karla Faye could become his own Willie Horton. The analogy is arresting. In a notorious campaign commercial during the 1988 presidential election, George W.'s father used the black rapist Willie Horton, who reoffended while out on furlough, to great effect against his opponent, the mild-mannered, technocratic Massachusetts governor, Michael Dukakis. Governor Bush's father did not hesitate to rouse the most deep-seated prejudices of white Americans in his ubiquitous Willie Horton commercials, which put the criminal's brutish features on television screens. Booth thinks the Tucker case is merely a temporary problem for Bush and that once the execution is over it will be swiftly forgotten. Surely something is wrong when the decision a politician takes about whether someone should live or die is driven by its anticipated impact on his polling numbers.

George W. Bush is a political phenomenon. He is a Republican governor who knows how to appeal to the right wing of his party through tough stands against gun control and teen pregnancy and in support of prison work gangs. But he also knows how to reach out to Hispanics and blacks and is much better at drawing them into his circle of supporters than are run-of-the-mill Republicans. Bush is never embarrassed about talking publicly about the virtue of prayer. When he is under pressure, it is to prayer that he turns. And that goes down well with Texans of all political stripes.

It wasn't always that way with the Texas governor. Karla Faye Tucker and George W. Bush share one thing. Both turned their lives around after a rocky start. George W. was a hard-living, aimless frat boy at Yale. After graduation, he drove his Triumph convertible hard and loved to party in his apartment. He drank a lot, he admits. He won't say whether he used marijuana or other illegal drugs. "I made a lot of mistakes in the past; I'm just not going to itemize them," Bush told a *Newsweek* reporter in the spring of 1997.[3] In 1977 Bush met and married Laura Welch, a deeply religious west Texas school librarian who motivated him to take up the study of the Bible and to talk about religion in public—something he now does at the drop of a hat.

Born again, Bush has become a harsh critic of what he labels the values of the 1960s generation, which he was part of. "The culture of my generation—if it feels good do it, and be sure to blame someone else—failed," he says. He claims the time has come for people like him to take on "the mantle of responsibility for our country." But the rugged self-reliance that has become his hallmark sharply contradicts his own life story. While he served in the military during the Vietnam War, his service was limited to flying F-102s in an Air National Guard Unit in Houston. He never flew outside Texas. The ladder he climbed in life was held for him by his father and his father's friends. Connections helped him make good in the Texas oil business. Businessmen impressed with the fact that his father was vice president and then president helped him out in the oil industry and assisted him in buying a chunk of the Texas Rangers baseball team. He borrowed $606,000 in 1989, and when the team was sold in June 1998, he received $15 million for his share.[4] By the time he had to decide on Karla Faye's appeal for clemency, Governor George W. Bush had already acquired front-runner status in the yet-to-be-run race for the Republican presidential nomination in 2000.

I drive Booth over to the office of David Botsford, Karla Faye's Austin lawyer, who holds a press conference on the sidewalk outside his office, which is in an old house on a street of houses converted into low-rise quarters for lawyers and doctors. Botsford is in passionate form, although he seems wired and fatigued. His words seem to be coming from some depleting well of adrenalin. He is responding to the announcement by Victor Rodriguez, chairman of the Board of Pardons and Paroles, that Tucker's appeal has been rejected. Botsford

says Texas has no mercy. He comments on Rodriguez's statement that Tucker lied to him. Rodriguez, the chief of police
in Brownsville, Texas, before Bush made him head of the
Pardons Board, had gone to see Karla Faye in prison at
Gatesville weeks before the execution. It was the first time
that Rodriguez, a cold man who is used to murder and executions, ever visited a condemned inmate. After his visit with
Karla Faye, he quotes her as saying that she did not recall the
details of the murders. Later, she told someone else that she
did remember the murders. Rodriguez jumped on this supposed inconsistency to buttress his case against clemency. For
Rodriguez, this was enough to prove that Karla Faye lacked
sincerity. It's curious that a man who has had no qualms about
dozens of previous executions felt the need for this tawdry
excuse. Was he trying to convince the public, or was it his own
spine he needed to stiffen?

One effect of the large number of executions in Texas is that
they create momentum. Karla Faye's case for clemency has
nothing to do with a claim of innocence—she readily concedes
she is guilty of murder as charged. She asserts that she has been
redeemed and therefore is no longer the person she was when
she committed two heinous murders. The problem with that
argument is that even if it is true—and there is much evidence
to corroborate it—she isn't the only person on death row in
Texas to have seen the light. Others before her went to their
deaths proclaiming that they had been born again. They too
were deeply contrite about the crimes they had committed.
And yet their pleas for clemency never once won a second
look from Victor Rodriguez and the governor of the state.
Suppose Rodriguez and Bush actually wondered whether Karla
Faye had been transformed into a person who was essentially
good. How could they act on a perception that a fundamental rehabilitation had been achieved—surely a wonderful
thing when it really occurs? Blocking them from acting, or

even considering acting, are all the executions that have gone before. Undoubtedly, the most awful thing that could happen to an executioner would be to allow a scintilla of doubt to enter his mind about past executions. Macbeth put the terrible dilemma this way: "I am in blood stepp'd in so far that, should I wade no more, returning were as tedious as go o'er."

One piece of distasteful evidence, long after the fact, sheds some light on how George W. Bush deals with the pressure of executions. In the summer of 1999, the front-runner for the Republican presidential nomination was being interviewed for *Talk* magazine. On the way to the interview, Bush and the reporter were riding in a limousine. The Texas governor, according to the reporter, proceeded to mimic Karla Faye Tucker pleading for her life. Not surprisingly, the Texas governor's office denied that this ever happened.

Botsford tells the assembled media that he still has a number of legal balls in the air—a couple of them aimed at the Supreme Court, one at a state court in Austin and another at the U.S. fifth federal circuit court in New Orleans. One by one these balls will crash to the ground over the next thirty-two hours.

That evening, I drive down to the Governor's Mansion to join the candlelight vigil on the sidewalk next to the front gates. About seventy-five people, including three or four very young children, sing "We Shall Overcome." It feels like a time so long ago, the days of the anti–Vietnam War and civil rights movement. One man arrives with a poster of the woman who is to die tomorrow. The poster is signed, "Love, Karla Faye."

The effect of the candles in the warm early evening is peaceful. The crowd is quiet, respectful. At the center of the group talking to a woman activist in her fifties is Sam Jordan, an African American who is the director of Amnesty International's U.S. campaign against capital punishment. Jordan testifies before congressional committees in Washington and spends a lot of time on the road traveling to prisons where executions are imminent. I meet Jordan and talk about the campaign, telling him about the abolition of capital punishment in Canada, where the last execution took place in Toronto in 1962. Inside the gates, just outside the mansion, three men in suits stand talking next to a shiny black late-model car.

Tuesday morning, the day of the execution, I leave for Huntsville, which is about 150 miles away. On the drive I see herds of cattle. Here and there, oil pumps are lifting black gold to the surface. Huntsville is a town of three or four thousand residents, surrounded on its outskirts by fast-food places and minimalls. The town is full of ghoulish advertising on the day of the execution. Store windows feature signs promising "Killer Bargains," "Bargains to Die For," and "Karla Faye Tucker Killer Bargains." Journalists invade the town photographing the signs. Some locals are a little sensitive. One asks a journalist why she wants to take a picture. Another remarks that today is the town's "one-day local economy." When I go out to a café for a sandwich, the woman running the place is notably polite. There are other outsiders eating here as well.

A quick drive along the main east-west street brings you to the state prison, the town's raison d'être. It's a giant red-brick edifice with a guard turret on the front corner. The red is garish, as though flames have licked it. The huge clock over the center of the front door is a little slow. Across from the main building is a smaller building, where execution witnesses are kept before they are summoned across the road.

There are about twenty-five media trucks parked on a lot adjacent to the prison. They point their satellite dishes into the sky, ready to relay the news of what is happening here to audiences around the world. All the big U.S. networks are here, as are correspondents from many other countries, including Britain, Italy, and Japan. Bianca Jagger, the former wife of Mick, is here too. She is an opponent of the death penalty and has been vocal in her opposition to this execution. At 4:30 P.M., a brief press conference is held at the mikes by a prison official who brings us up to date on the few remaining legal efforts to stop the execution. I explain what has been said to a Japanese correspondent who doesn't understand English well.

Prison authorities have roped off a large grassy area right across the street for the media. In this area, cameras are in position for stand-ups, with the prison in the background. An officer in a large cowboy hat admits me to this area. A bank of mikes at the far end of the area is adjacent to the walkway between the building where the witnesses are held and the prison. It is from here that the representatives of the media are to learn what is happening as the hours pass. Rumors are the other source of information, and there are plenty of these. One rumor in the late afternoon sweeps through the media area to the effect that George Bush has called a press conference for 8:00 P.M. and that the execution is not to take place that day. No one ever knew the source of this rumor, but it was interesting to see it circulate among the supposedly sophisticated journalists.

In the media area, there is a temporary-looking little building with windows on all sides. Inside, someone has installed a huge bank of telephones from which journalists are filing their reports. Just outside the media area, two large crowds collect all afternoon. The group that opposes the death penalty sits quietly, handing out literature. Some of them are the relatives of murder victims who nonetheless oppose the death penalty. Members of Amnesty International are here from other parts of Texas and from other states. Later I see Sam Jordan again. He is quietly businesslike on the day of the execution, inured to vanishing hope, having spent many execution days standing in front of U.S. prisons.

There is also the pro–death penalty crowd. Their numbers swell, and they become more raucous as the afternoon turns into evening. They carry placards calling for the death of Karla Faye. Some signs display a pickax; others call for her to be executed by pickax. One sign reads, "Your last orgasm, Karla Faye." The pro-death crowd is mostly young and increasingly aggressive. They are lusting after blood, cheering the executioner in the same way that people have done for thousands of years.

A circus is developing on this warm afternoon in Huntsville, despite all the efforts that have been made to sanitize the execution. The state of Texas prides itself on handling executions with professional calm. They now take place at six in the evening rather than at the witching hour of midnight. It's just something we do at the end of a working day. If you want a list of those to be put to death over the next three months, just call the state prison at Huntsville, and a very cordial person in media relations will fax the list to you. It tells you the age, race and sex of the condemned, the county where he or she was sentenced to death, and the date of the upcoming execution. If you like, you can ask the prison to send you the menus for the last meals of recent inmates who have been put to death. Media relations will be happy to comply. On execution day, official witnesses, the friends and relatives of the condemned, and the relatives of the criminal's victims are greeted with civility at the prison gate and invited inside to view the proceedings from corridors that surround the death chamber.

In midafternoon, a cameraman for KTVT, who has had his camera set up with an ample shot of the prison, gets into a hot dispute with a cameraman who has set up beside him. "You motherfucker," he shouts. "You're taking away my shot." The two almost come to blows. Five prison guards run over to the scene. "Stop this profanity now," one of them shouts with a Texas twang. "Any more profanity and you're out of here." The old-fashioned word *profanity* lingers in my ears. They kill people in here, but profane language is not allowed.

Neither are cigarettes. When one inmate who was about to be put to death here last year requested a final cigarette, he was told that this was out of the question, that this was a "smoke-free facility." Death row inmates are also not allowed to touch someone from outside the building. Even on the day of her execution, Karla Faye is not allowed to touch or embrace her husband. Actually, she has never touched him, since they were married by proxy when she was already on death row.

At 5:00 P.M., we are informed that the two appeals to the Supreme Court have been shunted aside. Six o'clock draws near. The hour of death. The media people draw close to the mikes for news. They grow quieter with death in the air. Meanwhile the pro-death chanters are working themselves into an ever greater frenzy just down the slight hill away from the media area. Suddenly a helicopter appears overhead and begins to circle the prison. For the next half hour the noise of the helicopter makes it very difficult to hear anything from the microphones. I meet an American whose girlfriend is here doing a report for Le Figaro in Paris. For a few moments, as we talk about France, the execution, the helicopter, and the snarling pro–death penalty crowd disappear.

At about 6:20 P.M., the witnesses walk out of the building to our left and across the street and up the front steps of the prison. I recognize Ron Carlson, the brother of the woman killed, who has forgiven Karla Faye and accepts her now as "a sister in Christ" and has steadfastly opposed the execution. The group of guards on the front steps, wearing large white cowboy hats, steps aside to allow the witnesses to enter to view the grisly event. The guards in the white hats are sepulchral.

At about 6:50 P.M., the first witness appears at the mikes in front of us. My heart sinks as I see him approach. Karla Faye is dead. The helicopter still circles in the dark sky above, and it is difficult to hear. From below comes the sound of cheering and then the singing of the song one hears at the end of football and hockey games. "Nya, Nya, Nya, Nya, gooood-bye . . ."

A few hours later in my hotel room in Houston I learn the details of the decision to execute Karla Faye and the scene in the execution chamber. The high point of the drama was George Bush's announcement in Austin that he was not going to grant a thirty-day stay of execution. He added that he has prayed for Karla Faye and for her victims. He said he was leaving it to "a higher authority" to judge her. With this pusillanimous, buck-passing comment, the last hurdle was cleared.

Strapped to a gurney, Karla Faye was wheeled into the execution chamber. She spoke first to those in the room where people close to the victims waited. She apologized for her part in the murders. She turned then for her very last remarks to the other window. Behind it were her husband, family, and friends—including Ron Carlson. She offered her love and the promise that she would see them again. The execution commenced. She was declared dead at 6:45.

The next morning I see another television interview with Richard Thornton, the husband of Karla Faye's female victim. His large, dark face appears on the screen. His jowls are partly covered by a black beard. He looks hatefully into the camera. When asked what he had thought of Karla Faye's apology the night before, Thornton scowls and describes the words she spoke to the relatives of the victims as a "canned little speech," nothing like the loving things she said to those near and dear to her. He gives no quarter. His attitude to Karla Faye, long set in stone, remains implacable.

Thornton's role in the media drama of the past couple of months has been crucial. He appeared on numerous television shows, including *Larry King Live.* His position was that his wife had never received any sympathy or mercy from Karla Faye and therefore Karla Faye should get no mercy. His was a biblical attachment to the notion of an eye for an eye.

In Houston, on the day of the slayings, June 13, 1983,

Thornton and his wife, Deborah, had a quarrel and he threw her out of their home. She left and encountered Jerry Lynn Dean, a former lover of Karla Faye Tucker. Later in the day, Deborah phoned her husband to ask if she could return home, but Thornton said she could not. Deborah went to the home of Jerry Lynn Dean. A while afterward, Tucker and her current boyfriend, Daniel Ryan Garrett, arrived at the house to steal Dean's motorcycle. They found Deborah and Dean in bed. Tucker and her boyfriend used the pickax, which happened to be by the side of the bed, to hack the couple to death.

On the morning after the execution, Thornton dispensed advice to the relatives of crime victims. Go and attend the execution, he said. It will make a world of difference to you. He claimed people said he even looked different now that it was over.

As for Karla Faye, in the last days of her life, she showed that she was indifferent to the choice being made by her executioners. To her, the path she was following was that of the Lord, and she would follow it wherever it led. Even though I do not count myself a believer, her simple conviction that in the lethal injection chamber she would be "going home" has left its mark on me.

I cannot get around the fact that the one real break Karla Faye ever had was her years on death row. There, for the only time in her life, she was able to escape from her terrible past. And then, when her transformation was complete and she had become an exemplary person in the eyes of so many, she was put to death.

The immediate effect of Karla Faye's execution is to open the door to yet more executions, in Texas and elsewhere in the United States. If she could be turned down for commutation, considering her clear case of redemption and rehabilitation, so could anyone.

There are now about thirty-five hundred people on death row in the United States. The evolving judicial regime makes it likely that within a few years there will be, on average, an execution a day in the United States. By December 15, 1999, the number of executions for 1999 had reached ninety-six, by far the highest total in any year since the resumption of executions in the United Sates in 1977.[5] When it comes to executions, the United States is heading away from the consensus in other advanced Western countries, which is to end capital punishment. Instead, the United States is putting itself in the company of such countries as Iran, Iraq, and China on the issue.

Two main rational arguments are advanced by the proponents of executions: those executed can never kill again, and executions deter others from committing capital crimes. Needless to say, the first argument is faultless, but it is not very important. That's because the difference between execution and life imprisonment, with no chance of release, is negligible. The proposition that executions deter future murders has always been the center of the rational case for capital punishment. And yet the many empirical studies conducted over many decades in various parts of the world have shown no compelling evidence that the threat of executions causes would-be killers to stay their hand. If anything, there is evidence that socially and demographically similar jurisdictions without the death penalty tend to have somewhat lower murder rates than those with capital punishment. There is even evidence that in the months following a highly publicized execution, there is a small but perceptible tendency for the murder rate to increase.[6]

The steep rise in the number of executions in the United States in recent years is driven by passion. Some might object that the raucous crowd whose members held obscene signs and shrieked for the death of Karla Faye expressed a synthetic, not a real, passion. I don't buy this. The hate and the emotional heat were too intense for this explanation to stand. It was as if those in the death-penalty crowd were using the fact that a woman was about to be put to death to work themselves into a state where they could leave the norms of society behind them. They were seeking freedom from restraint. To them, the blood in the air was intoxicating, liberating.

Only a very small percentage of American murderers are executed. In the United States, those whose lives end in death chambers are chosen through a highly politicized lottery in which some people are much more likely to draw the death ticket than others. One hundred thousand Americans are in prison for murder, but although the number being put to death is rapidly rising, from five in 1983 to seventy-four in 1997, only a tiny percentage of those found guilty of murder will ever be executed.

Those who win this unluckiest of lotteries are invariably the poor, the undereducated, and those from broken families. The rich are never executed in the United States, not ever. And there is a very strong taboo against putting women to death, particularly in Texas. As the dean of an Ohio law school who studies the death penalty put it, "Texans just don't treat their women that way." The main reason Karla Faye's case attracted so much national attention is that since the resumption of executions in the U.S., only one woman has faced the executioner. If women are much less likely to be executed than men, black men have a much greater chance of drawing the death ticket than white men. Thirty-nine percent of those executed between 1977 and 1995 were black, even though blacks constitute only 12.6 percent of the American population.[7]

The execution lottery is cruelly skewed in other ways. It makes a great difference in which state or even in which county the murderer commits the crime. You are much more likely to be executed if you kill in Texas, the site of half the executions in the United States in 1997, than in other states. And your odds against facing execution improve if you commit murder in a county that is too poor to afford to prosecute a capital case. It costs much more for the legal process that sends a murderer to the lethal injection chamber than it does to convict him to spend his life behind bars.

The frequency of executions has been increasing during a period when the number of violent crimes in the United States, including murders, is declining. Through their judicial appointments, during their combined twelve years in the White House, Ronald Reagan and George Bush pushed the law courts sharply to the right. By the autumn of 1991, these two presidents had transformed the Supreme Court and had filled over half the country's 837 federal judgeships.[8] A consequence of a conservative bench has been to speed up the time it takes to travel from death sentence to execution by removing some of the steps in the appeals process.

If right-wing politics distills the passion, making it a more potent political force, what is the source of the passion? In western Europe and in Canada, the death penalty has been abolished, despite some strong popular support in its favor. To an extent, in the countries where capital punishment has been eliminated, it is a case of political elites exercising their judgment and authority, even when the public does not agree. But there is more to it. Division and hatred in those societies is not as ferocious as in the United States. It is the desire of people to draw sharp lines between themselves and others that motivates executions. The death penalty is the ultimate expression of social exclusion. It draws an absolute distinction between decent society on one side and the condemned outcasts who are to be deprived of life.

There are many lines of conflict in a society that lead to the desire for the exclusion of some by others—class, religion, and gender, to name some of the most important. In the United States, the most significant has been race. The desire to exclude others along racial lines has been a potent force in American

life since the first European settlements in the seventeenth century. The ultimate expression of exclusion was slavery and the
slave trade, a scar so deep in America that it left its mark in the
American Constitution, which notoriously counted slaves as
being worth three-fifths of a person when calculating representation in the U.S. House of Representatives. After slavery
was abolished, as a consequence of America's greatest war,
exclusion based on race imposed a system of racial apartheid
on the South that endured until the 1960s. Fear and exclusion
based on race is still a hurricane force in American life.

The summer of 1998 is deadly in Texas. Day after day, the temperature in Dallas exceeds one hundred degrees. The poor
who have no air conditioning, especially the aged among them,
are suffering. The death toll from the savage heat rises. On July
15, when the temperature in Dallas hits 112 degrees, Governor
George W. Bush, America's top executioner, sanctimoniously
tells a television reporter: "This is a serious situation in Texas
and we must all pray for rain."[9]

# part two

# MAKING IT
# IN AMERICA

# OLD AND NEW WEST

ALEXIS DE TOCQUEVILLE noted in 1835 the peculiar ferocity of Americans in their quest for material betterment:

> It is strange to see with what feverish ardor the Americans pursue their own welfare; and to watch the vague dread that constantly torments them lest they should not have chosen the shortest path which may lead to it.
>
> A native of the United States clings to this world's goods as if he were certain never to die; and he is so hasty in grasping at all within his reach, that one would suppose he was constantly afraid of not living long enough to enjoy them. He clutches everything, he holds nothing fast, but soon loosens his grasp to pursue fresh gratifications.[1]

"Making it" is the great American passion. It is a passion that at times threatens to subsume all the others, giving the United States the feel of a one-myth culture, in which, as the popular saying has it, whoever has the most toys when he dies, wins. One of the great paradoxes of American life is that while the gap between rich and poor is greater in the United States than in any other advanced country, no one is as committed to the virtue of upward mobility as are Americans. Changes in the ways Americans "make it" have proven to be fundamental turning points in American history. Today, America is undergoing an immense economic shift, which is creating new winners and vast numbers of losers. The transition from the industrial economy to the information economy has led to legions of new corporations and superrich moguls, while it has consigned many long-established corporations and their owners to degrees of oblivion.

President Calvin Coolidge's famous maxim from the 1920s that "the business of the United States is business"[2] can hardly be improved upon as an assertion of the first principle that contemporary America operates on.

The question of who's making it and who's not in contemporary America was the focus of my trip to Nebraska, Wyoming, and Colorado.

Page, Nebraska, is tucked away in America's heartland. When I ask Bud, a farmer whose land lies just outside Page, if he knows all two hundred people in town, he says he figures he knows everybody within ten miles. When the crops are tall in the fields, northeastern Nebraska has the shimmering look of a green, gentle sea. The drive to Page from the west took me first through ranch lands where every now and then cattle were huddled together in the hot sun beside small pools of water. I went for miles up and down the rolling hills without seeing a single vehicle. The towns are few and far between. With their farm equipment depots on the edge of town and their old main streets, general stores, and little restaurants, these towns appear as though they are out of an American scene from decades ago. Even the slick advertising billboards of the bigger centers are absent.

Accompanying me on this voyage across elysium is a wacky

but lyrical program on Nebraska Public Radio called *Christmas in July*. Outside it is so hot that the cattle are in danger of perishing, but I am listening to the world's finest choirs and orchestras playing Christmas music. "Stille Nacht."

I am traversing this wonderful country en route to Page to attend a reunion of the Ickes family, whose members I am not even distantly related to. This substantial wing of the family—Harold Ickes was secretary of the interior in the Roosevelt administration in the thirties and his son Harold Jr. held a high office in the Clinton administration—is descended from a Nebraska couple who lived near Page during the tough times of the Great Depression. Their eight offspring and the children, grandchildren, and spouses of the eight are gathering for the fourth time in fifteen years.

When I arrive at the farm where the reunion is to be held, I receive a warm welcome. The Ickes descendants have been told by a friend of mine who is part of the family that I am an author writing a book about the United States and that I have come to record the stories of their lives. There are about 125 people present, including several who are in their late eighties as well as an array of toddlers, great-grandchildren of the original Ickes couple.

Most of those present have been farmers or have had close associations with farmers all their lives. This is a red-meat crowd—every meal from morning to night at the great open-air barbecue operation features beef. Vegetarians and chicken lovers do not fare well here. Neither do those who like a glass of wine with their steak: not a drop of alcohol is served during the entire reunion. Despite a little gossip by some about others at the reunion and about some who have not attended, there is remarkable affection and goodwill among those present. The descendants are a strikingly handsome lot, from the straight-backed elderly folk to the teenagers and children.

One of the shrewdest is Soren Sorensen, who is known as Junior, even though he is almost eighty. He is tall with a long face and the large hands of a man who has worked on a farm all his life. He has the gentle yet strong manner of someone who knows about the physical world but doesn't need to dress himself up in pretensions about manliness. This week the newscasts in America have been full of alarm about the heat wave that has seared the country. In Nebraska three thousand cattle have died because of the heat. The ranchers have been working day and night watering them down, to keep them standing in pools of water, and to prevent them from huddling too close together. Farther east the heat wave has wiped out the corn crop for thousands of farmers, pushing many of them into financial ruin.

Soren tells me that he is not too worried about Nebraska corn, the crop on his land and the dominant crop in this part of the state. The growing season got off to a slow start this year, he says, so the heat wave will speed things up, and unless something goes wrong in the next few weeks, it'll be a good crop. He conveys this information with the resigned, philosophical air of one who has seen good seasons and bad.

The real problem for the farmers, Soren tells me, is low prices for their crops. Low prices are driving family farmers out of business. The big operators, the agribiz companies, can still turn a profit despite low prices, he continues. It isn't that the family farmers haven't worked hard and invested in improving their land. Most of the land around here is irrigated by means of wells, which have been sunk on each farm. Big money is spent spreading inches of water each season to every corner of the crop. This huge effort has trebled, even quadrupled, output per acre and has dramatically increased the value of the land. But still the farmers are fighting a battle that they are losing. As in others parts of the country, the abandonment of local rail lines has added to the woes of many farmers who now have to truck their crop at higher cost to more distant rail shipment points.

Farmers like Soren have a habit of thinking dialectically in ways that confound city dwellers. When I mention the weather to Soren, he changes the subject to the prices farmers get for their crops. When I mention prices, he wants to talk about irrigation. The reason for this habit of mind is the conundrum that when crops are bountiful, oversupply drives down prices; when crops are poor, prices are higher, but farmers don't have much to sell. And these days, while many farmers are being ruined by heat waves and droughts, others are producing bumper crops. The supply-and-demand equations still work, but no matter how they come out, it seems that the farmers are doomed.

As Soren talks to me in his measured voice, we are sitting at one of the long tables at the reunion eating watermelon. The sun is sinking in the west, its last embers lighting a rosy fire across the sky. The heartland feels so bountiful on this warm evening, but Soren isn't the only person who tells me about the slow disappearance of the way of life that has made the Midwest one of the world's great breadbaskets. A woman about sixty-five years old, who has spent many years of her life writing a weekly column for a local newspaper, makes the point that what has kept farmers on the land is their love for their way of life. No one in his right mind would work so hard for so little income, she says.

Sybil, one of the daughters of the original Ickes couple, is a ball of fire who is determined in her flamboyant way to fight for the cattle ranchers who are also up against threats from outside forces. She is writing a book about the saga of one group of ranchers who settled in western Nebraska near the town of Gordon in 1896. The ranchers, who hailed originally from West Virginia, made the trek to Gordon, where there was vast potential ranch land. Sybil's nemesis is Ted Turner, the

CNN mogul who has taken a big interest in her part of the country, both in western Nebraska and in neighboring Wyoming. Turner's dream—his nightmare fantasy, in Sybil's eyes—is to reclaim a great swath of land from cattle ranchers across the heart of the country from Texas to the Canadian border and to populate it with giant herds of buffalo. (Although the number of buffalo is a fraction of what it was in the mid-nineteenth century, it has been rapidly replenishing in recent decades.) Sybil says Turner wants to obliterate the whole history of the homesteaders, their homes, their way of life, and that is why she is writing a history to reclaim and affirm their experience.

Sybil's son, a rancher from Wyoming, is a tough-looking, wiry guy. He has resolved to show environmentalists that cattle are not the enemy and that cattle ranching can go hand in hand with sustaining an intact ecological system. He says cattle have to be managed properly, and he claims he has been winning converts among environmentalists who used to believe that the only solution was to remove cattle from the ranges of Wyoming. He has a wry view of Ted Turner's crusade to repopulate the plains with buffalo. He thinks Turner doesn't appreciate that the buffalo have changed from the time more than a century ago when they roamed the range in great migratory herds. In those days, he says, the buffalo were kept on the move by their fear of predators. Today, the buffalo are essentially tame and the predators are no longer present in large numbers. The result, says this environmentally conscious cowboy, is that today's buffalo are much like cattle—they stay put where they are on the land, and they overgraze unless they are managed. He adds with a smile that the main difference between cattle and buffalo in terms of their impact on the land is that the buffalo are "politically correct."

One unforgettable character at the reunion is Millard, a businessman who now lives in Arizona. He is still an active rodeo

cowboy even though he is almost eighty years old. Millard
participates in rodeo events where two partners compete
against other teams. The rule for these teams is that the combined age of the two members must exceed one hundred.
Usually this means a fifty-two-year-old and a forty-eight-year-
old team up, but because of Millard's age, his partner is in his
early twenties. Millard ropes the steers and the young guy jumps
off his horse and ties them. A winning combination. I wish I
could see him in action, but he won't be performing at the
reunion.

Not all the people who have come to the reunion are farmers, ranchers, or old rodeo cowboys. Dennis, a practicing
Mormon, who is divorced, drove to Page from Salt Lake City
with his two daughters and his new fiancée. During Richard
Nixon's presidency, Dennis, at the age of twenty-nine, was the
youngest ever assistant secretary of the interior. He is a true
entrepreneur, moving restlessly from field to field, making
money in each one of them. He is moving into a new Internet-
related business. While others at the reunion are relaxing in
long conversations with people they have not seen for years,
Dennis is restless, driving into town for soft drinks or on his
cell phone checking on his businesses.

Fred, about fifty, is a doctor who lives in Seattle and specializes in diseases of the lungs. He seems perfectly acclimated
to life in the Pacific Northwest and does not long to return to
the Arcadian fields of his Nebraska forebears. He likes the new
Seattle, especially since it has rocketed upward from the bad
times it experienced in the 1980s to the boom days of the city
as a high-tech center. Another participant at the reunion who
is not a farmer but who did stay in the region is Mary Emma,
a retired schoolteacher from nearby Norfolk, the town where
Johnny Carson grew up. In her eyes the former talk-show host
is a wonderful guy. He came back to Norfolk years ago to fete
his former grade-school teacher when she celebrated her one

hundredth birthday. Without fanfare he has donated large sums of money to the town to help out with its schools.

What I was seeing on that warm summer evening was the last of an America of family farmers—the America idealized by Thomas Jefferson and by William Jennings Bryan, the great Nebraska orator-politician of the turn of the last century. Bryan, known as the "boy orator of the Platte," was the greatest political leader ever to come out of Nebraska. When he spoke at the Democratic convention in 1896, where he won the party's presidential nomination, he issued a passionate warning about the financial interests, with their gold standard, that were threatening to crush America's farmers: "Burn down your cities and leave our farms, and your cities will spring up again as if by magic; but destroy our farms and the grass will grow in the streets of every city in the country. . . . You shall not press down upon the brow of labor this crown of thorns, you shall not crucify mankind upon a cross of gold."[3] A century after Bryan's speech stirred the vast legions of America's farmers, the details of the debate about the gold standard were long forgotten. His true cause was to rally America to the defense of the family farm. At the dawn of the twenty-first century, the cause still moved many people, but the battle was all but lost.

West of Page, the same pressures that are destroying family farms across the corn belt are also at work, wreaking their havoc on the cattle ranchers. And as the Old West is dying, a new one is being born.

Somewhere in Nebraska, there is a geographical, sociocultural line between the Midwest and the West. One woman, who is a sociologist of the West, told me the crucial divide is between the Midwest, which receives more rainfall, and the West, which is drier and requires irrigation. When I tried that definition on the farmers at Page, they weren't much impressed by it. There is plenty of irrigation in eastern Nebraska, they said, and eastern Nebraska is clearly in the Midwest. But western Nebraska is a different matter. Here the country is like a tabletop tilted at an angle. As you go west, you climb toward Wyoming. The climb is so steady that you hardly notice it. In western Nebraska, between North Platte and Ogallala, you cross from Central Time to Mountain Time. When you get here, you're in the West. The cornfields that stretch across eastern Nebraska and Iowa and Illinois are far behind. Ahead is the great plateau of Wyoming.

The altitude rises as one drives into Wyoming along the I-80 from Nebraska. Cheyenne, the state capital, which is only forty miles beyond the border, is more than 6,000 feet above sea level. I stop driving fifty miles farther on, in Laramie, where the altitude is just above 7,100 feet. I go for my morning run just north of Laramie on the great plain where you can see for tens of miles and pick out small details in the clear thin air. My legs feel strong, but my lungs are hot and pressured. I'm working to get enough air.

From the plain north of Laramie, there is a clear view of the Snowy Range Mountains about thirty-five miles to the west. These mountains actually soar to 12,000 feet, but because the plateau at Laramie is so elevated, they don't appear to be nearly so high. When I drive through the Snowy Range and stop at the high point along the highway, at about 10,500 feet, even a brief climb above the parking spot leaves me feeling clammy and a little short of breath.

Laramie is a bare-bones Western town. Its downtown looks like a movie set with its stand-alone brick-and-cinder-block buildings. Vehicles, mostly pickups, vans, and aging American cars, move slowly along the wide streets. The fact that Laramie was built as a way station en route to somewhere else still overshadows the center of town. Right down along the edge of First Street run the railway yards. When the first transcontinental railway hit Wyoming in 1867, the towns of Cheyenne, Laramie, and Rawlins sprang like mushrooms from the great plateau. The Union Pacific made Laramie. On the bare plain around the town, it is captivating to watch the mile-long trains hauling their loads either east or west. In the center of Laramie, there is a walkway across the tracks. You can stand up above the trains, watching them shunting up and down in the yards. If you are in luck, a great monster of a train will slide beneath your feet on its way to Denver or Salt Lake City. The romance of the trains attracts Laramie natives and outsiders to this spot. Perhaps it's not so much romance but despair that draws some people here to the edge of this hard little town to dream of an escape to somewhere else, anywhere else. Wyoming has one of the highest suicide rates in the United States.

The big industry in Laramie, if I can call it that, is the University of Wyoming. The Laramie campus, UW's only one, is the town's biggest employer. The presence of thousands of students, academics, and full-time university employees creates the basis for Laramie's ample liberal counterculture. Identity is a big question in this town. You encounter the raw edges of the town's culture war wherever you turn—represented by the mystique of the cowboy.

*Mystique* is the right word to use, because the cowboy culture has metastasized far beyond anything related to the men who actually work on ranches. In some ways Wyoming has a better claim to being the true locus of cowboy culture than any other state, though certainly Texas, New Mexico, and others have strong claims to make. There were cowboys working in Mexico and the Southwest long before there was settlement in Wyoming, but it was Wyoming's version of the cowboy—an English-speaking, dashingly independent figure adept with horses and master of the plains—that captured the imagination of America.

The real age of the great cowspreads of Wyoming lasted only a couple of decades, from the completion of the transcontinental railway in 1869 until the devastating blizzard of the winter of 1887–88 that wiped out the herds of many of the cattlemen.[4] But if the cowboys freely roamed the range as transitional figures in the process of settlement, they made an indelible imprint on the American mind and more pointedly on the concept of manhood that still prevails in much of the American West. A cowboy on a bucking bronco has been featured on Wyoming license plates for decades. The state's link to the cowboy ethos is strengthened by the legends of scouts like Jim Bridger and Kit Carson and most of all Buffalo Bill Cody, the pony express rider, buffalo slaughterer, and showman who once scalped an Indian in a skirmish.

Nearby Cheyenne is hosting its annual Frontier Days festivities, and I decide to attend. The rodeo bills itself as "the daddy of 'em all." Having bought myself a handsome black cowboy hat (made in Mexico), I find my seat in the stands. Before the competitors ride into the stadium in the grand parade, the show begins with a tribute to America. A young woman rides in carrying an enormous U.S. flag. She reins in her horse right in front of the center of the stands. The emcee, who has already captivated us with his manly Western twang, begins to sing as the young woman on horseback holds the huge flag aloft. "Gawd bless America again," sings the emcee. "Wash her pretty face . . ." the song goes on. The Stars and Stripes ripples in the soft breeze as he intones in a deep voice with just a touch of used-car-dealer smarm that America is the freest country in the world, and that its armed forces have kept it that way for 220 or so years.

Before the cowboys do their stuff, out come the girls, a dozen of them on horseback. Wearing Stetsons, the girls each carry a big flag, but these are corporate, not patriotic, banners. Each flag bears the logo of a corporate sponsor and these flags are saluted by the emcee one by one. He calls the girls "dandies" and the crowd gives them a big hand. Then the dandies ride off to let the men do their work.

Professional rodeo cowboys and the clowns and riders who back them up have a lot of grit. No one can take that away from them. Clinging to the back of an angry, raging bull and trying to stay there for eight seconds and then getting out of his way after being thrown to the dirt is no tender occupation. Late in the afternoon, one of the rodeo bull riders stays down in the dirt, and the members of the medical staff, about fifteen of them, all wearing cowboys hats, run out onto the field. The poor guy lies still as the medics work on him, preparing a stretcher. The emcee is going on about how tough a life this is and that we've got to feel for a rider who gets hurt and has to stay off the circuit for a while. These guys don't get paid when they can't work, he reminds us.

Several times in the course of the show, the dandies ride back out with their corporate flags. Pretty girls, tough men. The roles in this pageant are very clear. Manly, free, violent but tender, ornery and lovable, the cowboy is the worker-troubador-romantic of American mythology. He is an anti-dote to unions, feminists, hippies, book learning, gays, and government.

On Second Street in Laramie, a block from the railway tracks, pretty close to the motel where I am staying, there is an ugly little bar called the Fireside. On the outside wall of the establishment is the image of a garish red flame licking at the building. One night in October 1998, Matthew Shepard, a gay college student of slight stature, was enticed to leave the Fireside by two young men, Russell Henderson and Aaron McKinney. In a pickup truck, the two men robbed Shepard and beat him with their fists and a Smith & Wesson .357 Magnum. They drove him to the plain just outside town, lashed his hands behind him, and tied him to a fence pole. There they resumed the savage beating, leaving him with bruises between the legs and elsewhere, where they kicked him. Shepard was still clinging to life when Henderson and McKinney drove off. The next morning, about eighteen hours later, the police discovered Shepard, unconscious. Five days later, he died.

Though the perpetrators of this hideous crime were quickly disowned by the people of Laramie, in truth in many ways they were not so different from a lot of young men—manual workers with tough-luck, but not particularly unusual, backgrounds. Like too many other young men, their struggle to define themselves as virile involved a virulent hatred for gays. What distinguished them from others is that they pushed their gay-bashing impulses to a violent, pathological extreme. Understandably, towns like Laramie deeply resent being placed on the couch by analysts and the media in the wake of a heinous murder. Why should the people of Laramie be saddled with some kind of collective blame just because two psychopaths happened to do their dirty deed on their terrain?

One evening at sunset, I run along a road that traverses the windswept plain just north of Laramie, and there I meet a long-time resident of the town who has left Laramie for greener pastures. He is back for a few days visiting family and friends. We sit at the side of the road, watching the sun go down, and he tells me about deep rifts in Laramie. When he was growing up here in the 1960s, there was what he called a cowboy-hippie divide. His father taught at the university, and he was clearly on the hippie side of the division. Every year during Laramie's Frontier Days annual festival, my interlocutor stayed well away from anything to do with the great cowboy bash. I still had my cowboy hat with me from the rodeo in Cheyenne, and it was clear that he did not regard it as a badge of civility. As a kid, more than once, he came home from Frontier Days with a bloody nose. The Cowboy Bar, located on Third Street in the center of town, was a place this man always avoided. In fact, he routinely crossed the street so as not to walk past it. He tells me that fights were no rare thing in Laramie among the teenagers, especially between the cowboy types and Latino kids. Indeed, on the night they left Shepard for dead, McKinney and Henderson ran into two Latinos, Emiliano Morales and Jeremy Herrera. They got into a fight with the two that was broken up when the police arrived.

The cowboy-hippie divide in Laramie can be seen in the stark differences between the Cowboy Bar and the Coal Creek Coffee Company, located only a few blocks away on Grand Avenue. If the Cowboy Bar exudes the macho image celebrated at rodeos, the Coal Creek Coffee Company is a big, comfortable place where you can get all the latte and biscotti you want, just as though you were in Seattle or New York or anywhere else in urban America. Inside, you will find a grab bag of customers, the local cops, counterculture types, lesbian couples, tourists, and people who want somewhere to read, talk, or play chess. At Coal Creek, I picked up the July 13 copy of a locally written coffee-shop news sheet featuring a lengthy article in which the editor, Dennis Parkhurst, warned about the danger of religious fundamentalism to America. He compared it to the "insane hatred that lived in the public mind of the German citizens at the time of the rise of Hitler," concluding that it was the "same kind of hatred that motivates the abortion-clinic bomber to act as he does."

About halfway between the Cowboy Bar and the Coal Creek is a large bookstore with shelves that are well stocked with the latest best-sellers, but it also has an entire stand devoted to an endless selection of magazines about guns and ammo and gun advocacy. For sheer selection I've never seen anything like it.

I spent my last night in Laramie at a barbecue. In the summer about forty university people get together once a week for a potluck supper at a little wooden house on First Street right across from the railway tracks. No one appears to be living in the house right now, but it is owned by friends of this crowd. Some of these people teach at UW, others are graduate students there, and the rest are not really affiliated with the university but are friends of friends that have been adopted into the group. I talk for some time to a guy, whose name I never learned, who was born in a small town in Arizona that has since been swallowed up by suburban Phoenix. When he was growing up—he is about forty—there were still occasional rattlesnakes on the streets. He came to Laramie planning to complete his Ph.D. in the social sciences, but things didn't go as he'd hoped and he ended up instead working at UW as a part-time janitor, where he now earns $14,000 a year. His personal situation has turned his mind to what is happening to a lot of people in Laramie. His credit cards are maxed out, and he has caller ID so he can keep an eye out for calls from creditors. He believes the middle class is a vanishing species in Laramie, that at the top end there are a few people who are very well off, but that there are more and more people working at low-paying service-sector jobs.

This man, who has thought a lot about the social structure of Wyoming, talks about a "new colonialism in the West." His is not the vocabulary of the cowboy-hippie separation, but in some ways his language gets much more to the point about what is happening in Wyoming. He sees a state that used to be a part of the Old West, by which he means a region with an economy based on primary products, the two key ones being ranching and coal mining. As a result of strip mining, Wyoming today produces more coal than West Virginia. Seen this way, forgetting cultural stereotypes, the cowboys have much in common with the coal miners.

The Old West, he contends, is being overshadowed, indeed subjugated, by the new. In Wyoming, the new Westerners are the wealthy, mostly from California, who have come to the state to purchase "getaway" properties where they can come to relax and unwind. The center of getaway country, which is transforming the economy of Wyoming, is the northwestern corner of the state around Yellowstone and Grand Teton National Parks. The town of Jackson, once a sleepy cowtown, is now a burgeoning tourism center. Not surprisingly, the well-to-do who are flooding into Wyoming to play are driving up land prices. And the newcomers don't like the ways of old Wyoming. Certainly, they like to envelop themselves in the myth of the cowboys, he hastily adds. And they even fancy themselves as ranchers when they set up "ranchettes" for themselves. And they don't approve of the raw Wyoming of the past. They get upset when they see guys driving through town in pickups with firearms. And they disapprove when people celebrate from time to time by blowing off great supplies of fireworks.

My friend the janitor at UW believes there are great problems in America today having to do with the rise of a small number of wealthy people who run everything. But he doesn't have much use for the theory that there are too many guns around. He says that it's harder to get a gun in America today than ever in history. He doesn't much like what he sees as the all-too-interfering state. In this, he is repeating a theme that is everywhere in evidence in contemporary America. What makes him different is that he doesn't think the direction of American capitalism is good for Wyoming, or for that matter, for the world. He believes America has created a huge world empire that is much like the British empire. And he thinks the division of the world between rich and poor will someday provoke a great war.

Others at the barbecue echo the complaint. Tourism is becoming the state's leading industry, but it doesn't pay well and it allows outsiders to control you. There is no doubt that these people feel they are being battered from the outside by money, by power, by a changing society. They feel it and they don't like it. The problem is they're not sure what to do about it. At some level, perhaps they're not even sure they want to do anything about it. As elsewhere in my travels, I am encountering people who don't believe the much-ballyhooed great prosperity of the moment is doing them any good. But even if Laramie hasn't been blessed by much of the leaven of new wealth, places not far away have certainly felt it. Fewer than three hours away by car, Denver has been rocketing upward, as everyone at this gathering in Laramie is well aware. What to do? Defend what's left of the autonomy of a forbidding place like Laramie where the air may be a little too thin for most Americans? Or come down to a slightly lower altitude, both literally and figuratively, to get a piece of the new prosperity?

One man at the barbecue is drawing conclusions that are both more negative and more political. Rick is a home renovator in his mid-forties who has traveled widely in the world but who has always called Laramie his home. He believes that Americans are hopelessly hooked on their drive for more money and more things. He thinks this potent materialism is unstoppable, that there is no basis in American thought for any sort of effective counterforce. Rick says he has run into social democrats in other countries, and he is inclined to think the way they do about society. But he cautions that Americans have "no sense of the state or the public sector," no inclination toward acting on behalf of collectivities and not just individuals. Rick is thinking of leaving the United States, perhaps for Canada.

Perched in the foothills of the Rockies, Boulder, Colorado, is located about forty-five miles from Denver. In the long run, that may be a little too close for comfort to the mushrooming metropolis. But Boulder is still far enough from the exurban offshoots of the big city to be its own place—and a very exclusive and desirable place it is. After I'd run for days in Laramie in air that remained noticeably too thin, Boulder was a treat. Its five thousand feet in altitude, two thousand lower than Laramie, let my lungs relax as I ran. Small wonder that athletic teams are often trained in Laramie, then moved to lower altitudes for competition.

A big educational, high-tech, and recreational center, Boulder is a yuppie town. The contrast with poor old Laramie could not be more pronounced. Right in the center of the city is a pedestrian mall, flanked by the name shops you'd find in Beverly Hills. Big, comfortable coffeehouses abound. The populace is tanned, fit, and fashionable.

From the pedestrian mall, I wander over to the Boulder Farmers' Market, one of the most self-conscious markets I've ever seen. In Boulder, organic food is the name of the game. Shoppers in the market scurry off to their vehicles carrying bags of organic delights. Off at the side of the market, I find a little political gathering attended by some of the most well-turned-out, healthy-looking people I've seen this side of Martha's Vineyard. Lo and behold, these comfortable people, in their light summer suits and frocks and Gucci shoes, are Boulder's liberals. The gathering is for a candidate for the Boulder City Council by the name of Françoise Poinsatte. She is a thirty-nine-year-old Democrat, and her brochure lists her record of activity in various and sundry civic organizations. Her platform takes a mildly anti-developer line, asserting that Boulder needs careful growth, not unregulated explosion, and that this desirable goal can be achieved through comprehensive planning. Poinsatte also wants Boulder to be a city that retains its diversity, by which I guess she means that it should not become exclusively an enclave for the rich. In fact, it already looks as if it's well down the road to being exactly that.

The well-dressed, attractive candidate is chatting with a small group of supporters. I find a carefully coifed dark-haired man off to one side. He turns out to be Poinsatte's husband. He is amiably low-key as he tells me about the campaign and their goal of keeping Boulder a manageable, community-centered place. By his side is a young man with the definite look of a political operative. He says that today in Boulder there are far more jobs on offer than there are people willing to take them. I figure that's always been the lot of upscale places—they tend to drive their proletarians out of town and then they have trouble finding peons to do the service-sector jobs. So it was when I lived on the Côte d'Azur, so it is in Boulder. I inform the young man that I'm from Toronto, and he fires back, "I once flew to Cuba from Toronto." I guess these really are Boulder's liberals.

Just as I am leaving this crowd, I pass two men who are chatting portentously. Both are carrying bags full of organic corn. The man who is talking is in his thirties, thin, with a stylish suit and tie, and he is wearing a button for Françoise Poinsatte. "Just as California is ground zero for national issues," he says importantly, "Boulder is ground zero for municipal issues." Now I feel grounded.

That evening, in light rain, I decide to take a drive out past the house where Boulder's horrific, nationally notorious murder took place. The killing of JonBenet Ramsey, the six-year-old beauty queen, on December 24, 1996, remains unsolved years later. The little girl was strangled in her family home at 755 Fifteenth Street. The police investigators famously bungled the case when they allowed the little girl's mother and father to wander around the crime scene, creating the potential for evidence tampering. The pathetic crime, with its lurid overtones of child exploitation, still provides weekly fare for the tabloids. Every few months, Larry King assembles yet another panel to gossip about who did it—JonBenet's mother, her father, or someone else—and about whether charges will ever be brought.

For some reason this part of Colorado, the new frontier for the newly affluent, seems to be a spawning ground for sensational crimes. The next morning I set out for the site of the most sensational of them all, the killings at Columbine High School, in Littleton, Colorado, on April 20, 1998.

It is July 29, 1999, precisely one hundred days since Eric
Harris and Dylan Klebold took the lives of twelve students
and one teacher and then completed their rampage by turning their guns on themselves. I drive around the perimeter of
huge, sprawling Denver with its stark skyline. This is a
magnificent urban setting with the foothills of the Rocky
Mountains rising above the mile-high plateau where the city
is located. Everywhere there are billboards for John Elway's
car dealership featuring a toothy picture of the former Denver
quarterback. Far past the city center, I approach Littleton,
which is right on the doorstop of dramatic mountain peaks.

It must have seemed to be the pot of gold at the end of the
rainbow for the young families in the sports utility vehicles,
Jeeps and station wagons—mere cars are rare here—who
migrated to this new community on the edge of the foothills.
The main thoroughfares in Littleton are wide and clean.
Something is missing on them. Pedestrians. Almost no one
walks along these streets, which gives the whole place a
strangely detached quality. It is as though the large late-model
vehicles that are sliding up and down the thoroughfares are
remotely controlled. The houses in the neighborhoods that
surround Columbine High School are large, amply appointed
dwellings on curlicue streets that lead nowhere.

Columbine High is on wide Pierre Street. Off to one side
is a park, where a couple of people are playing tennis. The
school itself, which before the shootings would have appeared
completely unremarkable—a big formless-looking suburban
high school—is still swathed in the bandages of red plastic
strips strung along the side of the street to keep people out.
Construction workers are toiling to get things ready for the
resumption of classes in mid-August.

What went wrong here? What caused this perfect American
paradise to implode? From the first moments after the guns
stopped firing, these questions echoed around the country.
On the afternoon of the shootings, I was driving across Toronto

with my fourteen-year-old son, Jonathan. Jonathan, who is something of a history buff, said he thought the event might have something to do with the fact that the date was April 20, Hitler's birthday. Naturally, I dismissed his idea as fanciful. It later turned out that Jonathan was exactly right.

If the timing could be explained easily, the motivation for the massacre remained much tougher to unravel. Discussion soon focused on the presence of cliques at Columbine High School. Harris and Klebold were said to be a part of a marginalized group in the school, called the trench-coat mafia, a loose-knit collection of students whose trademark was the black trench coat. If you want to see an idealized version of what they were supposed to look like, there is a scene in the 1998 film *The Matrix*, in which a man and a woman in the required gear gun down a large number of people. Some thought Harris and Klebold were influenced by the film.

The media quickly decided that the members of the trench-coat mafia felt picked on and despised by others in the school, particularly Columbine's athletes. As the two killers entered the library, which was crowded with students, they were reportedly in high spirits. "Who's next?" one of them is alleged to have said. "Who's ready to die? All the jocks stand up. We're going to kill every one of you."[5]

In the aftermath of the shootings, the cliques in the school were closely investigated. Widely canvassed was the theory that the jocks received special treatment, were the favorites of the school administration and the other students, and got away with rule breaking that would not have been tolerated in the case of other students. Stories surfaced about gay students being harassed at Columbine. A boy named Tom Ibison, who now says he is gay, was reportedly tormented at the school for being overweight. Classmates shoved him, threw food at him, and called him "faggot." Another kid, Joe Stair, who was a friend of the two killers and was close to the

# CORPORATE GURUS AND
# REVEALED TRUTH

I N 1971 Z EV S IEGL EMBARKED on the adventure of a lifetime.
Siegl and two friends, all of them residents of Seattle, founded
an enterprise that has since grown into an American giant. In
1998, when I met him, Siegl was no longer riding the corporate rocket upward. He was the general manager of Star Soils.
But he remembered the glory days.

At the beginning of the seventies, Siegl and his friends were
idealistic, ambitious, and confident. As he tells it, they had
been influenced by the zeitgeist of the sixties. They were young
and they believed they could do whatever they liked. One night
at dinner, the three friends discovered that two of them had
bought coffee by mail order in the previous couple of weeks.
It dawned on them that they were not the only young, hip people who shared a passion for really good coffee. They decided
to go into the coffee business. Although they knew little about
commerce, they threw themselves into their project determined that they would never compromise on quality. Their
guru, where coffee was concerned, was a Dutch immigrant
by the name of Alfred Peet who lived in the San Francisco area.

Peet had come to the United States after the Second World War. He was steeped in the coffee-making lore of Java, in what was the Dutch East Indies, later to become Indonesia.

Siegl became the first employee of the new company, which was named Starbucks. He tied on an apron in the company's first store and dispensed the very first coffee beans to the customers.

For the Pacific Northwest, the late twentieth century turned out to be a period of creativity—many new companies with innovative product lines were developed. Seattle was the launchpad for Starbucks and Microsoft and later Amazon.com, and nearby Portland for Nike.

Siegl sees the Pacific Northwest as a region with special characteristics that explain its business success over the past three decades. The region has been a magnet for young adults from elsewhere. Siegl, originally from New York State, was one of them. Full of confidence and enthusiasm, he and his partners thought that if they couldn't make it in coffee, they would turn to something else. Too many people in the East were cynical, Siegl reflected. Here in the Pacific Northwest, there was more idealism, a commitment to quality, a determination not to compromise.

Siegl and the other founders created a thriving local business selling dark roasted coffee beans to an expanding and discerning clientele. He stayed with the company until 1980, which was before the arrival of Howard Schultz, the New York business impresario who transformed Starbucks from a cultish coffee-bean retailer to a continental giant. In his autobiography, *Pour Your Heart into It,* long for sale in Starbucks outlets across America, Schultz relates the story of his pilgrimage from New York to Seattle.[1] In the manner of the "feel good" business success memoirs of the new gilded age, Schultz tells how he discovered the little coffee company in Seattle and decided he had to devote his life to building it. Even though the

management at Starbucks was very unsure about him, he ultimately talked them into taking him on board. Getting into
management was only the beginning of Schultz's struggle to
redesign the company in his own image. His great discovery,
the revelation around which he rebuilt Starbucks, came during a visit to Milan. He was visiting espresso bars in the Italian
metropolis and watching the baristas who served caffelatte to
their customers. It came to him in a blinding flash, like Moses
receiving the Ten Commandments from the Lord—Schultz
would open coffee bars across America. American baristas,
dispensing dark coffee with a strong aroma, would serve latte
just the way they did in Milan.

On his return to Seattle, Schultz told his colleagues at
Starbucks about his idea of opening coffee bars instead of simply selling the beans. The others at the company were resistant
to the new idea, but Schultz persuaded them to allow him to
open a small espresso bar in the Pike Place Market in Seattle.
On an unseasonably cool morning in Seattle in April 1984,
Schultz opened Starbucks at the market two hours earlier than
usual. The great experiment was about to unfold. As Schultz
declares in his memoirs, "As far as I know, America was first
introduced to caffelatte that morning."

Recently, I spent an hour or so hanging around that first
Starbucks outlet on a sunny Saturday morning. A plaque of
the sort that you see at Plymouth Rock announces that this
was the company's first store. The place itself is lovingly maintained to look exactly as it did in the days of that historic
caffelatte.

Siegl is philosophical about the role played in the economy by people like Schultz. He concedes that perhaps Schultz
or Bill Gates have some superior abilities that contribute to
the remarkable commercial success of their endeavors, but
Siegl sees this as the age of the "new robber barons." He
believes that what distinguishes men like Schultz and Gates

from others is an "enormous drive to dominate." Siegl is a classy guy. He doesn't show resentment toward Schultz; maybe he doesn't even feel it. But I interpret his social Darwinist remarks about entrepreneurs like Schultz and Gates as an invitation to think critically about the way such personalities insist on having everything their own way.

As far as Siegl is concerned, Schultz deserves plenty of credit for how well Starbucks has done. Siegl is impressed that the company maintains its uniform quality standards in hundreds of outlets across North America. There are few industries, he reflects, where the biggest company is also the industry leader. He believes that Starbucks will score even more success when it takes its American formula for serving Italian-style coffee to Europe. Starbucks will figure out how to adapt to the particulars of the British and French markets, he thinks.

But Siegl sees contenders on the horizon in the coffee business, which takes us back to Alfred Peet, his original inspiration. Peet, now in his eighties, lives in Berkeley, California. In his maneuvers to take over Starbucks in the 1980s, Schultz did not gain control of Peet's, Alfred's own company, although Starbucks had once controlled it. Today Peet's is expanding, taking advantage of the very sophistication among West Coast residents that launched Starbucks. Peet's now has fifty stores in the San Francisco Bay area and has been considering outlets in other parts of the United States.

As I look at Siegl in the boardroom of a waste-management company in an unimposing building in Seattle's south-end warehouse district, I can see what an impressive person he is. He has a certain forceful optimism about him. He did it once, maybe he can do it again. And then he starts talking about composting, his current enthusiasm. If we can just figure out how to get the compost back to the people whose lawn originally produced it, he says. . . .

What strikes me about the Starbucks story is that at its center is something quintessentially American. Let me call it "the founder myth." In developing Starbucks, Howard Schultz has become a legend, someone whose achievements are separate from those of other mortals. Schultz, who is part pitchman, part prophet, is not the only entrepreneur in the Pacific Northwest who has made himself a legend.

The greatest of the new giants, of course, is Microsoft, and Bill Gates, its creator, has grown another myth. His revelation—the equivalent of Schultz's on his trip to Milan—was his appreciation that software mattered more than hardware, the key to his colossal rise at the expense of IBM.

In his autobiography, *The Road Ahead,* Gates talks about how he and his partner, Paul Allen, understood the meaning of the new small-size computer chip in a way that those running the big companies did not: "In the short term, the computer establishment was right . . . But Paul and I looked past the limits of that new chip and saw a different kind of computer that would be perfect for us, and for everyone—personal, affordable, and adaptable.

"Computer hardware . . . would soon be readily available. Then, software would be the key to delivering the full potential of these machines. Paul and I speculated that Japanese companies and IBM would likely produce most of the hardware. We believed we would come up with new and innovative software."

Then the pace picks up as we come to Gates's description of the creation of the software: "Paul and I didn't sleep much and lost track of night and day. When I did fall asleep, it was often at my desk or on the floor. Some days I didn't eat or see anyone. But after five weeks, our BASIC was written—and the world's first microcomputer software company was born. In time we named it 'Microsoft.'"[2]

Jeffrey Bezos is a New York–based financial analyst who moved to Seattle in July 1994 to follow his lodestar. The result was the world's premier e-commerce company, Amazon.com—and another founder myth. Like Schultz and Gates, Bezos was a man possessed. In the early 1990s, when Bezos first saw the World Wide Web, he had a vision of a boundless new realm for retail over the Internet. He quit his New York job and headed for the West Coast with his wife, MacKenzie.

Outside Seattle, they rented a modest two-bedroom house and converted the garage into a work area. To save money, he bought three wooden doors at Home Depot, and using two-by-fours and angle brackets, he fashioned the doors into desks for the fledgling enterprise. Almost everyone he talked to about the idea of selling books online thought he was crazy. He is fond of saying, "If I had a nickel for every time a potential investor told me this wouldn't work . . ." He usually follows this line with a wild, uncontrolled laugh.[3]

I'm in Portland, Oregon, to check out another of the giant corporations to appear in the Pacific Northwest over the past couple of decades. The corporation is Nike and the myth of its founder, Phil Knight, is second to none.

Nike's plush headquarters is a few miles west of Portland at Beaverton in beautiful green countryside. Over the driveway into the complex is a huge arch with a single symbol—the Nike swoosh and nothing else. Lying directly ahead is the Steve Prefontaine Building, named after the legendary Oregon runner who died in a car crash in the mid-1970s at age twenty-four.

My first impression of the Nike complex is that it is luxurious and a little spooky. Everywhere in these quiet buildings, the cheerily efficient people are all wearing a piece of clothing with the swoosh on some part of their anatomy. The young woman delivering missives from one building to another, who shows me to my first destination, has the swoosh on her socks. Plenty of shoes, not surprisingly, on the denizens of these hallways, have the swoosh, and white cotton T-shirts with a small swoosh are favorites.

The swoosh's ubiquity is disconcerting. It's not often that everyone in a large office complex wears some common symbol.

It all made more sense when I met Nelson Farris, Nike's director of education, in his comfortable office in the Dan Fouts Building (named after the famed quarterback). It is reassuring to meet a runner my age who has been working for Nike since the early days of the company. He serves me caffelatte and we chat, talking about running and discussing the rise of Nike from its pioneering days to its present incarnation as a global corporate power.

Farris sees the early days at the company as a time when Nike "kicked the ass" of its big-time competitors, such as Europe's Adidas. Nike rose, he says, by breaking all the rules, by exhibiting the free spirit one associates with the Pacific Northwest. The conventional wisdom in those days was that the company was in the "footwear" business and should align itself with the dress-shoe manufacturers in the eastern United States. Instead, Nike, the upstart from Portland, ignored the eastern shoe manufacturers and adopted as its mission to serve athletes. Nike's idea was that "runners would make running shoes for runners."

The key to the realization of this idea was Bill Bowerman, who founded Nike along with Phil Knight. Bowerman was the coach of the famed University of Oregon track team. After a stint in Australia, he brought the idea of aerobic running as an aid to training back to the United States. "Bowerman was behind the running craze of the 1970s," Lee Weinstein, Nike's communications director, told me later over lunch in the pleasant deli at Nike's headquarters. And Bowerman personally invented America's most famous running shoe, the Nike Waffle Trainer. Impressed by the need for a light shoe that provided cushioning, he borrowed his wife's waffle iron, poured rubber into it—and the rest is history. Out of the kitchen utensil came a sole from which protruded little square studs with a tiny dot at the end of each one.

The shoe was created in 1971 and every runner, in those heroic days of the sport, knew about the Waffle Trainer. Beginning in 1974, when it became the top-selling training shoe in the United States, I bought a new pair every six months and ran in them until the waffles were worn smooth—the signal to buy a new pair. I was not the only runner in the late seventies to be dismayed by the news that the Waffle Trainer had been superseded by a spiffier, more expensive shoe, the Nike Internationalist.

Phil Knight had been a fine middle-distance runner at the University of Oregon, with Bowerman as his coach. Bowerman, the idea man and initiator of the legendary shoe, teamed up with Knight, the athlete turned business visionary. In its early days, Nike took the needs of the runner very seriously in the design of its running shoes. "In those days," Farris says, "designing shoes was an art. Today," he adds, "it's both an art and a science." Farris tells stories of every wacky idea imaginable being looked at seriously in the quest for the better running shoe. The result of both listening to runners and experimenting was unprecedented strength and flexibility—seemingly extreme opposites—in the shoe. Farris describes the originators at Nike as runners who were also "risk takers." Nowadays things are much different in the way Nike designs new shoes. That's where science comes in. In Nike's state-of-the-art lab at Beaverton, Farris says that every centimeter of a shoe is tested for both strength and flexibility. Similarly, rigorous testing is done on the fabrics Nike uses in its line of athletic clothing.

About twenty-seven hundred people work for Nike in its

Beaverton complex, and about two thousand more are employed by the company in other locations in the immediate vicinity. Farris tells me that about 70 percent of the Beaverton employees run on the trails around Nike's HQ or work out in the weights room. Nike built running time into my schedule the day I visited Beaverton, but I had already gone for my daily run in downtown Portland early in the morning.

Nike rose along with the American running craze, and it has suffered whenever the zest for running has receded. In the early 1990s, Farris explains, the American interest in running declined somewhat. While famous events like the Boston and New York Marathons held their numbers, smaller marathons shrank in size and some were even canceled. Nonmarathon races were also affected. But, according to Farris, in the past few years there has been a renewed interest in running. The numbers are coming back.

Farris admits that the company culture has evolved as a consequence of this enormous growth. In the beginning, everyone was a generalist, he remembers. With size came the transition from "doers to managers," from generalists to specialists. With that change came the problem of a "line of sight" from each employee's individual role to the larger goals of Nike. To ensure that a line of sight is sustained, the company holds conclaves of its employees, akin to an "annual renewal of vows," to reconnect everyone to Nike's mission. The idea, Farris says, is to use these employee "boot camps" as a way to rededicate Nike to its core values, which have to do with serving athletes.

In Beaverton, we glimpse only the superstructure of Nike. Like the proverbial iceberg, most of the bulk of the huge operation is beneath the surface, or more properly beyond the Pacific in the Asian plants where Nike's products are manufactured. Nelson Farris admits that the roiling controversy in recent years about working conditions in these plants and the remuneration of employees has affected morale in Beaverton. There have been times, he says, when employees have not been "sure about my company."

The executive I talked to about the volatile subject of the company's labor practices in Asia was Vada Manager, Nike's senior manager for U.S. corporate communications. If one secret of Nike's rise to great corporate status was its bold initiative of runner-designed shoes, its other great secret was its almost total reliance on Asian labor from the very beginning. Phil Knight's first venture before the creation of Nike was the import of Japanese running shoes into the United States. In 1962 he went to Japan, where he met with executives of the Onitsuka Tiger company, explaining to them that he represented Blue Ribbon Sports (BRS), a name he made up on the spot. Back in the United States, Knight and Bowerman shook hands and contributed $500 each to the fledgling venture. BRS became the exclusive United States importer of Tiger shoes.

For the rest of the decade, BRS marketed Tiger shoes in the United States, with Knight acting as chief businessman while Bowerman came up with improvements to the design for the shoes. With this arrangement, the revenues of BRS grew from $8,000 annually in 1964 to $1.96 million annually in 1972. Conflict and legal wrangling with Tiger in 1972 led to a break and the formation of Nike, named after the Greek goddess of victory. By 1979 Nike had achieved a 50 percent share of the U.S. running-shoe market. The following year, Nike went public. In the early eighties, Nike International was established to handle sales to a market that extended to forty countries. In 1984 Nike revenue reached $919.8 million. Then, after a few rocky years, Nike revenue soared to more than $2 billion in 1990. The rest of the decade was growth, retrenchment, and renewed growth. In 1996 the company's revenue skyrocketed to $6.47 billion, putting it in a league of its own vis-à-vis other global sports-apparel companies.

But Nike's labor practices in Asia have become a stubborn issue, the public consequence being a loss of sales in the U.S. market. Vada Manager reflects Nike's concern about the issue. He welcomes me warmly to his office, and as soon as I am seated he flips a switch so he can tape our conversation. Manager explains to me that Nike does not own Asian plants, that it signs agreements with the companies who make products for it to ensure quality and to make sure that Nike's labor practices are adhered to. In each plant where Nike products are made, Nike people are present to see that the products do not contain defects. The company maintains an eleven-person unit to keep an eye on the labor practices in the Asian plants. Manager travels regularly to check out the plants in China, Vietnam, and Indonesia, often arriving, he explains, without letting the plant managers know in advance that he is on his way.

He tells me that the managers in the Asian plants are indigenous to the region, many of them from South Korea and Taiwan. He admits that there have been some lamentable incidents in which managers have mistreated employees. When such cases have come to light, however, he insists that Nike has moved quickly to deal with the offenders. In one notorious case where employees were forced to run around the factory in the hot sun as a punishment, the Taiwanese manager was terminated and deported from Vietnam with Nike's support. These incidents, Manager says, are not typical of the experience of plants where Nike shoes are produced. He asserts that jobs at these Asian plants are highly prized. Eighty percent of the employees are women—not because women are docile, he insists, but because women are generally more adept than men at stitching shoes.

He paints a picture of young women (in their early twenties) from rural areas, coming to work at a plant for a few years. There is evidence, he says, that these women are often able to save between 30 and 40 percent of their earnings. This money is typically sent back home to help out their families, or it is saved so that when the women have completed their stint at a plant—usually for several years—they are able to return home, where they can start their own small businesses. I wonder about these astonishing savings. Manager tells me that while the average per capita income in Vietnam is about $240 a year, at a Nike plant workers make between $55 and $60 a month. That's less than $15 a week. Americans, despite their high-flying economy, save only a very small proportion of their incomes. One has to marvel at someone whose income is 1 percent of that of a middle-class American income ($360 a year compared with $36,000 a year) saving ten times as much of that income (40 percent as compared with 4 percent). It's all a bit like *Alice through the Looking Glass*—the wretchedly paid save, and the better paid cannot put away a penny.

At the conclusion of our hour together, Manager asks if I have ever visited one of the Asian plants where Nike shoes are manufactured. When I reply no, he says I might benefit from seeing a video about the factories and the women who work in them. He pops the video in the VCR and we see young women walking into a large, well-lit, clean-looking factory. We see close-ups of female workers stitching shoes. At another point, there is a look at the wooden dormitories where workers are housed and then a close-up of one woman brushing her teeth.

Howard Schultz, Bill Gates, Jeffrey Bezos, and Phil Knight are revered. In all these cases, the gurus and their early and heroic feats are a crucial part of corporate lore, recounted lovingly by executives of the companies today. Such founding myths are central to the American ethos, as they have been at least from the era of the American Revolution. The seminal American myth, of course, is that of the founding of the United States, substantiated by the Declaration of Independence and the

Constitution. Even more than the Declaration, the Constitution is understood as transformative. Before the authors gathered at Philadelphia, the oft-told story goes, the newly independent United States was foundering. Fractious state governments were fomenting disunion, predatory foreigners were taking advantage of American weakness, and American society was fraying as evidenced in shocking events like the Shays's Rebellion of 1787 in Massachusetts. Ahead lay the abyss. At Philadelphia, though, a remarkable group of men gathered, and when their deliberations were completed, the most perfect governing instrument in the history of the world had been fashioned.

The propensity for proliferation of founder myths is quite particular to Americans. In Britain, the emphasis is on the pedigree and longevity of institutions, even relatively new ones, rather than on a sudden revelation of a company's founder. Canadians are incapable of honing and sustaining American-style founder myths. Perhaps, for better or worse, we don't take ourselves seriously enough. The idea of Canadian corporate executives praising the founder of the company and his moment of creative genius, its essence continuing to be at the heart of the company's mission, might embarrass a Canadian, or provoke an irreverent, ironic remark.

# 9

# GREED, GLUTTONY, GOD, AND
# THE AMERICAN DREAM

*Make money, be proud of it; make more money, be prouder of it.*
—Henry R. Luce, 1937

*The New York Stock Exchange:
a part of what makes this country tick.*
—Commercial on CNN, 1998

IF THE TWENTIETH CENTURY is looked at as a contest between Freud and Pavlov, then the clear winner at the beginning of the new millennium is Pavlov. Forget the neuroses, the Oedipal complex, and the damage your mother did to you when you were two. Never has American society been so fixated on the concept of stimulus-response. It is the advertiser's mantra. Human beings are understood and treated as a bundle of unlimited appetites. And a vast number of Americans are going along for the ride, or for the satisfaction of their drive for more.

Never in the history of the world has there been a society with such a compulsive drive for More. Not only does More satisfy our innermost needs, but it is virtuous, at times approaching the heroic. In the late 1990s, when so much of the world was slipping into the Asian economic contagion, with economies like that of Russia on life-support systems, it was the plucky Americans, consumers and investors, who saved the day. Quarter after quarter, American consumers, defying rising levels of personal debt, were out there spending and spending, keeping the economic wolf from the door and ensuring the creation of millions of new jobs. And American investors, whether large institutions or individuals chasing hot stocks or mutual funds, kept on plowing their capital into the stock market despite periodic spine-tingling plummets in stock prices and frequent forecasts of doom and gloom. It seemed difficult to argue with the proposition that greed was greasing the wheels of progress.

Of the people I know well—Europeans, Canadians, Caribbeans, Americans—it is the Americans who are most fixated on stuff. Ring their bell on the subject of stuff and they definitely salivate. When I visit Americans, the conversation is never far from the next expedition to get more stuff, and to get it at a bargain price. Let's go to the suburban mall and visit all the great stores there. My acquaintances in suburban America will go downtown to accommodate visitors from out of town, but the nearby mall has everything they want and a lot they never knew they did—furniture, knickknacks, designer clothing, bookstores with comfortable chairs and a coffee bar, and great and varied food. Not many days pass when they do not visit the mall.

I can't get over the capacity of Americans to shop, shop, and shop some more, to go home and arrange their acquired treasures, and then plan for the next outing. The deal is that you work hard, that you dedicate yourself to your job, business, or professional practice. Depending on your circumstances, you may make a lot or a little. And you pay relatively low taxes compared with people in other advanced countries. What you

have, you spend on stuff. Never has stuff been as cheap relative to incomes as in America today.

The other side of the deal is that you ask no questions about
larger matters, about ultimate issues, about meaning, community, and the future of society and the planet. Goals are
finite, personal, daily. Americans live in a state of capitalist
existentialism. It's a fusion between the personal radicalism
of the sixties and the materialist bedrock of the longer American
experience. America was once Protestant in a serious way,
with the emphasis on saving and work to achieve a distant end.
The emphasis then was on discipline and deferred gratification.
Today, people are ready to work hard, perhaps as hard as ever.
But there is no deferral of gratification. *Consume now* is the
mantra. One way that is evident is in the evolution of the
American diet. Americans are eating more and more, and that
is creating a serious new health problem for them, the problem of obesity. However politically incorrect it may be to
acknowledge it, gluttony has forced its way into our consideration of contemporary American society.

One evening on the outskirts of Atlanta, I dined at OB's
Real Pit Bar BQ. It's a family place with an almost entirely
white clientele. At OB's, steaks, chicken, and turkey legs are
smoked outside in the pit. The portions are huge. When my
chicken and potato arrived, the chicken was literally hanging
off one end of the plate. The steaks I saw were similarly oversize. The turkey legs were too big and too greasy to contemplate. OB's Real Pit Bar BQ serves Southern-style food in
portions that are fully in keeping with the contemporary
American drive for More. It is as though More cleanses you of
your sins. Restaurants in the South, indeed across America,
are serving epic portions.

In the mass-food, fast-food sector in the United States, the
battle for customers has now become combat over quantities
served. In many fast-food chains, you get free refills of what
are already mega-size servings of soft drinks. One chain in a

lot of states from the North to the South is Cracker Barrel, where travelers weary from hours on a boring interstate are welcomed into an atmosphere of ersatz colonial cheeriness. Hostesses in costumes left over from shooting *How the West Was Won* greet you at the door and usher you through the general-store-style front area, which is full of articles for sale. Here you can buy your daughter a T-shirt emblazoned with the words GRITS—Girls Raised in the South. Then you are shown into the dining room, with its large fireplace, turn-of-the-century photos of industrious American life, and decor centered on what looks like sawn lumber. The first time you see a Cracker Barrel, the warm, cozy pioneer feel may charm you. The third or fourth time, you are more likely to be impressed by the industrial precision with which each one of these places is made to look absolutely identical in Pennsylvania or Georgia.

My first time in a Cracker Barrel in northern Ohio, the waitress rushed back to my table while I was still halfway through my gigantic chicken salad and had only touched my barrel-size soft drink to offer me a refill of the drink. Main courses are as daunting as the salads, and what I find hard to believe is the number of patrons who go on to order dessert without flinching.

In many parts of the country, in an apparent effort to lure hapless customers with large portions, McDonald's has come up with an option called "supersizing." Signs invite people to supersize their orders: "If we don't recommend a supersize, the supersize is free!" For an extra 79 cents, an order for a cheeseburger, small fries, and a small Coke grows into a cheeseburger, supersize fries (more than double the regular order), and supersize Coke (forty-two ounces instead of sixteen, with free refills). The enhanced offering contains more than 1,340 calories compared with 680 in the smaller version. The additional calories, in the form of fat and carbohydrates, bring the meal to over half the daily recommended caloric total for teenagers.[1]

It is not just the chains that promote abundant calories.

I remember a restaurant in North Platte, Nebraska, where the idea is to eat handfuls of peanuts before your main course arrives. You shell the peanuts and toss the shells on the floor. Meanwhile, the waitresses refill your bottomless soft drink.

Shape it any way you like, but the fact is that obesity is a burgeoning issue in American society. A few years ago, one-quarter of Americans were obese—more than 20 percent above their ideal body weight. In a few years, experts predict one-third of the people of the United States will be obese. The physical character of the American population is changing rapidly, radically, and is a cause for worry. In one sense, obesity is a disease of affluence and labor-saving technology. Almost all Americans can afford to eat as much as they could possibly want. Indeed, no population in the history of the world has ever spent a smaller percentage of its average per capita income on food than Americans do. In addition, over 70 percent of the American labor force is now employed in the sedentary service sector. Those in traditionally more physically demanding fields—manufacturing, farming, and mining—are outfitted with labor-saving technology that has drastically reduced the number of calories a day that they burn on the job. Historically, bosses had to pay their workers enough for them to replenish their bodily strength so they could keep on working. Since physical labor required plenty of calories to sustain workers, this fact put a limit on how little bosses could pay their workers.

All of a sudden this calculus, which played such a central role, no longer applies. In the United States, the simultaneous reduction in the number of calories required to sustain the average man or woman coincides with a fall in the price of food. All industrialized countries are having the same experience, but America in particular, for a number of reasons. Not only is the price of food cheaper in the United States than in western Europe, Japan, or Canada, but the American system of production of food is more industrialized than that in other advanced countries. Food production on a large scale has undermined traditional patterns of food consumption to a greater degree than elsewhere, a trend exacerbated by the explosion of fast-food establishments in the United States. Americans eat out more than any other people on the planet, and that has had a very material impact on the diet of the nation.

In other industrialized countries—France is a good example—traditional menus and a high propensity to eat prepared meals at home have kept the full impact of fast-food restaurants at bay. McDonald's is on the rise in France, but the French still regard a trip to Macdo, as they call it, as something of an event, an outing to a special place. Per capita, there are many times more McDonald's in the United States than in France. And the French are distinctly thinner than Americans, as a trip to any French town will quickly reveal. Go to New Orleans and then walk along the Promenade des Anglais in Nice if you want a real shock in the display of alternative body shapes. Actually, the comparison is the same between any American and any French city.

One exception, however, is Martha's Vineyard, the island playground of the affluent just off the coast of Massachusetts. The cost of transit to the island and the high price of accommodations ensure that visitors are mostly from the upper classes. During a visit, when I went for my daily run along one of the beaches, the slender, fit vacationers I saw were like no other American crowd. Obesity, it seems, is not an affliction of the rich in America.

That anomaly aside, obesity is the great American epidemic of our time. In 1999 William Dietz, the director of nutrition at the Centers for Disease Control, stated that "this is an epidemic in the United States the likes of which we have not had before in chronic disease."[2] It is a safe bet that over the next couple of decades, the cost to public-health budgets in the United States as a consequence of obesity will far outstrip the costs due to HIV. And as was the case with other epidemics in history, understanding and confronting this one involves deeply difficult social and political factors. Health, fitness, and diet are class and gender issues in the United States, and obesity lies in a complex of larger matters.

Meanwhile, the flip side of the actual tendency to obesity is the marketing, through advertising and the media, of an idealized female body that combines big breasts with skinniness. The pallid, bony, childlike woman is the desirable object and objective in magazines, billboards, and in the popular press and film. Appropriately, many people have expressed concern about this completely unrealistic body image foisted on American women. The price girls and women pay for eating disorders, fostered by cultural pressures, can be death.

At the dawn of the millennium, American capitalism has got its braggadocio back. It makes no apologies for itself, as it did during the Cold War. During those decades, even though almost all Americans identified with their system against the Soviet one, the idea nevertheless existed that there could be an alternative, that American capitalism was not the only possible way of doing things. Victory in the Cold War has changed that. Now Americans feel that their way of life is all there really is on this planet. It may take other peoples a long time to savor the full fruits of American civilization, but they're all heading in the same direction. With the exception of China, which is a source of growing unease for Americans, America's adversaries or potential adversaries are not dignified as representing alternative ways of life but are understood as rogues led by megalomaniacal dictators or as countries that are locked into a hopelessly inward-looking nationalism.

Without ideological adversaries—those who actually

threaten its way of life—American capitalism has lost all its defensiveness. It is fully itself again, as it has not been since the 1920s. There is an unselfconsciousness today in the American insistence that the unabashed individual pursuit of great wealth is the engine that drives humanity forward to an ever more materially prosperous future. In December 1998, in that triumphalist spirit, *Time* magazine unveiled its list of the twenty greatest business titans of the twentieth century. Nineteen of the twenty were American and only one of them was a woman. When you consider that between 1945 and 2000, the U.S. share of global economic output shrank from 50 to 20 percent, it's evident how much *Time*'s list was an exercise in American narcissism. The most remarkable fact of the last half of the twentieth century was the construction of wealthy, advanced, powerful economic engines in western Europe, in Japan, and in other parts of Asia. This reality, responsible for the shrinkage in relative American economic output compared with the rest of the world, is reflected in *Time*'s list only in its inclusion of Sony's Akio Morita.

Imagine a list that ranks American crime boss Lucky Luciano as one of the world's twenty business titans of the twentieth century but includes no one from Britain, Germany, and France and only one Asian. Couldn't, for instance, Ferdinand Porsche of Porsche and Volkswagen have made the list? What about Gianni Agnelli, the Italian auto magnate; Paul Sacher, the Swiss pharmaceutical wizard and renowned symphony conductor; or Lilliane Bettencourt, the titan of French cosmetics? Most revealing were the lyrical praises sung to American business titans by Norman Pearlstine, *Time*'s editor-in-chief:

It is no accident that our list is almost entirely American. . . . If the 20th century was, as Luce . . . said, the American Century, it was largely because our system, espousing freedom of markets and freedom of the individual, rewarding talent instead of

class and pedigree, bred a group of leaders whose single-minded
fixation on getting rich—and creating great products in the
process—led to unheard-of levels of productivity and prosperity. . . . Other countries may have had the capital, the natural
resources or the skilled workers needed to industrialize, but
their economic and political systems usually favored consensus
management and faceless bureaucrats while denigrating the kind
of individual initiative required to take an idea and turn it into
an industry.[3]

Thank you, Lucky Luciano.

To me, the phrase that stands out as the centerpiece of this
interpretation of the past century is "single-minded fixation
on getting rich." There it is—the engine that propels humanity, separating the real heroes from the drones, who more likely
than not turn out to be "faceless bureaucrats." At the end of
the twilight struggle of the twentieth century, the conclusion
in the mind of Norman Pearlstine was that "capitalism not only
won, it turned into a marvelous machine of prosperity, led by
people who could take an idea and turn it into an industry."
Capitalism had triumphed and it was no reproach to say that
Greed had won.

The zeal of the evangelists at home is matched by the mis-
sionary fervor of Americans abroad to convert the world not
to a particular brand of Christianity but to the corporate values and practices of the United States. Customarily, when we
think of the extension of the power of empires, we think of
the use of military might, the imposition of political will by
force. Today, American capitalism is remaking the world in its
image, using the American example to rewrite the rules about
how commerce is practiced, thereby creating huge upheavals
in the ways other people live.

In western Virginia, near the Appalachians, where a car-
racing meet was about to be held, I saw a billboard that read,

"Before the race, why not drop by for a conversation with Jesus?" What would Jesus have to say about Greed as the reigning goddess of contemporary America? Would he endorse raging material ambition—the drive for copious wealth—as the way back to a contemporary Garden of Eden? Would he have thought Norman Pearlstine was right on with his materialism, or would he have found it crass, vulgar, a sure sign that the human race was wandering in the ethical wilderness?

We have to square two facts about contemporary America. The United States is the most materialist country in the West, but it is also by a long margin the most religious. The overwhelming majority of Americans believe in God and think that God matters. This differentiates them hugely from the French, for example, where church attendance is extremely low, nominal Catholicism is the norm, and it is thought tasteless in almost all social settings to bring God's name into a conversation. In the three and a half years I lived in France, while I attended church with my friends occasionally, I can't recall anyone ever mentioning God to me.

In the United States, quite the reverse is the case. God turns up all the time. Most of my American friends and acquaintances accept as a matter of course that they believe in God. Many of them attend church regularly and send their children to religious summer camps. As far as I can see, this doesn't stop them from doing cocaine, having extramarital affairs, and treating their employees hard-heartedly, even brutally. Some of the religious Americans I know are not on speaking terms with their parents.

Throughout history, from society to society and religion to religion, the Almighty has worn many faces. He seems to represent very different kinds of morality. He has espoused slavery and has lent aid and comfort to slaves in their struggle for freedom. He has been a stern paternalist; alternatively, she has marched hand in hand with feminists. At times, God has encouraged asceticism, inspiring the truly devout to take vows of poverty; at others, God has supported material striving, ready to welcome the successful into the company of the elect, while shunning the slothful and the weak.

What kind of God do contemporary Americans believe in? There are important differences in the qualities of God in America—from the compassionate, inclusive, forgiving deity of African-American belief to the exclusionary, judgmental, formalistic Almighty we encounter in white fundamentalism. Episcopalians and Baptists have quite distinct versions of God, as do the varieties of Islam and Judaism on offer in the United States. Basic disagreements about abortion and birth control rack American theology.

That said, it is possible to construct a contemporary, mainstream, popular American God (one who is not attached too closely to any particular sect or religious leader) and to contemplate the values He stands for. First, it is reasonable to conclude that He must be very tolerant of huge gaps in income and wealth between rich and poor. While standing foursquare behind charity for the less fortunate, He obviously admires the profit motive. He doesn't seem to have too much difficulty with the death penalty, and He isn't very upset when U.S. military force is used abroad. On billboards and on television commercials and religious broadcasts is an approachable, personal deity. One commercial often shown on CNN advertising a publication titled *Power for Living* features sports heroes and other celebrities. Reggie White of the Green Bay Packers and Heather Whitestone McCallum, a former Miss America, tell their stories and then assert that what has helped them most through good times and bad has been their "personal relationship with God." The commercial is effective because it reduces God to a human scale, holding out the hope that you can have a "personal" relationship with Him. What is more, the people making the pitch have all made it—they are attractive, rich, and successful. You can make it too. The commercial reminds me of those football players who fall on their knees and pray after they score a touchdown or who kneel in a circle with their teammates at the beginning or end of the game. Apparently, God can help you score touchdowns. He might help push your mutual fund along. Who knows? Far from being a distant Jehovah, a great, angry ruling deity, America's God is a little God, a friendly helpmate, a problem solver, a good-luck charm.

I became intrigued by the ad for *Power for Living* and wanted a copy of the publication so I could find out just what is meant by a "personal relationship with God." I tried the 1-800 number in the commercials, but I couldn't access it from Canada. A friend in Seattle called the number for me and asked if the promoters of the publication would mail it to me in Toronto. They said no, they could not send the booklet to Canada, though they couldn't explain why. So my friend had it sent to her and forwarded it to me.

The book, written in plain language, is full of brief, inspirational stories about how various people came to God. In one chapter, "How to Get Right with God," the author, whose name is Jamie Buckingham, tells us stories of his terror of the unknown as he grew up. When he was a little older, he continues, a friend who was to accompany him on a hunting trip failed to show up at a meeting place. Afraid to spend the night alone in the wild, Buckingham succeeded in finding his way back to his cabin. Amazingly, he felt no fear through the night, and when he emerged from the cabin the next morning, he experienced the world coming alive in the early dawn, went out in the glade, and spotted a "magnificent buck. He was standing head erect, his rack of horns crowning his regal head." Then the revelation came to Buckingham: "He and I were part of the same creation—citizens of this marvelous garden of nature."[4] Here is a God who helps you through the night and helps you deal with your deepest fears.

Billboards urging you to be reborn in Christ or to prepare

yourself for Christ's return are common these days in all parts
of the United States, but there are more in the South than in
any other region. I can't help wondering what such devout
Americans would do to Christ if he actually showed up. Would
southern conservative evangelists like Jerry Falwell welcome
this strange, revolutionary character into their midst? Would
Pat Robertson give up his power and wealth to follow this
Jewish prophet who respected and ministered to the disad-
vantaged, preached love for all members of humankind equally,
and claimed to be the Son of God? I can't help thinking that at
least some of the fundamentalists would be in the front lines
of contemporary crucifiers in the event of the Second Coming.

One hot Sunday in April, I'm driving north across North
Carolina on crowded Interstate 95. People are rushing to get
back home to places like Philadelphia and New York after a
school vacation. Suddenly the northbound traffic comes to
a halt. Somewhere ahead is a big problem so we creep along
for about half an hour. That gets me to an exit, to who knows
where, and I take it.

I find a Burger King, which is already crowded with people
fleeing the interstate. While I eat a chicken burger, the manager goes around from table to table explaining that a couple
of tractor-trailers have collided on the I-95 a few miles north
and that one of them has jackknifed and is blocking the traffic.
He tells everybody how to find a secondary highway for the
next hundred miles. I follow his advice, and soon I am cruis-
ing along past scrubby fields and shambling single-story wooden
homes that turn up in clumps along the side of the road every
couple of miles. Up ahead the sky is turning dark, with huge
clouds billowing far up into the heavens. That morning just
before I left my motel room in Savannah, Georgia, a TV weather
forecast warned of severe thunderstorms and possible tornadoes that day in the Carolinas. It's been in the back of my mind,

not least because earlier in the week severe tornadoes tore through Oklahoma and Illinois, reducing housing subdivisions to rubble and leaving about forty people dead.

It's still sunny where I am, but I watch the building storm clouds as I head north. I start fiddling with the radio dial to see if I can get a weather forecast. On both the AM and FM bands, all I can find is country music and evangelical religious broadcasts. There is no news, no weather anywhere. Surely at the half hour, I will find something, but no. Then at the hour, I try again. Still nothing. By now there are clouds overhead, and I appear to be driving into a black tunnel. The storm clouds ahead have an ugly yellow tinge. It feels as if the sky is about to explode. I leave the radio on a gospel station. As I drive, thinking only about the weather, hymns play in the background. Suddenly the music is interrupted by an announcer who tells us in a flat voice that a tornado warning has been issued for a number of counties in North Carolina. He proceeds to read off the list of counties. They mean nothing to me as a nonresident and I don't know one from another.

All hell breaks loose. The cloud bursts and a wall of water descends. This isn't rain—a waterfall is crashing on my car. I have just reached the ramp at Interstate 40 and turn northwest. The deluge continues as I hear a powerful bass voice singing, "Yes, we will gather by the river, the beautiful, beautiful river. Yes, we will gather by the river. . ."

There's nothing else to do but drive slowly as the water pounds down, and I listen to this deep voice. Up ahead the sky is starting to clear. A minute later the rain stops. The hymn is reaching its wonderful climax. I look around me at the fresh, wet pickups and cars emerging into the sunlight.

# BEAUTIFUL *LOSERS*

**C**HARLESTON, WEST VIRGINIA, a small town as state capitals go, comes equipped with the mandatory Capitol dome, a knockoff of the Capitol in Washington, mother of all such domes. I have occasionally wondered what archaeologists, thousands of years from now, sifting through the ruins of this civilization, might make of what is left of the great dome and all the other smaller domes around America. Might they conclude that these were the temples of some strange faith, where high priests conducted their rituals? And would they be far wrong?

Most of Charleston is pretty rundown, with modest wooden homes, many of them in evident disrepair. Not too far from the dome on a commercial street, I find a terrific old-fashioned restaurant, the Blossom Dairy. With its big blue booths and wraparound lunch counter, the place is right out of the fifties. Waiters and waitresses are genuinely friendly with an unforced Southern style of hospitality, serving great burgers, milk-shakes, and mushroom soup. When I tell my waiter, who lives about fifty miles south of here in coal-mining country, that

I plan to drive to Matewan, the legendary site of miners' wars with the coal companies, he asks me, "Why do you-all want to go down there?"

West Virginia is the heart of Appalachia. The social order in this mountainous territory was vastly different from the slavocracy that dominated old tidewater Virginia. The new state was quite free of the rising industrial and commercial interests of both North and South. The original white settlers of the territory who arrived in the 1820s and '30s first established a largely self-sufficient economy. The settlers consumed most of their own farm produce and hunted the plentiful game in what was then a sparsely populated region.

South of Charleston is a claustrophobic landscape of rising mountains divided one from the next by narrow valleys. I was prepared to see the scarred faces of mountains that have been strip-mined in the hunger for coal, but I was not ready for the sheer scale of devastation to the mountains and ridges of West Virginia, south from the state capital all the way to the Kentucky border. Mile after mile, the earth and top layers of rock have been scraped and blasted away. Ugly tracks run up remaining cliffs. On bald rock, there is sometimes a top cover of scruffy trees planted over the mined areas.

The latest technique for getting out the coal is called mountaintop removal. It is a stark term, to describe a shocking procedure—tearing off the top of a mountain. To prepare for these giant explosions, coal companies drill holes in the mountain, each of which will contain three hundred pounds of explosives. When all the holes have been drilled, all personnel leave the site. The explosion fires rock more than eighty feet in the air along a line five hundred feet long. The contours of mountains are permanently altered. West Virginia is now a battleground between those concerned about the terrible threat to the environment and those who argue that mountaintop removal provides jobs. Recently a court order to stop Arch Coal from proceeding with one mountaintop-removal project drew hundreds of angry protesters to the federal courthouse in Logan in the heart of West Virginia coal country. A caravan of dozens of cars and pickups, emblazoned with the words "I Love Coal," circled the courthouse in a display of rage against the judicial blocking of the project. The slogan is up-front, in your face—if you don't love coal, then screw you. It's a more desperate war cry than the cool motto "I Dig Coal" that appeared on license plates in the 1970s.

Ironically, coal miners' jobs are disappearing as methods of extraction grow more efficient and, in the case of mountain-top removal, more awesomely destructive. Of all the procedures employed, this one uses the lowest number of workers per ton of coal extracted. Companies like Arch are expert at portraying opposition to mountaintop removal as simply anti-coal. One of their most famous tactics is to use miners, whose positions are highly vulnerable, as the front men in public demonstrations, like the one in Logan, on behalf of future projects.

In addition to being a hard, material place, Appalachia is a state of mind. The mountain heartland is America's counterpoint to Microsoft, the Internet, and Wall Street. Here is where the real speaks to the virtual. The heart of the new economic paradigm lies in communications. Iron and coal, the key resources in the old industrial economy, are far from the front shelf of today's economy. Appalachia is irredeemably about the old, hard stuff that still makes the world go round to a much greater extent than people like to think. The narrow valleys in West Virginia are crowded with rail lines. Here I see the long trains, with their dozens of cars, carrying the black gold to the rest of America.

I am driving through the southern corner of West Virginia, approaching the Kentucky border. My destination is Matewan, which sits on the West Virginia side of the Tug River. On the other side of the small river is Kentucky. The road to Matewan goes over a mountain and then down into the valley where bloody battles were once fought. Matewan is a very small town, overshadowed by a looming mountain and a wide swath of railway tracks dedicated to hauling coal out of this narrow valley. Now more a museum than a town, Matewan has had a savage experience that encapsulates the history of Appalachia. Indeed, on the main street of the little town, I find a museum where the history of the region comes vividly to life. The curator is a young guy, a native West Virginian, with a master's degree in history. We spend a wonderful couple of hours talking about the history of this little town, which has been the scene of searing conflicts since the late nineteenth century.

The first settlers of the Tug Valley had plenty of land and were largely self-sufficient, but in the decades following the Civil War, new and potent pressures assailed the traditional mountaineer society from within and without. Population growth meant that new generations of mountaineers mostly had less land than their fathers. On top of this, market capitalism, which was extending across America, was reaching into remote corners of Appalachia. Outside interests saw money to be made in timber and a couple of decades later in coal. As entrepreneurs pushed into the region, the mountaineer culture was subjected to painful stress. Naturally the newcomers, who were bringing modern capitalism to the region, thought they were superior to the locals with their mountain-bred ways. The activities of the capitalists drove up land prices, and many of the mountaineers sold their holdings, leaving their sons without property.

Into this troubled landscape in the late nineteenth century wandered the Hatfields and the McCoys and their hangers-on. Their feuding became the stuff of legend in the daily newspapers of the time. Every American has heard of the Hatfields and the McCoys. What made them infamous was the novel communications technology that was part of the new capitalism of their day. The daily newspapers were fighting it out for circulation, and many of them sent correspondents into the mountains to get the sensational story for their readers—that the Hatfields and the McCoys were lawless mountaineers who became embroiled in a blood feud that they were powerless to stop.

The feud began in the stormy decades following the Civil War, a conflict that had bitterly divided the mountaineers between those who sympathized with the North and those who backed the South. The Hatfields and the McCoys lived on opposite banks of the Tug River, the McCoys on the Kentucky side, under the sway of their famous leader, Randolph or "Old Ranel." The leader of the Hatfields, William or "Devil Anse," and most of his clan lived on the West Virginia side. Although there was an earlier encounter, the first major clash occurred in the late 1870s, when a Hatfield was accused of stealing a hog from a McCoy. Bad feelings continued after the acquittal of the Hatfield in court, erupting when two of Old Ranel McCoy's nephews killed one of the witnesses from the trial. This murder was followed by another trial, with the McCoy nephews acquitted on grounds of self-defense.

Hatfield-McCoy mayhem was spiced with romance at about the same time. Roseanna, the dark-eyed daughter of Old Ranel McCoy, fell in love with Johnse Hatfield, the son of the leader of the rival clan. Twenty-one-year-old Roseanna lived with eighteen-year-old Johnse for a while and became pregnant. During her time with young Hatfield, Roseanna learned of a plot by three McCoys to kill her lover. Roseanna rode her horse on a harrowing moonlight journey to warn Johnse, thereby saving his life and giving future literary crafters of the legend a romantic and thrilling chapter to incorporate. When Roseanna had had enough of swaggering Johnse and his family—she discovered that Johnse had married her cousin Nancy McCoy—she returned to her side of the Tug River and moved in with an aunt.

Next came a battle between members of the two families on an election day—election days being often wild and woolly occasions in the Tug Valley. The upshot of the battle was the fatal wounding of Ellison Hatfield, brother of Devil Anse, who died three days later. Ellison's death led to a furious reprisal by Devil Anse against the McCoys. The leader of the Hatfields was holding three McCoys prisoner, and with about twenty men he took the prisoners across the Tug River to the Kentucky side, tied them to some paw paw bushes, and shot them dead. The episode is known to feud historians as the Paw Paw Massacre.

Anger about the massacre built for years in Kentucky. In 1887, the state offered rewards for the arrest of the Hatfields who had been involved. Freelance detectives and Kentucky posses invaded the woods on the West Virginia side of the Tug in an effort to capture the Hatfields to win the reward money. Pitched battles led to the killing of one Hatfield and the capture of nine others. West Virginia struck back, offering rewards for the capture of the invading McCoys, but the Hatfields had their own plans. They crossed into Kentucky, burned down the house of Old Ranel McCoy, killed two of his children, and beat his wife as she tried to go to the aid of her dying daughter.

At this point, ten years after the original feud began, the Hatfields and the McCoys became a national sensation. Newsmen mingled with private armies in the mountains to get the story out to a shocked nation. Both West Virginia and Kentucky threatened to send their militias into the battle zone. In September 1889, nine Hatfield supporters were tried in a Kentucky court for their part in the attack on the McCoy home. Eight of them were sentenced to life in prison. The ninth, Ellison Mounts, was sentenced to die for the murder of Old Ranel's daughter. A few months later, Mounts was hanged.[1]

In the 1890s, the Hatfields and the McCoys became as famous as Al Capone did forty years later. Devil Anse Hatfield morphed into a kind of aging mountaineer philosopher. Writers beat a path to his door and passed his musings to the nation. The legend of the Hatfields and the McCoys did more than entertain Americans. It taught them a lesson about primitive, lawless hillbillies in a mountainous corner of their country who needed to be saved by progressive ideas and economic development from the outside. The hillbillies were backward people, the popular view had it, whose ignorance and poverty generated endless feuds among them. The best thing that could happen to mountain society was for the rising timber and coal interests to move in, develop the place, and shine the light of progress on its benighted inhabitants. In recent years, an alternative interpretation has been advanced, which stands the conventional wisdom on its head. In the most comprehensive study of the famous feud, the historian Altina L. Waller has concluded that it was not the primitive character of mountaineer society that provoked the violence, but rather the intrusion into the region of outside forces that engendered the crisis.

Her portrait of the mountaineer society shows that although it was not as wealthy as other parts of America, it had schools, courthouses, and churches. Its denizens, including some Hatfields and McCoys, tried to make their living in the rising timber business. While they often suffered misfortune, they were sometimes successful. Indeed, Devil Anse Hatfield managed to turn himself into a moderate business success by the time the feud was ending. Their struggles were played out as the timber interests were moving in and reducing the society of the Tug Valley to economic servitude. Waller stresses what other sensationalized accounts ignore: that there were very long gaps between the episodes in the feud and that the combatants often used the procedures of the courts, rather than violence, to deal with their grievances. She concludes that "the feudists were struggling with the same historical forces of capitalist transformation that had been changing America

since before the American revolution. . . . They . . . were beset
by social and cultural tensions as they attempted to accommodate or to escape or to resist being drawn into first a national,
then an international, economic system."[2]

Waller's analysis of the feud illuminates what came next in
the life of Matewan and the surrounding region. As the economy of the region shifted to timber and then more decisively
to coal, the little town was once more overwhelmed by bloody
conflict. Subsequent struggles pitted the miners and their union
against the coal companies and their goons. John Sayles's unforgettable film *Matewan* tells the story of the 1920 massacre in
the small town when coal-company goons shot it out with coal
miners and a local police chief by the name of Sid Hatfield.
Matewan's mayor, two miners, and seven coal-company detectives were killed. Hatfield, a relative of the storied Hatfields
of the past, emerged as the local hero who stood up to the coal
bosses. But not many months later, he too was gunned down
by detectives working for the coal interests.

The climax of the class war in West Virginia, much less well
known than the Hatfield-McCoy feud and the Matewan massacre, was the conflict in the mountains that erupted in
1920–21, in part in outrage against the assassination of Sid
Hatfield. At its climax, thousands of miners in three counties
rose in armed rebellion against the coal bosses. They faced not
only the police, militia, and federal troops, but bombers of the
U.S. Army Air Corps, sent in to put down the uprising. While
the bombers made menacing sorties over the rebellious miners, no bombs were actually dropped. In the end, the miners,
who were prepared to fight it out with the bosses and their
goons, were not ready to fight Uncle Sam's troops. Many of
the miners had fought in the trenches in the First World War,
and their patriotism compelled them to put down their arms
when the federal army showed up.[3]

I left Matewan still thinking about a comment by the

Matewan museum curator. We were musing about the great economic boom, currently under way in America. I asked him if this region of West Virginia and neighboring Kentucky had felt the boom. "We've heard all about the boom," he said. "But for some reason, it doesn't seem to have made it here."

# AMERICAN PYRAMID

I F YOU DON'T MAKE IT IN AMERICA, it's because you're just bloody stupid. Or perhaps lazy, or a woman, a black, an Hispanic, or an Indian. But unless you have one of these strikes against you, as the majority of Americans do, there's no reason for you to fail to make it to the top. How powerful and enduring that idea is, facts notwithstanding. Maybe that's the real reason that the suicide rate is so high among white American males over the age of fifty. If you're over fifty and you're a white male and you haven't made it the way you thought you should have, life can be depressing.

Unlike Europe, where the presence of social classes has been acknowledged for centuries, America has resisted the idea that its citizens are divided into more or less permanent groupings that bestow power and wealth on some while withholding it from many more. The belief that America holds out a unique promise of upward mobility to those who dare maintains a powerful hold on the imagination, not only of Americans but, through television and Hollywood movies, on the world. In our era we can call it the myth of Donald Trump, who

symbolizes the guy who makes it, loses it, gets it back, and
flaunts it, flanked by beautiful blondes. Where else but America
would a Donald Trump be considered by some qualified to be
a viable candidate for the presidency of the United States?

In the past, it was called the Horatio Alger myth. Alger was
a mid-nineteenth-century New England writer who wrote
dozens of inspirational stories about poor boys making good
by working hard, scrimping and saving, and sometimes mar-
rying the boss's daughter. Only in America, the moral was
relentlessly repeated, could poor boys aspire to anything and
everything. Everyone knows the names of men who've made
fortunes on their own—John D. Rockefeller and Andrew
Carnegie in the heyday of the robber barons, Bill Gates, in fact
the son of a doctor, in the age of the cyber capitalists.

The myth of the poor boy who makes good and becomes a
captain of industry is seductive. The only problem is that it has
about as much to do with reality in America as the prospect of
winning the lottery. One of the secrets of the great success of
American capitalism in the 1990s was that the earnings of the
majority of wage and salary earners increased very little during a time when fabulous fortunes were being amassed and
productivity was on the rise. The fortunes of the wealthiest
Americans are so gigantic that they bear comparison with no
previous ruling class in world history. And those fortunes have
been expanding explosively. When *Forbes* magazine published
its list of the four hundred wealthiest people in America in the
autumn of 1997, the average superrich person on the list had
a net worth of $1.6 billion. Two years later, that figure had shot
up to $2.6 billion.[1]

More shocking still is that the combined net worth of those
listed on the Forbes 400 was $1 trillion, not much below the
Gross National Product of Italy. These four hundred individuals, .00015 percent of the population of the United States,
had net assets equivalent to the net assets of the 170 million

least wealthy Americans, or 63 percent of the U.S. population. (These figures include home ownership assets, by far the
largest component of the assets of most American families.)²

The poorest 11 million households in America, with a population of about 30 million people, actually have negative assets,
that is to say they owe more than they own. On average, the
net debt of these households is $6,852. Indeed, the mean net
wealth of the poorest 85 million Americans is a little less than
zero. It is only when you get above the level of the 85 million
poorest people in the United States that you start to encounter
net assets that are at all appreciable. The next 29 million
Americans on the way up have net assets per household, on
average, of $36,711, including the money they have put into
the ownership of their houses. Then the next 45 million
Americans as we move up the wealth pyramid have assets per
household, on average, of $72,456. By now we have accounted
for 190 million Americans, or 70 percent of the population of
the United States. Even at this level we are very far from anything you can call real wealth.

It is worth pointing out the racial and ethnic differences that
stand out as we make the climb to this point. By the time we
reach this level, we have already tallied 68.5 percent of whites.
Above us still are the remaining 31.5 percent of whites. But
at this point, we have accounted for 91.9 percent of blacks,
leaving only 8.1 percent of African-American households with
assets above this level. We have included 89.4 percent of
Hispanics, leaving only 10.6 percent of Hispanic households
with higher net assets than this. Indeed, 25.6 percent of black
households and 24.3 percent of Hispanic households have zero
or negative net worth, compared with only 9.8 percent of
white households. Shedding further light on this is that the
median net worth of white households is $45,740 (meaning
that 50 percent of white households have net worth less than
this, and 50 percent of white households have net worth greater

than this). In stark contrast, the median net worth of black households is $4,418, and of Hispanic households, $4,656.

The next step on our climb up the pyramid is the 50 million people who live in households with an average net worth of $158,223. Then as we head up toward real wealth come the 19 million people whose households have an average net worth of $342,327. In the final category are 7.6 million Americans who live in households with an average net worth of $864,932.

We have climbed all this way but we have not yet encountered the superrich, in an atmosphere far more rarefied than that breathed by the merely very affluent we met in the last group. The rich and the superrich, in fact, constitute a small proportion of the 7.6 million Americans who are a part of this category.

Let's take a closer look at the individuals at the very pinnacle of the pyramid, the superrich who are celebrated in the annual Forbes 400 list. In the 1999 list, Bill Gates was again number one, awesomely so. The founder of Microsoft in the space of two years more than doubled his net wealth from about $40 billion to $85 billion. His feat was the greatest personal accumulation of capital in the history of the planet in such a short period of time—actually in any period of time. Astoundingly, the personal fortune of this one man is now equivalent to the net wealth of the 100 million poorest Americans, including the investments they have in their homes.

The meteoric rise of Bill Gates's fortune came during a time when Microsoft was under a legal cloud. A court ruling in April 2000 that Microsoft had violated U.S. antitrust laws left the company facing possible proposals by the U.S. Department of Justice that it be split into two or more companies, separating the software unit from the Windows operating system business. This legal assault coincided with a period of severe volatility in the stock market in which the value of technology stocks was hammered. As the value of Microsoft's shares plummeted in the early months of 2000, so too did the fortune of Bill Gates. By late April 2000, *Time* magazine concluded that his net wealth had declined to $62 billion. Others put the figure even lower.

In second place on the Forbes list in the autumn of 1999 was Paul Allen, cofounder of Microsoft. He came in at a cool $40 billion. Two years ago, Allen was stuck in third place on the list with assets of $17 billion. Riding the huge wave of his tech stocks, Allen also managed to more than double his immense fortune in only two years. Falling to third place from second two years ago was the legendary Warren Buffett, the sage of Omaha, Nebraska. Buffett, who has long been renowned as the most savvy investor of them all, a pro's pro, did less well than Gates and Allen. He increased his net wealth by $10 billion, from $21 billion to $31 billion, between 1997 and 1999. Next on the list, improving his position from sixth place two years ago, is Bill Gates's best friend, Steven Ballmer, the self-styled Napoleon figure who operates the business side of the Microsoft monolith. Ballmer increased his net worth from $8.3 billion in 1997 to $23 billion in 1999.

Microsoft has spawned a whole school of mini-superrich minnows who swim alongside Gates, the barracuda. Indeed, the Microsofties, from the billionaires right down to garden-variety millionaires, have been transforming Seattle and its environs in ways that provoke mixed reactions from the citizens. Part of the rite of passage of new ruling classes, from the ancients to the moderns, has been to construct gargantuan monuments, and among these there have always been castles or mansions in which the great man lives. Building mega-mansions on the shores of Lake Washington, where pleasant upscale suburban Seattle neighborhoods are located, is a favorite Microsofty pastime. Bill Gates, of course, led the way with the construction of his forty-thousand-square-foot futuristic palace on the eastern shore of the lake. Guests to the Gates home are given electronic pins so that as they walk about, lights come up as they approach and go down as they pass. Even more unnerving, the guests can watch screens transmitting who knows what to them during their peregrinations. This reminds me of Elvis Presley's proclivity for outfitting Graceland with jukeboxes so guests could listen to—what else?—"Hound Dog" or "Don't Be Cruel."

Also located on Lake Washington is Charles Simonyi, a high-ranking Microsoft programmer, who was said to be worth $1.5 billion in the Forbes 400 list for 1999. His mansion is tastefully more diminutive than that of Bill Gates. It is a glass-and-steel twenty-two-thousand-square-foot dwelling that boasts a computer lab, an indoor gym, a sixty-foot-long lap pool, and a heliport. His bedroom features a revolving bed, which is synchronized with window shades for him to get the best of Seattle's dull and dreary dawns.

Perhaps the brainiest Microsofty is Nathan Myhrvold, worth a mere $650 million, according to the Forbes 400 list for 1999. Myhrvold has styled himself as Microsoft's renaissance man, with interests that go far beyond the business concerns of the software giant, which perhaps explains why he is now on a long-term leave from the company. He loves books, gourmet cooking, expeditions to dig for dinosaurs, scuba diving, and racing cars. The twenty-thousand-square-foot mansion he's building on Lake Washington will feature a one-thousand-square-foot kitchen. His house is to be round, three stories high, with 120-degree windows that open onto the lake. A wine room, a media room, and a gym with a basketball court are part of the plan.

Not surprisingly, with billionaires and multimillionaires building on the shores of Lake Washington, the mere upper-middle-class mortals who had previously lived in the neighborhood are finding property values rising to Olympian heights. Old houses, including the house Gates grew up in, a lovely Cape Cod–style home by the lake, are being torn down to make way for the new castles of the new mega-rich.

In general, the techies did very well on the Forbes 400 list in 1999. There were seventy-one moguls on the list who derived their fortunes from technology and software. It is the techies, the masters of the new globe-girdling cyber magic, who have set the tone for American capitalism in the new millennium. As others have suggested, the techies have raised the tone of the superrich from the lurid and destructive image of the junk-bond dealers who came to prominence in the 1980s. With Bill Gates as their point man, techies have done more than anyone else to give American capitalism its hopeful, future-oriented face. To some extent, though, this new look of American capitalism has resulted from a conjuring trick no less difficult to contrive than the cyber universe itself. The theme of the 1999 Forbes 400 list was "the billionaire next door," the idea being that there are now so many billionaires that they no longer all live in a cloistered corner of Manhattan. We are being encouraged to feel warm and cuddly about the new nerdy billionaires. Bill Gates in his oversize sweater is just so huggable.

The problem with this attempt to normalize extreme wealth is the underlying fact of the immense inequality that is at the very center of American life. I've presented the figures on the chasm that separates the superrich from the rest of the American population. The figures also show that the majority of Americans are very far from being rich themselves. Selling the idea that America is a very rich country, in the sense that most Americans are rich, is a great lie, a whopper. And yet, even after you've seen the cold, hard numbers that make the nonwealth of the majority of Americans very plain, something of the great lie sticks, subtracting hugely from the impact the facts would otherwise have. Why does the great lie, which shields Americans and the rest of the world from the vast inequalities of American life, have such staying power?

It should not surprise us that people from nonwealthy backgrounds, who have acquired great fortunes, tend to be imbued with an unshakable conviction that capitalism is the best of all possible social systems. In Bill Gates's best-selling book *The Road Ahead,* the man who made more money than anyone else in the history of the world said that Adam Smith would have been pleased by the way capitalism had shown its advantages over other systems during the 1990s.[3] It would have been remarkable indeed had he not reached this conclusion, but others also buy the conclusion uncritically. The crucial point about social classes is not merely that they exist objectively but that social behavior is influenced by their existence. In other words, consciousness about class matters as much as the objective fact of class.

People often go to New York to invent a new life for themselves, to launch their careers, to make their fortunes in the city that remains the financial capital of the globe. I am driving to New York in late March to check out an endangered species, America's socialists, a small coterie of individuals and groups whose central conviction has always been that divisions between the classes is the most telling fact about a society. The occasion is the annual meeting of the Socialist Scholars in Manhattan who will be discussing Karl Marx's *Communist Manifesto* 150 years after it first saw the light of day in 1848.

The Socialists will be meeting at a college not very many blocks from the World Trade Center. I have decided to stay in Jersey City, which is right across the Hudson from Manhattan. My route takes me down the west side of the Hudson past the exit to the George Washington Bridge, from which you can enter Manhattan at about 180th Street.

Where I am driving on the Jersey side, the landscape approximates my idea of hell on earth. Freeways with rusting bridges merge and converge as I pass through endless industrial sites, some functioning, others rotting. From time to time, there are pond-size pools of liquid of a metallic blue-green hue beside the freeway. The road takes me over bridges that cross other bridges, tracks, and bits of towns that signs allege exist along the route. At last, I am approaching Jersey City, where I exit and am fed into mean streets and a dingy commercial district. At least this looks like a real place, with crowds of people on the sidewalks. As it turns out, my motel is only a couple of hundred yards from the yawning mouth of the Holland Tunnel. If I hadn't turned quickly into the motel parking lot, I would have been sucked into this underwater route to Manhattan.

Later I learned that Jersey City leads the United States in car thefts and that the car most often stolen is the Toyota Camry, the car I am driving. Fortunately, a friend has lent me the Club, which I fasten onto the steering wheel of my car each time I park it.

After an hour's respite in this dingy motel, it's time to face the reds. If Karl Marx had been alive today, the drive through the Holland Tunnel from Jersey City to Manhattan might have inspired an opus on class divisions in contemporary capitalism. Everything I witnessed on the horrific Jersey shore is a giant service platform for Manhattan, discreetly separated by the Hudson.

It feels good to be on the upmarket side of the water, where the socialists are set to gather. Inside the large, modern college building, I am immediately surrounded by literate, aging, talkative American socialists. There are book tables everywhere. Socialist beards are thrust toward each other. Slowly, we head for the main conference hall where the weekend reflections on the *Communist Manifesto* are set to begin.

On the platform is a panel of distinguished American and European socialists. A couple of the Americans, Harry Magdoff and Paul Sweezy, were well-known elder statesmen of American socialist thought decades ago, when I was a kid. I'm delighted they're still with us. Marx hadn't been dead all that long when they were born, so maybe they can provide some genuine insight into the life and times of the *Manifesto* over the past century and a half.

When the highly articulate speeches and reflections have

been going on for about an hour, I realize that I am finding
them very odd. It is not that they are deficient in eloquence or
humor, it is that they seem to be so lacking in any connection
to time or to place. Except for being vaguely set in a post–Cold
War context, these orations are tied to no particular locale or
social struggle in any recognizable way. These could be socialist declamations from the moon, for all they have to do with
earthly realities of any sort.

Pessimism hangs in the air of these speeches. We lost. They
won. This is the general gist of the messages we are hearing
at a historical moment when things are looking decidedly
upbeat for the American variety of capitalism and rather
somber for the hard-line socialism favored in this hall. From
time to time, the speakers pay homage to Marx for the astonishing brilliance of the *Manifesto,* including lavish praise for
the way he managed to foretell globalization and to analyze
it luminously a century and a half before it happened. One
has to admit that his forecast that control of capital would
be ever more concentrated in fewer and fewer hands isn't
looking too bad right now. The speakers are kind enough to
leave out Marx's forecasts that didn't turn out so well.
Nobody mentions that Marx would have been as down in the
mouth as those on the stage to learn that, 150 years after his
*Manifesto,* the working class was as far from revolutionary
zeal as ever.

What gives the session its peculiarly abstract air, of course,
is that we are in Manhattan, the heart of capitalism, in a country where almost no one would admit in public to being a
socialist. In France, Germany, or Canada, where socialists
actually play a role in politics, the speeches would have been
at a lower altitude, making contact from time to time with
concrete realities in their countries. Only in America where
nobody gives a fig what these socialists think would the people on the platform convey the impression that they were

speaking for all the socialist struggles in the world. Such are the joys of spending time with a roomful of generals who have no foot soldiers.

While the session is still under way, during periodic trips to the rest room I run into some fellow Canadians I know who invite me to a wine-and-cheese affair that is to be held in a Soho flat. After the session, rain blows through the streets as about a dozen of us walk to the site of the party, which is located on the upper floor of a warehouse, now refurbished as a trendy apartment with a high ceiling. By the time we arrive, the place is packed with middle-aged socialists, and Harry Magdoff is in a large wing chair with a crowd of interlocutors pressing in on him. Fine ruby red French wines are flowing from a table at the far end of the open-plan apartment. Rotund comrades holding two glasses of the precious liquid aloft squirm awkwardly through the crowd to reach their companions.

The highlight of the session on the following day comes when Michael Moore, the impudent filmmaker, much renowned for his creation *Roger and Me* and one-time star of *TV Nation,* climbs onto the platform. Moore, who is pudgy, wears his trademark Detroit Red Wings cap. In his guise as the true representative of working-class Americans, Moore informs the socialist literati that their best bet would be to put aside their copies of *The Nation* or *Das Kapital* to take a trip to the movies. He announces that the year's leading films such as *Good Will Hunting* and *Titanic* are all about the class struggle. It's out there, he says, ordinary Americans resisting the ruling classes. Funny you hadn't noticed it, he tells an audience whose eyestrain does not come mainly from watching Hollywood extravaganzas. The comrades, who are not much amused, squint at him in neuralgic displeasure.

With Moore's advice that it is time to get out and experience the masses still ringing in my ears, I left the conference to see Manhattan, which certainly looks better than it did a few years ago. Construction cranes are much in evidence. The

miracle of squeezing new structures into existing structures—
always Manhattan's speciality—continues. The street people
of New York, particularly those asking for a handout, are much
less in evidence than in former years. Where have they gone?
Has the city government removed them? To where? It's still
early in the miracle that the Republican mayor, Rudy Giuliani,
has supposedly wrought in Manhattan. In later months, we
learn much more about the police brutality and the roundups
of the indigent that have accompanied the cleanup of the
metropolis. Nonetheless, it feels safer to walk the streets of
Manhattan than it only recently did. As in much of the rest of
the United States, the violent crime rate is down, in part at
least as a consequence of changing demographics. As the population ages, the proportion of the total made up of the most
violent component—young males—has declined. Despite the
change for the better, the United States remains by far the most
violent of the advanced industrial countries.

By the time I get to Times Square, it is dark and the mighty
neon gods are beaming images of female pulchritude to the
masses below. Maybe this is where Michael Moore should have
directed the socialist scholars. Products like Revolution and
Contradiction, whose names would surely have warmed Karl
Marx's heart, are displayed by heavenly bodies. Perhaps if Marx
made a sudden return today, he would conclude that sex-
ploitation, not religion, is the opium of the people.

Sunday morning, I wake up in my dingy motel room in Jersey
City, ready to head back to Toronto. I look out my window to
discover that a thick blanket of fresh snow has covered this
dilapidated town. And the snow is still falling furiously. After
going for a run in the splendid surroundings where hardly a
moving vehicle is to be seen, I pack up and drive to the freeway. Perhaps I am being repaid for my negative reaction to this
part of New Jersey during my inbound trip. The place has certainly been given a facelift of a sort. It has become an arctic
wonderland, much more like the shore of Hudson Bay than

the shore of the Hudson River. For miles on the treacherously
slippery road, I do not encounter a single other vehicle. During
the two hours it takes me to get back to the New York State
Thruway, there is little evidence that I am driving through a
stretch of America's great megalopolis.

There have been times in American history when those who
feel they are the victims of the power of a superior social class
have expressed their outrage through trade union and political action. The closing years of the nineteenth century saw class
tension as the entrepreneurs of the second industrial revolution, which followed the Civil War, opened factories to supply
the new national market that was now within their grasp.
Industrial workers in the Northeast and Midwest, many of
them immigrants from Europe, worked long hours in wretched
conditions for low rates of pay. Workers were beginning to
organize into unions, some of them relatively conservative,
such as those in the American Federation of Labor, led by
Samuel Gompers. But some of them were radical, even revolutionary, like the Knights of Labor and the Industrial Workers
of the World (IWW). In the face of worker organization, bosses
fought back when they hired goons and thugs to intimidate
those involved in the drive to expand unions. Violence and riots
were not infrequent occurrences in the last decades of that century and the first decades of the twentieth century. In May 1886,
the most famous of these incidents, the so-called Haymarket
affair, erupted in Chicago. As part of the widespread movement
in support of the eight-hour workday, several thousand people
attended a meeting at Haymarket Square. Toward the end of
the meeting, which was being patrolled by a contingent of 180
policemen, a bomb went off in the midst of the police, wounding 66 officers, seven of whom later died. The police fired into
the crowd of demonstrators, killing several people and wounding about two hundred.

The police response to the terrible events of that night was to arrest eight anarchists in Chicago, even though they had no evidence that these persons were guilty of planting the bomb. The anarchists were charged with having incited murder through the propagation of their ideas and their writings. In the sensational trial that followed, the anarchists were sentenced to death. Meetings of protest against the sentences were held all over the world. Despite the protest, a year later, four of the condemned were hanged, one other committed suicide, and the three others remained in prison.[4] The Haymarket affair heralded a period of repression and backlash against unions and working-class agitation, but it did not stifle the growing movement.

Working-class agitation in the United States led to the brief rise of a number of socialist political groups in the country. Although immigrant workers were central to this agitation, the movement spread to American-born working people as well. In the election of 1912, Eugene Debs, the Socialist Party candidate, received 900,000 votes for president. Socialist agitation continued during World War I and in the 1920s. Despite the return to prosperity during the twenties, the distribution of income and wealth in the United States was extremely uneven. Millions of workers and their families remained desperately poor and the movement for change continued. Working-class campaigns provoked an extremely harsh reaction. In the atmosphere of the "red scare" of the twenties, local and state police and the FBI became active agents of repression. Hundreds of immigrant workers were rounded up by police, held for long periods in seclusion, and deported from the country following secret trials. In this highly charged atmosphere, two anarchist working men from the Boston area, Nicola Sacco and Bartolomeo Vanzetti, were arrested and charged with having perpetrated a holdup and murder at a shoe factory. They were tried and sentenced to death. For seven years, as legal appeals took place, the case was followed all over the world. As their execution date neared, millions of people were convinced that Sacco and Vanzetti were innocent and that they were being victimized because they were foreigners and anarchists. In August 1927, with protests on their behalf reaching a crescendo, the two died in the electric chair.[5]

During the Great Depression of the 1930s, American capitalism itself seemed to be tottering and in danger of collapse. This time capitalism had to be rescued by a son of the wealthy who became the champion of ordinary Americans, although his name was reviled in the homes of the rich, whose very fortunes and enterprises he did so much to safeguard. Franklin Roosevelt opened the door to the notion that private enterprise alone could not be relied on to ensure social well-being. Roosevelt's New Deal accepted the idea that the government was responsible for ensuring that people had work and that in the face of misfortune their minimum needs would be met. These crucial changes to the principles on which the American system rested were reinforced by the experience of World War II, which illustrated that a national mobilization to win the war was also a national mobilization to put people back to work.

Like people in other industrialized countries, Americans held on to the lessons of the Depression and the war for about a quarter of a century after 1945. While corporate America profited hugely from the economic activities of this era, the income gap between those at the top and those at the bottom in American society actually closed a little. The majority of Americans were acquiring some measure of prosperity and, along with it, middle-class hopes and aspirations.

The 1970s was a decade of transition, marked by crises that negated the Great Social Compromise on which post-FDR America operated. Inflation, triggered by the Vietnam War, undermined the effort to run a countercyclical fiscal and monetary policy in which government spent more, reduced taxes, and lowered interest rates during recession and cut back spending, increased taxes, and raised interest rates when the economy was in danger of overheating. Under the pressure of vast increases in the price of oil, the economies of industrialized countries, including the United States, were battered simultaneously with slowing growth and rising inflation. Stagflation, as this was called, seemed to contradict all that had been learned during the postwar decades.

Slowing economies produced another dramatically destabilizing effect. The social programs that had been put into place during the postwar decades to help people during recessions suddenly became much more financially burdensome. With unemployment higher as a permanent condition, welfare-state programs cost much more at the same time as tax revenues failed to grow because of reduced economic growth. Out of this vicious cycle came the government deficits, which were to long plague the United States and the other advanced countries.

It was the new and unaccustomed world of the 1970s that opened the way for the destruction of the Keynesian compromise of the postwar decades. Central bankers and bondholders were at the center of the revolution that occurred with lightning speed at the end of the seventies. Paul C. Volcker, chairman of the Federal Reserve Board, was the unlikely revolutionary who launched the United States on a tough regime of tight money and high interest rates. Not only did his new stance at the Fed wring inflation out of the American economy, at the cost of a severe recession, it also helped defeat Jimmy Carter in the presidential election of 1980. Ronald Reagan came to power in part thanks to Volcker. Deregulation in the eighties, driven by Reagan in Washington and Margaret Thatcher in London, did much to usher in the age of globalization, whose key elements were free capital flows, freer trade, and worldwide systems of production and marketing by major corporations.

The eighties revolutionaries, at the Fed and in the White House, prepared the way for the private-sector impresarios of the nineties who have brought us the new world of computers, the Internet, and the dot-com companies. In the "new economy," wage and salary earners have much less bargaining power than they had in the old industrial economy of the postwar decades. For one thing, companies can threaten to shut down plants in the United States and head for greener pastures where wages, benefits, environmental expenditures, and workplace investments are much less expensive. A large part of the new economy has nothing to do with high tech but with deregulation, which allowed companies to flee from the United States.

But the high-tech revolution and the transformation it has wrought are also very real, comparable in historical terms to the way the automotive industry remade America in the 1920s. The revolutionary technology, whose potential became clear during the 1990s, completed the transformation begun with the monetarism and deregulation of the late seventies and early eighties. Profoundly innovative technology is both creative and destructive, bringing to mind the great Austrian economist Joseph Schumpeter's concept of "creative destruction." When cars and trucks were built on a vast scale in America in the 1920s, new industries were created and pools of capital were invested in them. The steel, glass, rubber, petroleum, and chemical industries were transformed. Highways were constructed and city layouts dramatically altered. Here was economic creativity on the monumental scale. Along with it, however, came massive destruction. Railroads had reined in American transportation for many decades, during which roads were little more than dusty pathways. The rise of cars and trucks displaced rail, turning profitable companies into money losers, ushering in three-quarters of a century of rail-line abandonment. As always with creative destruction, the new investment rendered much of the existing investment if not worthless then worth much less.

The new technology of the 1920s pointed toward a more productive, more affluent society. But the transition to that better future was anything but smooth. It was chaotic and disruptive. Not the least important of the causes of the Great Depression of the 1930s was the rise of the automotive industry and the consequent ruin visited on other sectors. As it turned out, the better world foretold in the revolution wrought in Detroit was not fully seen until the 1950s, following a decade of wrenching economic turmoil and a world war.

The new technology that reordered American commerce in the 1990s was no less an exercise in creative destruction. Microelectronics radically altered industrial production techniques. And personal computers and the Internet spawned nothing less than a new American economy. Similarly, the personal computer and the Internet have changed the commerce of the world. Personal computers have revolutionized every office in America. And it was not so long ago that many experts predicted there would never be a mass market for personal computers. It was Bill Gates and his associates at Microsoft who comprehended this revolution, though it took them a long time to figure out that the Internet would be of colossal importance. But Microsoft played catch-up with all the clout of a monopolist when it developed its Internet Explorer and then pushed aside competitors by providing the program as part of the sale of its dominant Windows operating system.

By the beginning of the new millennium, hundreds of millions of people around the world were hooked up to the Internet. Capturing the attention of even small proportions of humanity became an exceptionally alluring business prospect. Out of the cyber universe came a new business entity—e-commerce. Yahoo!, AOL, eBay, and Amazon.com are a few of the amazing corporate names that have been spun out of the ether. As the most powerful search engine on the World Wide Web, Yahoo! commands an audience of tens of millions, numbers that would make all the great television networks of the world quake. It's not an orderly audience to be sure, but it is an audience to whom advertising is being sold on the Net at ever-rising rates. And unlike the audiences of the great television networks, Yahoo!'s is multiplying the way the buyers of Model T Fords once did. Yahoo! is like a latterday CBS, a network presiding over a huge audience.

It is eBay and Amazon.com, though, which expose the heart of e-commerce with all its creative and destructive potential. Amazon.com started out selling books online. Headquartered in a warehouse in an anything but trendy area of south Seattle, the company had a tiny staff, but it had an idea whose time had come. The company could sell books online to a worldwide clientele, providing the convenience of ordering at home. You could sit in your apartment in Menton in the south of France, as I once did, find the Amazon.com Web site, browse, find books you want, and order them. So what if I was hundreds of miles from a first-class English-language bookstore. Most of Amazon's customers did not have such requirements. You could be sitting in your apartment in Manhattan, only blocks away from the nearest Barnes and Noble outlet, and still decide that it was more convenient to browse and order from the online warehouse in Seattle.

Amazon's other secrets had to do with real estate, investment in stores, and staff. The mega-bookstores, outfitted with their attractive coffee bars, that have become ubiquitous in the heart of America's great cities and shopping malls, have been highly successful in driving out the smaller bookstores of the past. But their achievement was based on the investment of billions of dollars in the acquisition of prime real estate and in the design and construction of their proud stores. When I saw

the old warehouse that headquartered Amazon.com in south
Seattle, with its bright inexpensive banner hanging down the
front, I had to laugh. Forget about investing in expensive real
estate or building fancy stores and a staff. All you need is some
technical people to run a first-rate online system and a staff to
put a list together, keep it up to date, and deal with customer
inquiries. I am not suggesting that these are simple matters,
requiring no innovative and creative solutions. Perhaps the
real virtuosity of companies like Amazon.com is displayed in
how they run their gigantic warehouses, hardly the stuff "new
economy" dreams are made of.

Launched from the start as an online company whose man-
date was to act as an auctioneer for all manner of goods and
services, eBay went Amazon.com one better. The company
did have to bar certain goods from auction, such as guns and
human organs. With a few exceptions, though, the world was
eBay's oyster. From a base of a few hundred thousand shoppers, eBay quickly expanded to supply purchases to millions
of people. People who held stock in the company at the beginning soon grew wealthy on their holdings. Top managers at
eBay discovered overnight that they were billionaires. Pierre
Omidyar of eBay was estimated to be worth $4.9 billion by
the Forbes 400 in the autumn of 1999.

By summer 1999, Amazon.com figured out that there was
no particular virtue in limiting itself to the sale of books. The
company made the move implied in the kind of commerce it
had pioneered and became a general auctioneer of goods and
services along the lines of eBay. Not that Jeffrey Bezos of
Amazon.com needed to make the move because his net worth
was suffering. In autumn 1999, the Forbes 400 estimated his
fortune at $7.8 billion. The same year, *Time* magazine named
Bezos its person of the year. Since then, however, the fortunes
of Bezos, and other dot.com magnates, have shrunk precipi-
tously in the great tech-stock meltdown of 2000–01.

The productivity advance as a consequence of e-commerce is audacious and significant. A worldwide market has been established by the online giants, and it is a market that wipes out the differences between Manhattan and the outback of Australia: e-commerce has both centralizing and decentralizing effects. On the one hand, new corporate giants spring forth to handle the business and in the process they destroy much of the value of billions of dollars of investments that have been built up by their non-online competitors. That is the centralizing face of e-commerce. On the other hand, e-commerce wipes out much of the advantage of location in prime places in great cities or in their surrounding suburbs. It opens the door for individuals and small companies located in little towns or cities to sell online under conditions essentially the same as those of people in large commercial centers. That is the decentralizing side of e-commerce. This decentralizing side is not particularly egalitarian in its effects because the corporate juggernauts emerging at the heart of e-commerce are where the real clout and economic opportunity lie.

The new world of e-commerce, which is only beginning to signal its long-term effects, is an immense force for "creative destruction." Over the next decade or two, it will do no less than reshape the service sector of the American economy. It is not difficult to foresee that e-commerce will prompt large numbers of job losses in the traditional retail sector of the American economy. Competition between online retailers and actual stores will not lead to the demise of the latter. It will lead, however, to a shift in the market from a labor-intensive sector to one much less labor intensive. Traditional retailers will respond by going online themselves to meet the new challenge. For example, Barnes and Noble has met the threat from Amazon.com by setting up its own online book-retail operation. Meeting the challenge of e-commerce with an e-commerce response, however, tends to further reduce the number of people employed in the retail sector. Traditional retailers can also be expected to respond to the online challenge by enhancing the services they provide in their stores. While you can buy a book online, there is much pleasure to be had when you go into a large bookstore, browse the shelves and sit in the armchairs provided, then take a pile of books into the coffee shop in the store for further consideration. That said, the shift to e-commerce will be large, and its effects on employment in retailing are likely to be dramatic. Just as for decades railroads laid off employees after the rise of the automobile, for a long time to come America can expect layoffs in the traditional retail sector.

The story doesn't end there, however. Defenders of e-commerce will rightly point out that the new form of retailing they have pioneered increases productivity, requires less labor, and should therefore benefit consumers not only with greater convenience but with substantial savings. In theory, savings to consumers leaves more money to be spent or invested elsewhere. This means that jobs lost in traditional retailing should be replaced with new jobs, perhaps in entirely new sectors of the economy.

Broadly speaking, there is truth in this response. The problem is that the transition, as in the case of the fall of railroads and the rise of autos, may be far from smooth. There is no guarantee that people who lose jobs in one sector end up finding work in other sectors. The transition from the industrial economy to the service-sector economy in recent decades was difficult. All you have to do is visit rust-belt cities in the Northeast and Midwest, where manufacturing plants have closed down, to see this with your own eyes. If you live in Buffalo, Syracuse, or Rochester, where tens of thousands of blue-collar jobs have been lost, it isn't much help that Boston has flourished with the rise of new service-sector employment.

In addition, there is no guarantee, indeed no likelihood, that the new jobs will appear as quickly as the old ones are lost. The process of creative destruction is highly uneven, and involves lags in time, which may prove devastating to individuals and communities. In extreme cases, they can prove devastating to whole countries, as they did in the 1930s. At this stage, it is not possible to predict how disruptive e-commerce will turn out to be. It would be prudent, however, to watch out for storms along the way.

Indeed, we are already witnessing the class struggle developing within the e-commerce companies themselves. As it turns out, Amazon.com, usually thought of as being on the cutting edge, is also exhibiting one of the oldest and least progressive features of capitalism—the subjection of its employees to a vicious regime of work speedup. Most of the media attention about Amazon.com has focused on the youthful, brash tycoons who launched the company. Not much attention has been paid to the vast majority of the company's employees—there are more than five thousand of them—who toil in low-paying service positions. The majority of people who work for Amazon.com do not have creative jobs and cushy stock options. They make about $10 to $13 an hour and their job is to answer the e-mails of customers who have forgotten their passwords or who require information.

These galley slaves of the new economy can be forgiven for thinking the drive to do things faster and faster is largely aimed at getting them to sweat harder. At Amazon.com, an employee who grinds out 12 e-mails an hour is regarded as first class. But someone who answers fewer than 7.5 e-mails per hour for any extended period could face job termination. It turns out that much of the fabled productivity in this sector is achieved on the backs of low-paid workers, doing mind-numbingly boring jobs. Gretchen Wilson, twenty-four, an organizer with the Washington Alliance of Technology Workers, has been involved in a drive to unionize the employees at Amazon.com. She charged that the company has been waging "a classic, by-the-book, anti-union campaign right out of the 1930s."[6]

If Seattle has become a symbol of new technology and the new economy, in November 1999 it also became a symbol of resistance to the globalization agenda being fostered, not least by corporations such as Amazon.com, Microsoft, and Starbucks that rose to prominence in Seattle. Under the auspices of President Bill Clinton, the United States hosted a meeting of the members of the World Trade Organization (WTO), whose goal was to launch a new multilateral round of global trade negotiations. The meetings themselves turned out to be a debacle. But it was what happened on the streets that announced a new stage in the conflict over globalization. Fifty thousand demonstrators, representing labor and environmental organizations and other groupings of activists, fought the WTO agenda in the streets, in the so-called Battle of Seattle.

While much attention was focused on the violent activities of a few of the demonstrators, the largely peaceful protests announced to the world the presence of a coherent body of opponents of the official American line on the WTO. Most of the protesters were young, giving the event major generational significance. The culture was changing.

In April 2000, the new movement used the techniques that were developed in Seattle to attempt to shut down meetings of the International Monetary Fund (IMF) and the World Bank that were to be held in Washington, D.C. Finance ministers and central bankers from twenty-five countries were to attend. As in the Seattle protests against the WTO, the dozens of organizations involved in the mobilization found common ground in their opposition to what they called the "corporate agenda" of the IMF and the World Bank. These institutions, according to their critics, have contributed to the suffering of the people of the world's impoverished countries

rather than to the amelioration of their conditions. To qual-
ify for loans, the critics said, the IMF has insisted that recip-
ient countries dismantle social programs and adopt policies
that open the door to inflows of foreign capital and imports,
typically at the cost of increased joblessness. The World Bank,
they maintain, provides capital that benefits Third World elites
and multinational corporations, while often directly assault-
ing the majority of the people through such projects as the
construction of dams that lead to the flooding of the territory on which communities, towns, and farms are located.

I arrived in Washington early on Sunday, April 16, when
the biggest protests were planned. Hundreds of demonstrators had been arrested over the past few days and the
authorities had announced the closing to vehicle traffic of an
area in the center of the capital stretching ten blocks from
north to south and nine blocks from east to west. Inside the
closed area were the buildings housing the IMF and the World
Bank, the White House, and the Ellipse, the giant open space
south of the White House where demonstrators planned to
assemble for a parade later in the morning.

Walking across the bridge from Georgetown toward the
closed area, I encounter two D.C. policemen in riot gear—
knee pads, visors, and gas masks and carrying nightsticks. One
of them warns me that it might not be too safe to enter the
battle zone.

A couple of blocks farther on, I come to one of the hotels
where delegates to the meetings are staying. Police form a line
across its front. Delegates in their dark blue suits, wearing
name tags, are waiting for shuttle buses to take them to their
meetings. That is, if they can make it through the blockades
that have been thrown up by demonstrators.

I am now entering the zone where demonstrators and police
keep a wary eye on each other from behind their barricades.
The police, holed up behind portable metal fences, aim to

prevent demonstrators from making it to the sites of IMF and World Bank meetings.

The majority of the demonstrators at the intersections are in their twenties, and almost all of them are white. They have come dressed for the occasion in jeans, fatigues, and loose-fitting shirts and sweaters. Many of them are outfitted with gas masks or bandannas soaked with vinegar to diminish the effect of tear gas or pepper spray. They have set up their own barriers in the center of intersections to prevent delegates from reaching their meetings. They have tied brightly colored rows of string from lamppost to lamppost across streets to slow down traffic and to block the police. At some intersections, they have piled mattresses around the perimeter and have picked up parked cars and positioned them to block the roads. In the middle of these intersections, twenty or thirty kids are sitting on the pavement, chained together in a circle, with their arms inside pieces of plastic pipe. All this is intended to make it very difficult for the police to separate them and drag them away to paddy wagons.

At one street corner, a long line of protesters, linked arm in arm, chant, "This is what democracy looks like. This is what democracy sounds like." While I am watching the chanters, I notice a man in an expensive dark suit crossing the intersection with several well-dressed companions. I have seen that face before. Then it clicks. Laurent Fabius, the finance minister of France is out for a stroll. Fabius, elegantly attired as only a member of the Paris elite can be, nods to the demonstrators, and a few of them try out a few rusty French phrases on him. The Socialist finance minister is not afraid of the kids on the street. He belongs to a party whose leading members cut their teeth in the great demonstrations in Paris in 1968, when 10 million people went on strike in opposition to the government of Charles de Gaulle.

At the next intersection, a parade of animal rights activists weaves through a throng of protesters. They chant slogans and carry bright puppet caricatures of animals and their human foes to make their point. A block farther on is another little parade. This time, the protesters are carrying elaborate gizmos that depict how the IMF and the World Bank grind down the people of developing countries. Here and there a young person, outfitted as a turtle, strolls along. Many demonstrators are carrying placards that read "Shut Down Capitalism." Overhead, a helicopter circles continuously over the battle zone.

One of the strengths of the new activists is their diversity. Trade union members, university students, anti-poverty activists, environmentalists, socialists, anarchists, supporters of Ralph Nader for president, feminists, and opponents of the death penalty are all here. While they have their own axes to grind, they can coexist under the broad tent of the anti-corporate agenda. Beneath the seeming chaos of this mobilization, there has been a great deal of organization. The Washington protests have been planned for months by a network of groups that communicate through Internet Web sites. Planners have divided the war zone in Washington into eight pie-shaped areas, assigning their forces particular sectors. On the streets, they communicate by cell phone and through the dispatch of bicycle messengers. Many of the activists here have undergone training in nonviolent tactics and in how to keep their cool while being assaulted by police with tear gas and pepper spray. At many intersections, "legal observers" are in position to act as potential witnesses in the event of violence or mass arrests. Many of the young demonstrators carry video cameras and still cameras so they can record what goes on. One of their goals is to establish alternative media for the coverage of these events.

As I approach one intersection, about a dozen protesters are moving out of the area. "What's going on?" I ask one young woman. "The police are getting ready to use tear gas, and I'm not equipped, so I'm leaving the area." When I reach the intersection, a highly choreographed scene is playing itself out. Police officers in riot gear are putting on their gas masks. On the other side of a barricade, not more than a couple of feet away, protesters with their backs turned to the police are calmly putting on their own gas masks and bandannas. I stick around for a while, but the tense standoff continues and no tear gas is deployed.

A little later, I come upon a scene at a street corner where a young woman is telling bystanders that a few minutes earlier policemen on motorcycles tried to break through a line of protesters. In the ensuing melee, she claims, one officer rode his motorcycle right over one of the demonstrators, a young man who has now been carried away.

Finally, I reach the Ellipse, the space south of the White House where thousands of demonstrators have gathered to go on a legally authorized march through the streets of the capital. A huge platform and sound system have been set up, and movement singers and inspirational speakers entertain the crowd. Michael Moore, who rained on the parade of the socialist scholars in New York, is the emcee.

There are no cops on the Ellipse, which is a peaceful oasis in the midst of the war zone. Many of the older demonstrators who have left the confrontations with the police to the twenty-year-olds have assembled here, but there are plenty of kids as well. Movement book tables have been set up. You can get literature on the IMF and the World Bank, the socialist revolution, and on the struggle to save the African-American journalist Mumia Abu-Jumal from being executed for a murder in Philadelphia his backers say he did not commit.

Later, as I walk back out of the war zone, I see Laurent Fabius once more. He still hasn't made it to his meeting. This time he is climbing into a van with about a dozen other delegates. In front and behind the van are police cars with their roof lights

blazing. Fabius is not smiling. A moment later, the little caravan heads off to try to get him to his appointed destination.
Just down the street, two D.C. cops are following eight or nine
anarchists dressed in black and carrying red-and-black banners. The anarchists are not smiling either. They climb into
their own van and head off toward the war zone.

The kids I saw on the streets remind me of the kids I saw in
Washington in 1965 when tens of thousands marched against
the war in Vietnam. But today's movement is more diverse
than its predecessors, its sensibility is more clearly internationalist, and its connections with activists in other parts of
the world are much more developed. It can no longer be said
that today's young activists are sixties wannabes. They have
created a new movement that has its own critique of the world
and its own approach to how to change the system. In short,
it has its own culture. Notably absent from that culture is the
bombast that was so much a part of the sixties movement and
particularly of its almost exclusively male leadership.

The kids in Washington went about their tasks in a calm,
professional way, ready for what the riot squads were prepared
to serve up and unfazed by the enormous power of the system
they were challenging. Just as Microsoft, Amazon.com, Bill
Gates, and Jeff Bezos have emerged out of the new capitalism
of the past couple of decades, so too has the new movement
of opposition to the corporate agenda. The kids who came to
Washington are united by their sense of alienation from the
culture of greed that is so integral to contemporary America.
Thirteen hundred of them were arrested in the streets of
Washington. They did not succeed in shutting down the meetings of the IMF and the World Bank, although they delayed
some of them. What they did succeed in doing was to focus
the attention of millions of people in many countries on the
nature of the new global economy and its institutions, and the
resultant social inequalities and threats to the environment.

part ★ three

# REPUBLIC TO EMPIRE

# GOVERNMENT OF THE PEOPLE

A FEW YEARS AGO, I was lunching in Manhattan with the senior executive of a prestigious multinational publishing company. Over glasses of wine, we were chatting about American politics when my lunch companion said something that shocked me. He told me he hadn't voted in the previous congressional election and didn't intend to vote in the presidential election later that year. In Canada, where three-quarters of adults vote in federal and provincial elections, it would be aberrant for a professional to tell you he didn't vote. This man explained that he had voted in the past, but he had given it up because he now believed that all politicians were essentially the same, that it didn't matter who you voted for.

In other Western democracies, middle- and upper-middle-class citizens vote in elections as a matter of course. Only in the United States is it socially acceptable for members of these classes to come right out and tell you that they don't vote. Indeed, among Americans who are working class and poor, it is the norm not to vote. Voting is the exception among the mass of Americans, not the rule. A potent example was the congressional election of 1994, in which only 39 percent of eligible adults bothered to vote. Just over half of these, 20 percent of eligible adults, voted for the Republicans, giving them control of both houses of Congress for the first time in four decades; thus, one adult in five participated in the historic turnover of power from the Democrats to the Republicans. Four out of five did not. Nonetheless, pundits interpreted the vote as an expression of the will of the American people.

Presidential elections are another story. You'd think that having the chance to participate in electing the world's most powerful political leader would motivate people to vote but, paradoxically, only about half of American adults bother to exercise their franchise. Indeed, participation rates among voters in U.S. presidential elections are lower than for the principal office of any other industrialized country.

One of the most arcane features of American politics is the way the president of the United States is chosen. In parliamentary democracies such as Britain or Canada, the prime minister is the leader of the party that commands the support of the majority of the members of Parliament (sometimes in a formal or informal alliance with other parties) following a general election. Party members in convention select leaders of political parties. In the United States, the presidential candidates of the Republican and Democratic parties have no real institutional links to the members of Congress in their parties. A losing candidate in a presidential election does not emerge as the leader of the opposition who then gets to rise in a daily question period in Parliament to hold the leader of the government to account. After Bob Dole, the 1996 Republican presidential candidate, lost his race against Bill Clinton, he went on to do Viagra commercials on television.

Republican and Democratic presidential candidates are picked through a highly idiosyncratic process that involves big money, media momentum, and a series of state primary and caucus contests through which delegates to the party convention are chosen. To fight each presidential election, cabals form around potential candidates. The goal of these "armies of the night" is to raise big sums of money, cash being the lubricant that enables the candidate to slide through the pre-campaign period, the primaries, the convention, and the election itself. The rules for the selection of delegates to the nominating convention vary bafflingly from state to state. In some states, voters can be registered as Republicans or Democrats and are permitted to vote in the primaries to select delegates who support one of the presidential candidates for their party. In other states, voters can participate in open primaries in which they vote for candidates in either party. In still other cases, delegates to party conventions are selected through attendance at caucuses, which are held at various places throughout the state.

In this system, in which some people's votes have considerable impact while other people's votes count for very little, money, media momentum, and success in early primaries and caucuses are tightly intertwined. The New Hampshire primaries and the Iowa caucuses occupy a highly symbolic position in the selection of presidential candidates in both parties. In a country with a population of 270 million people, that New Hampshire with its 1.2 million residents and Iowa with its 2.8 million[1] should play such a disproportionate role in choosing presidential candidates is indeed an oddity. Moreover, these two states, with a combined population of 4 million people, are not especially representative of the demography of the United States as a whole. New Hampshire has only twelve thousand Hispanic and seven thousand black residents. The state is overwhelmingly white. Iowa, home to thirty-nine thousand Hispanics and fifty-four thousand blacks, is also much more white in its demography than the U.S. average.[2] Neither state has firsthand experience with the problems of major metropolises. New Hampshire and Iowa are crucial to presidential candidates, especially those other than the front-runners, because they come very early in the process of delegate selection. New Hampshire jealously guards its coveted place as holder of the first primary through legislation that allows the state government to back up in front of any other state that tries to outflank it by scheduling an earlier primary date.

In both New Hampshire and Iowa, presidential candidates are in the business of retail politics. They go after votes one at a time. This is the place to see them up close. In July 1999, I had an opportunity to do just that.

When I encounter Gary Bauer, a family-values right-winger whose major focus has been on stopping abortions, he is on a lengthy campaign tour across Iowa in his bid for the Republican presidential nomination. His strategy is simple. If he can find enough votes in Iowa to put him high on the list of Republicans behind the front-runner, Texas governor George W. Bush, he could go on to become a major contender for the nomination. And in the event of a miracle, if Bush slipped, as front-runners sometimes do, Bauer could surprise the world and wind up with the nomination. To do that he has to stalk every last potential voter he can, up and down the towns and villages of the state.

On the day I observe the Bauer campaign in Iowa, the candidate is making four appearances. I decide to take in his act at the Boone County Fairground about forty miles north of Des Moines, the state capital. Bauer is due to arrive at the fair at two-fifteen. I get there about three-quarters of an hour earlier on an afternoon when the mercury has easily broken ninety-five degrees. Boone County's fair is pretty ho-hum, especially in the sweltering, humid air. I arm myself with a greasy, sweet and salty turkey leg, barbecued in the best Southern style. When I tell the woman who sold me the turkey leg that presidential candidate Gary Bauer is about to arrive, she says she's never heard of him. She adds that she never bothers to vote and that none of the politicians deserve her vote. Well, what do you think about the fact that he might be the next president? I ask. A few minutes later, I see that the news is having some effect on her, as she tells another customer that a presidential candidate is coming.

Most of the fair is devoted to displays of cows, steers, and pigs, but I soon find the exhibitor booths. Almost side by side are the local Republicans and Democrats. I ask a woman seated behind the red-white-and-blue bunting at the Republican booth to confirm that Bauer is to arrive at two-fifteen. She fixes me with the excited gaze of a political operative who thinks she has just discovered a genuinely independent, motivated Bauer supporter.

I go over to see the Democrats. Two of them, a tall young fellow and an older heavyset balding man, are standing behind their version of red, white, and blue. I strike up a conversation with the younger man, who tells me the Democrats outpoll the Republicans in this county. He explains that their strength is in the towns, among working people and union members. The Republicans dominate the countryside. Casually, I inform the young Democrat that Gary Bauer, the Republican presidential candidate, will be here to speak in a few minutes. "Never heard of him," he replies evenly.

Outside the single-story building where the Republicans and the Democrats have their booths, I position myself for the arrival of the candidate. A couple of spooky guys in suits, glued to their cell phones, are walking around the fairgrounds. Bauer's advance men, for sure. Nobody else in Boone County looks like that. A quarter of an hour later, Bauer's bus pulls up just outside the fair. The candidate's grand entrance is then held up for another ten minutes as a driver of a bus whose vehicle is outfitted to hold wheelchairs loads a man in a wheelchair aboard. At last, all is in readiness for Bauer. A sound truck rolls into the fairgrounds, and a smarmy deejay voice invites the thin heat-stunned throng to come up and greet presidential candidate Gary Bauer.

Right behind is the bus, all decked out in bright red, white, and blue with "Bauer for President 2000" emblazoned on the side. After it comes to a stop, about a dozen people file off, not a bad tactic since it gives the candidate a goodly percentage of the crowd he is about to address at the fair. Bauer steps off the bus. He is a diminutive man and is surrounded by much taller men and women. I'm only a few feet away from him and I can see that he has managed to appear very crisp in his white shirt and tie despite the heat that has wilted everyone else. His trick is that he is wearing a T-shirt underneath to soak up the sweat. Even though he looks a little fish-eyed, like someone who has just switched to contact lenses, he successfully conveys the impression that he is important.

The little knot of people around the candidate strolls past several black bulls, who are in the process of being hosed down, and heads inside the exhibit area. Bauer walks into the Republican booth. With a mike in hand, he speaks to the crowd of about thirty-five people informally but with a tone of authority. At once, he addresses the question on everyone's mind. Why does this little guy with the rather turtlelike head, a man who has never been elected to any public office, think he has the remotest shot at becoming the next president of the United States? He tells us that in 1964 he was sitting with his father, a janitor from Kentucky, watching Ronald Reagan on television. He told his father that someday Reagan would be president and that he, Gary Bauer, would work for him in the White House. Naturally, his father told him he was crazy, but two years before his father's death, he was able to show him that miracles do happen when he escorted his dad into his office in the West Wing of the White House during the Reagan presidency. Bauer was working as a special assistant to the president.

Bauer's defining issue is abortion. He sails into a diatribe against abortion and on behalf of the unborn. Winning a round of applause for this, he focuses the issue politically, taking aim at George W. Bush. When I am president, I will only appoint pro-life judges to the Supreme Court and the federal bench, he declares. I am very disappointed, he continues, that George W. Bush, when challenged by me to do so, refused to take the same position. Instead, Bush said only that he would appoint judges who are qualified.

From abortion, he turns to the plight of America's farmers, the second major theme he has been developing on his three-week-long search for votes in every corner of Iowa. This happens to be the week that a cruel heat wave has been destroying the crops of farmers, particularly in the East and parts of the Midwest. Iowa farmers haven't been as hard hit by the heat wave as others. What's killing them is the low price of corn. Bauer talks with compassion about farmers, but he's very sketchy when it comes to solutions. The brochure his supporters hand out, which has been written for Iowa voters, doesn't even mention farmers. Instead, the brochure places Bauer on the outer edge of the religious right wing of the Republican Party. Much of it deals with the abolition of abortion. This even comes up in his foreign policy, which calls for an end to Most Favored Nation status for China, until China "ends coercive abortion under the 'one child' policy." Bauer's other policies are a grab bag of the nostrums of the political right: a reduction of the income tax to a flat rate of 16 percent; an increased defense budget that would allow the United States to deploy a Star Wars anti-missile defense system; opposition to same-sex marriage; support for voluntary prayer in public schools; and permission to post the Ten Commandments on the walls of state facilities.

The candidate fields two questions from the audience. Asked what are his views on gun control, he replies that we don't need more laws and notes that the boys in Littleton, Colorado, who carried out the massacre at Columbine High School broke nineteen gun-control laws. Asked whether he is in favor of making English the official language of the United States, he declares that he is opposed to printing ballots in any language other than English. Bauer chats informally with well-wishers for a few minutes, while I try to disengage myself from the Republican woman who early spied me as a potential supporter. The candidate climbs back on the bus with his little party and heads off to another engagement.

The week that I saw Bauer in Iowa, three or four other candidates for the Republican presidential nomination were skulking about in the state. And Al Gore and Bill Bradley were to be back on the hustings there in a few days. When the candidates were not in Iowa, they were usually in New Hampshire doing the same thing, speaking to small crowds at state fairs, in restaurants, or in school gymnasiums. Odd though the process is, it is a heaven-sent opportunity for long-shot candidates, those who haven't yet come to national attention and who haven't raised gobs of money. Jimmy Carter, as a little-known Georgia governor, got the bounce out of New Hampshire that took him to the White House in 1976.

Bauer's dream did not come to fruition, however. He won only 6 percent of the votes in the Iowa caucuses the following winter, placing fourth in the field of six Republican candidates. A few days later in New Hampshire, he got 1 percent of the vote and dropped out of the race.

Seven months later, the contest for the Republican nomination was reaching its climax. The candidate who came out of New Hampshire as a serious threat to George W. Bush, the front-runner, was Arizona senator John McCain. At the peak of the sulfurous struggle between Bush and McCain, I got a close-up look at both candidates as they campaigned for votes in the Republican primary in New York State.

It is the last weekend before Super Tuesday in early March 2000, when contests are to be held in thirteen states, includ-

ing California, Ohio, and New York, to pick Republican delegates. The George W. Bush campaign, which enjoys the backing of almost the whole of the Republican Party establishment,
has taken over the center of the spacious new terminal at the
airport in Rochester, New York. In an hour, the Texas governor is to fly in from nearby Syracuse for a Saturday morning
rally. Hundreds of people have driven in from the suburbs and
nearby towns to greet the favorite in the Republican race. The
almost entirely white crowd, many of them parents with their
children, is as uniformly middle class a slice of America as I
have ever seen. Everyone is casually well dressed. There are
no punks, freaks, hippies, or poor people here. A middle-aged
man tells me that every local person who owes his or her job
to the Republicans is in the crowd.

In front of a big stage where the candidate is to speak, a
media area has been roped off. A first-class sound system is
pumping out soft rock and country music to the throng, which
waits affably for their hero's arrival. Right next to the side of
the stage is a fast-food outlet where I manage to get a table.
Everyone at the tables is wearing "Bush for President" stickers and has Bush posters. At the table next to me, a couple in
their early twenties, both of them wearing Bush stickers, are
making out in an inoffensive sort of way—Republican fore-
play, I think to myself.

Half an hour before Bush is to arrive, an emcee climbs onto
the stage and starts warming up the crowd. He calls out the
names of all the local cities, suburbs, and counties and gets
people to cheer when they hear theirs. He instructs us on
what to chant when "the next president of the United States"
arrives. Soon everyone is shouting, "Bush, Bush, Bush . . ." and
waving the red-white-and-blue Bush posters. One woman
has a homemade sign: "We love ya, Dubya." This crowd is more
good-natured than raucous.

At last, Bush and his party ride up the escalator behind the stage and climb onto the platform. With the Texas governor is his wife, Laura; the local county chairman of the Republican Party and his wife; the New York governor, George Pataki; and a surprise guest, Elizabeth Dole, the former presidential candidate who has endorsed Bush. Side by side, the members of the platform party look like prosperous peacocks, pheasants, and partridges that have been flushed out of the nearby brush.

We hear first from the gum-chewing county chairman, a plump man in a $1,000 blue suit. Then Governor Pataki, introduced as the "great governor of New York State," makes genial comments about the depth of character of the governor from Texas. The first really heartfelt cheer comes when Elizabeth Dole is introduced. She tells the crowd that in this election the swing voters are going to be middle-aged women, and they are going to be won over by the compassion of George W. Bush. This time the gender gap is going to work for the Republicans, she pledges.

Bush steps up to the mike. He thanks the genial crowd for bringing their children. They are the future of America, he says, and he is so glad to see them. I soon learn that this line about the children is like a loop of tape that Bush replays several times during the speech, every time the energy level falls. Bush unveils his educational platform, whose centerpiece is that if a public school keeps on failing to improve performance, he'll give parents the federal share of funding (which is not much) so they can send their kids to the school of their choice. As he speaks, the Texas governor undulates his torso a little in a soft-core assault on the mike. For punctuation, he raises both arms to the sides in a gesture that is more awkward than riveting. The crowd cheers for his promised tax cut, but their real lustiness is saved for his assertion that "America needs a sharpened sword. I will rebuild the United States military. The evil empire may be gone," he shouts, "but madmen and missiles are still there!"

Bush really connects with this. The rest of his speech is well received. But the people here are not burning with a passion to do much when they capture the White House and neither is their candidate. They want their man in and the other guys out. It is the most basic of political appetites. The fact that he doesn't look as if he wants to do much is the most reassuring thing about George W. Bush. This is a prosperous crowd and they want the government to leave them alone.

When the speech is over and Bush has finished signing the placards of those near the stage, I head down the escalator to the bottom floor of the terminal. I figure the Texas governor might come down this way and I am not disappointed. A few local policemen and a couple of security spooks in gray suits with earpieces accompany Bush as he makes his way slowly along a line of about seventy-five well-wishers. He takes time with people. He poses with girlfriends, wives, and children as proud men take snapshots of their loved ones with the candidate. The woman next to me is waiting for the governor, hoping he will sign her Bible. Five or six young guys tell Bush that they are members of the Yale fraternity he belonged to. He poses with them, looking a lot like their older brother. Bush enthuses as he meets a woman who tells him she is here with the four children she has adopted. He thanks her warmly for what she has done and poses for a photo with the children. As he passes me, I reach out and he grasps my hand.

Bush is going through the motions. He knows he needs every primary vote he can get. But he is doing it patiently and there are flashes of human connection as he smiles at someone and makes a few remarks. He is boyish, a little vulnerable, and one-on-one he is much more likable than in his flailing speeches.

Many hours later, after the sun has set on this windy March day, Senator John McCain's crowd gathers in a muddy park in Rochester. There are still a few patches of snow on the ground. In the center of the park is a Vietnam Veterans' Memorial. On a concrete lookout, searchlights flash flags of the United States Army, Navy, Air Force, and Marines with white light.

The organizers have brought a huge generator for the occasion. Below the lookout, a stage has been set up where Senator McCain will speak.

An hour before the senator's scheduled arrival, hundreds of people surround the stage and are backed up the side of the muddy hill toward the lookout. McCain's crowd is almost entirely white, but the makeup is different from Bush's rally. There are more factory-worker types, some young people who look as if they've seen a downtown recently, and a fair number of veterans. A few of the vets are a little kooky, shouting in guttural voices that they want McCain and then collapsing into peals of laughter.

Falling sleet is caught in the searchlights. All of a sudden, the generator groans and the lights fade and go off. A man from Schenectady explains that he is an engineer and he is going to help put the lights back on. The generator chugs and up come the lights, but there is another groan and out they go again. The lights keep fading out and bursting back. People are stamping their feet to keep warm, but they stay cheerful. A few are beginning to shout that John is late. We're all watching down the street for a glimpse of John McCain's famous Straight Talk Express. One of the organizers is worried about security and is walking back and forth with a state trooper, pointing out places along the rope line he thinks need watching.

Two buses pull into the parking lot. Close to a hundred media people with mikes, cameras, recorders, cell phones, and old-fashioned pads of paper file past the rope line where I have held on to a front-row position. A bit of music comes up from the main platform, but then it fades. Here come the senator and his wife, their faces caught in the glare of television lights as they walk along the rope line toward the flags at the lookout. The crowd is cheering. People's hands stab out toward the candidate in the darkness. He reaches for the hands, turns into the crowd, his face breaking into a brilliant smile as he accepts the best wishes of the crowd. He comes right up to where I am standing, catches me with his eyes, grasps my hand, and moves on.

All the way down the hill to the stage, McCain is touching people in the crowd, exchanging quips with them. His crowd is bigger than Bush's rally in the morning, and there's been no warm-up. After a few words from a congressman from New York State, McCain seizes the handheld mike. The senator from Arizona jokes about the cold night and warms the shivering crowd. He spies a woman in the front row with a copy of his book, asks her to hold it up, calls her a "great American," and promises that at the end of his speech he will sign every copy of the book people have brought with them. McCain's sterling credential is his years as a prisoner of the Vietnamese during the war whose veterans are commemorated in this park. He sails into the subject. "The United States is the mightiest nation in the world," he proclaims, "and therefore, the most powerful force for good." It is a proposition that makes me shiver, but the crowd cheers lustily. "I'm ready to be commander-in-chief and I don't need on-the-job training." He tells the crowd that he will rebuild the U.S. military and that one thing he learned in Vietnam is that young Americans must "never be put in harm's way unless the goal is victory." The crowd roars.

He pledges support for charter schools and bonus pay for meritorious teachers, both uncontroversial ideas for a conservative crowd. Then he dives into the maelstrom he has created in recent days, proclaiming: "Ours is the party of Abraham Lincoln, Theodore Roosevelt, and Ronald Reagan, not the party of Pat Robertson, Jerry Falwell, and Bob Jones." For the past few weeks, since the bitter fight he lost against Bush in the South Carolina primary, McCain has been attacking the power of the religious right in the Republican Party and lambasting Bush for visiting Bob Jones University. The university's founder was virulently anti-Catholic, and until a couple of days ago, the school's official policy has been to ban interracial dating. (The school has only a few nonwhite students.) McCain congratulates the university for its change of policy, which was announced on *Larry King Live* by its president, Bob Jones III, declaring that at least it has brought them "into the eighteenth century."

Pat Robertson's Christian Coalition supports Bush and has targeted McCain for defeat. It is more the power of the Christian right than the substance of their message that McCain resents. On the issue of abortion, his pro-life position is virtually indistinguishable from that of Bush and the Christian Coalition. On gun violence, like the Christian Coalition, the senator stresses the bad influence of Hollywood and violent video games, while opposing new gun-control legislation.

McCain takes aim at the friends of George W. Bush who have been pouring money into the campaign. Two wealthy Texas brothers have recently spent $2.5 million on a television ad that is running in New York, Ohio, and California. The ad shows a funnel of black smoke spewing up behind Senator McCain's head. The voice-over accuses the senator of promoting pollution, while it toasts George W. Bush as a friend of the environment—a dubious claim, considering that Texas has recently been named the most polluted U.S. state. McCain shouts, "George Bush should tell his Texas billionaire friends to take their money back to Texas."

On tax cuts, McCain tells the crowd that 38 percent of the Texas governor's proposed tax cut would go to the top 1 percent of income earners. "Donald Trump doesn't need another tax cut right now," he quips. The centerpiece of McCain's campaign has been his assault on what he calls the "iron triangle"— money, special interests, and legislators—that he says have taken over the political system to use for their own venal ends. McCain—the war hero who is now a maverick outsider—

vows that he will go to Washington, D.C., and clean out the special interests and give government back to the people. He's a latter-day James Stewart.

Miraculously, the generator keeps working through McCain's speech.

But Super Tuesday turns out to be the end of the road for the McCain insurgency. George W. Bush wins the three big prizes on that day—victories in New York, Ohio, and California. Two days later, McCain "suspends" his campaign.

The conventional wisdom among Americans is that their country has been endowed with the finest system of government in the history of humankind and that the Constitution of 1787 was, if not a direct gift from heaven, at least the product of the most distinguished political assembly ever convened.

In the mid-1980s, during a visit to the National Archives in Washington, D.C., I learned an important lesson about the mystique that attends the Constitution of the United States. The Constitution drafted in 1787 is the second, not the first, American Constitution. Its predecessor, created during the Revolutionary War in 1781, established a Confederation among the thirteen American states. It was this first Constitution that I had come to have a look at as part of my work on a film for the National Film Board of Canada.

The first thing I noticed on entering the National Archives, other than the guards with guns in open holsters, was the exhibit on the main floor of an original copy of the revered Constitution of 1787. It is mounted on a waist-high dais. Over its top is a bullet-proof glass bubble. We were informed by a guide that in the event of a nuclear attack on Washington, the Constitution would be dropped down a tunnel a quarter of a mile deep so that, whatever the fate of the human denizens of the metropolis, the work of the Founding Fathers would remain unscathed.

After checking in with officials, I was escorted up several storys to a documents storage section. An archivist took me into a room where rare documents are secured in metal tubes. He located one such tube, which he informed me contained an original copy of the Constitution of 1781. We walked into the adjacent room where the NFB crew had set up a camera and lights to film a brief sequence in which I would talk about the fact that Article 11 of the Constitution of 1781 explicitly invited Canada to join the new American union. I sat down at the table and was miked by the soundman. When we were all set, the archivist took the copy of the 1781 Constitution out of the tube and handed it to me. I was stunned.

"You mean you have no problem with my holding this document?" I asked.

"It's up to you," the archivist replied.

There I was, a foreigner with sweaty hands, being handed an original copy of the first Constitution of the United States. My years of training as a graduate student in history flashed through my mind. I couldn't do it. I insisted to the archivist and the somewhat baffled film director that the document be placed on the table, where I could refer to it during my on-camera comments without physically handling it.

The first Constitution was chiefly noteworthy for its marked decentralization. It gave the states most of the power and the national government very little. It lives in the shadow of the Constitution of 1787, which is treated with reverence. Indeed, most Americans have never even heard of the 1781 version.

Washington, the world's current global capital, is a giant transmitter of American values and traditions. The shrines of Washington create a sense of empire, of timeless, matchless power. In this sense, the city is like the center of previous great empires. So much of official Washington is constructed in neo-classical architecture that it would seem just for the United States to pay Greece royalties in return for the borrowing of intellectual property. The edifices, monuments, statues, and perspectives of official Washington create a sense of grandeur and power at the heart of a civilization. But not, it appears, for all Americans.

Not long ago, I sat next to the Vietnam War Memorial in Washington for an hour on a Saturday morning to see who was visiting the shrine. The weather was good, and the crowds kept coming, so that along the full length of the black wall on which the names of Americans killed in Vietnam are inscribed there was never a break in the throng. Only about one person in two hundred visiting the memorial that day was black, even though 25 percent of the fifty-eight thousand Americans killed in Vietnam were black and 65 percent of the population of the District of Columbia is black. Indeed, half of the 32 million Americans who are black live within five hundred miles of the nation's capital. Why were visitors from among them so dramatically absent?

Similarly, almost all the visitors to the Lincoln, Jefferson, and FDR memorials, the White House, and the National Gallery were white. The only blacks I saw at the National Archives among the crowds who had come to glimpse original copies of the Declaration of Independence and the Constitution of the United States were the guards at the doors. To whom does the phrase "We the people . . ." actually refer? For the white Americans who have come to the shrines that make up official Washington, what message is being inculcated? What do the Americans who visit with their families take away with them?

At the National Archives, visitors seeing original copies of the Declaration of Independence and the Constitution of the United States are glimpsing artifacts that represent the central creed of Americanism. These documents have a religious significance in the United States. They define that which is American, fencing it off from what is un-American.

The Constitution of 1787 defines what has become the most powerful office in the world, that of the president of the United States. Accustomed as I am to a parliamentary system of government, the American presidency has always struck me as both awesome in its potency and dangerously fragile. The presidency is Janus-like, with its two faces, that of democracy and that of authority. The conflict between the two aspects of the presidency has been there from the inception of the office in Philadelphia in 1787. Alexander Hamilton, the voice of plutocracy and centralized power in the newly founded United States, went so far as to advocate the election of the president for life. The Founding Fathers did not go along with this extreme suggestion, but they did create an office that reflected their own deep ambivalence between democratic decision making and the need for authority.

The Constitution of 1787 anchors the president, whose person embodies the executive branch of government, in the framework of a system of separation of powers. Congress passes the laws and the U.S. Supreme Court decides on their constitutionality. This leaves the president in charge of the operation of the federal government and, subject to the approval of Congress, with the power to appoint cabinet members, Supreme Court justices, and countless other officials. The president can veto legislation, subject to an override by two-thirds of Congress. The president has the authority to propose foreign treaties, which go into effect provided that he can win the approval of two-thirds of the Senate. And by no means least, the president is the commander-in-chief of the U.S. armed forces.

All constitutions reflect the political and social circumstances of their creation. The U.S. Constitution was written four years after the signing of the peace treaty with Britain that ended the American Revolutionary War. It was the work of an elite group of leaders who were able to carry out their

deliberations in secret. At the time of the Philadelphia conclave, the nascent United States was riven with sectional divisions and low-level political power struggles. Many New
Englanders thought they had little in common with the
Southerners. For their part, Southerners were determined to
defend the institution of slavery against assault from
Northerners, who feared slave revolts and favored the abolition of the slave trade. The government of New York State was
fiercely decentralist. Many politicians throughout the thirteen
states preferred to serve only at the state level in order to avoid
the taint of participation in the U.S. Congress or other national
bodies. The Philadelphia convention was not exactly a coup
d'état, but the trajectory of the United States' political organization was appreciably altered by the work of the Founding
Fathers, who pushed the thirteen states toward a much closer
union than that of the Confederation of 1781.

The presidency, as it emerged from Philadelphia, reflected
traditional American constitutional thinking as well as the limitations of the will to union of the thirteen states in 1787. James
Madison, the Constitution's key architect, was determined to
avoid what he saw as the potent oppositional threats of tyranny
and excessive democracy. Tyranny could result from a president
who took on the authority of a king, just at a time when
Americans were dispensing with the hated British monarchy.
Excessive democracy, Madison and the other framers of the
Constitution believed, would threaten the holders of property.
In particular, Madison loathed the way state governments had
come to the aid of debtors against creditors. He wanted a government that would defend the interests of the money-lending
class. To avoid the dangers of tyranny and rampant popular control, the drafters of the American Constitution placed their faith
in the separation of powers. The authority of the United States
government was to be vested in an executive branch, a Congress,
and a Supreme Court, each with its sphere of powers, each able

to restrain as well as enhance the actions of the others. Behind
the separation of powers and the notion of checks and balances
lay a well-understood sense of the kind of social order that existed
in America and that the Founding Fathers wished to foster.

The institution that was especially designed to protect the
interests of the propertied is the U.S. Senate, one of the most
singular legislative bodies in the world. Senators are the princes
of the American political system. Today, there are only one
hundred of them, representing a population of 270 million
people, which makes this one of the world's smallest legislative chambers in relation to population. Moreover, the Senate
strays about as far from the principle of representation by population as it is possible for a legislative body to stray. Since each
state has two senators, the votes of some Americans in choosing members of this body are far more potent than others.
Wyoming, the smallest state in terms of population, has
240,000 residents per senator, while California, the largest
state, has 16 million residents for each. A Wyoming vote in the
election of a senator is worth about sixty-six California votes.
The extraordinarily skewed nature of representation in the
Senate is driven home when we consider that the twenty-five
states with the smallest populations—and half the senators—
have a total of just under 42 million people, or just under 16
percent of the American population.[3] Moreover, it requires the
votes of only thirty-four senators, representing seventeen states,
to kill a constitutional amendment or to defeat a foreign treaty.
The smallest seventeen states have a total population of only
18 million people, or just under 7 percent of the American population.[4]

Unrepresentative upper chambers, designed to protect
elites against excessive democracy, have been common-
place in the English-speaking world. The British House of
Lords, which extended the power of a hereditary aristocracy
into the modern world, and the Canadian Senate, whose

members are appointed by the party in power at the federal level, are two examples. But the House of Lords, whose hereditary peers have now been all but banished, and the Canadian Senate have little power in relation to elected Houses of Commons. In the United States, however, the Senate, with its eighteenth-century pedigree, is as influential as ever. One thing that has changed since 1787 is that as a consequence of the Seventeenth Amendment to the Constitution, which went into effect in 1913, senators are directly elected by the people. Prior to that date, they were elected by state legislatures.

The unrepresentative nature of the Senate may be thought a merely abstract problem as most issues in American politics have been sectional or ideological in nature and have not tended to pit large states against small. However, as we anticipate the changes in store for the United States in the twenty-first century as a consequence of the rise of regional mega-cities and a vastly altered demography, the eighteenth-century Senate may prove a major roadblock to necessary social and political adjustments in coming decades. Imagine a future when both California and Texas, the two most populous states, have Hispanic majorities. Under such circumstances, it is not difficult to imagine issues concerning immigration, education, culture, and social programs that will pit predominantly rural and small-town states, with meagre populations, against big states in the Senate. Or suppose in coming decades that the American majority decides it needs a constitutional amendment to ban handguns and to overturn the gun-friendly Second Amendment. It is not hard to see how a coalition of senators from small states would line up to torpedo the change. And of course an amendment requires the adherence of three-quarters of the states as well as two-thirds of the Senate and the House. Again, small states would end up playing an outsize role.

The twenty-first century legacy of the revered eighteenth-century Constitution is that America has a system of government that renders decision making exceptionally difficult at the national level. The system through which Americans choose their presidents has become chaotic and unpredictable, and the cooperative meshing of the executive branch and legislative branch of American government has failed to the point that the elaboration of national policies has become extremely difficult. Robert Shogan, Washington correspondent for *The Los Angeles Times,* wrote: "This state of institutional belligerency makes it next to impossible, except during extraordinary periods, such as wartime or the immediate aftermath of a landslide presidential election, for either institution, the executive or the legislature, to establish policy goals and reach them."[5]

For many elements of American society, including most members of the economic elite, this is no big deal. The instinctual starting point for the economic elite is to assume that coherent collaborative state strategies are not crucial to the achievement of economic and social well-being. As long as the great boom that began in the early 1990s continues, this point of view is unlikely to be subjected to critical reevaluation. Only when America faces stiff economic competition once again from Europe, Japan, and perhaps China and India can the incoherence of American decision making be expected to become a matter for debate.

In the Western world, American politics is uniquely venomous. In other democracies, passion, exaggeration, hyperbolic rhetoric, and smears abound, but only in America does the battle against political opponents enter the realm of visceral malevolence. In Germany and Britain, politicians say very nasty things about their foes. In France, Gaullists hurl sulfurous warnings about the dangers of Socialist government. In Canada, the intense dislike of the separatist government of Quebec for Jean Chrétien, the prime minister of the country, is always on display. But a sizable number of Americans go an extra mile in their politics; extremely provocative actions and statements against electoral officials are typical.

The practice of character assassination reached a high point in the unprecedented political assaults against Bill Clinton.

The most virulent attacks on him were generated on the far right, particularly among white supremacists, those involved in militia movements, extreme opponents of abortion, and members of the gun lobby. In the June 1999 issue of *Soldier of Fortune,* Robert K. Brown, the editor/publisher, began his column on Clinton with one word: "Traitor." Brown went on: "It was a waste of time to focus impeachment proceedings on matters connected to Oval Office masturbation motivated by thong-snapping fat girls using cigars for unnatural purposes." Then he gets to the heart of his argument: "Clinton's complicity in Chinese espionage efforts should have been the focus of the impeachment. . . . Not long after the president's reelection, this column reported that DNC fund-raiser John Huang had received a top secret clearance at the request of Clinton and that he had phoned the Chinese embassy after top secret CIA briefings. That disclosure here and elsewhere, like the rape charges, didn't get much attention from the mainstream press or the American people. This matter, which can only be termed treason, should be fully explored—because the country is in grave danger." Brown looks the part of a Clinton hater. On the page with his column, you see a photo of his hard, tight-lipped face. White-haired, he is wearing a combat-style shirt and a military-style cap with lettuce leaves on the peak, which is emblazoned "Soldier of Fortune Magazine."

Clinton-hating was a much more revealing phenomenon than the gossipy media discussions of the president typically allowed. The American presidency is a fragile institution. That was the real import of the often farcical tribulations of Bill Clinton.

In the present gilded age when the New York Stock Exchange is more important than the White House, and the Federal

Reserve chairman, Alan Greenspan, is taken more seriously than the president, it was easy to regard the Clinton story as a light, if crude, entertainment. The media treated it as a sequel to the O. J. Simpson saga. But beyond the tabloid merriment, the Clinton affair entailed ominous signs about the future course of American democracy. What was novel in the war against Clinton was not the presence of a philanderer in the White House. It was that a significant number of politically influential Americans no longer accepted the spirit of accommodation of political opponents that is the essential basis for an enduring democracy. To such people—right-wing corporate executives and foundations, influential talk-radio hosts, and members of the Christian Coalition—American politics has become a war zone. As the former protégé of the ultraconservative William F. Buckley Jr., Michael Lind, who has abandoned the right for the center, warned in his book *Up From Conservatism,* "The only political movement on the right in the United States today that has any significant political influence is the far right."

Bill Clinton, the first Democrat to win two presidential elections since Franklin Roosevelt, has faced the fury of a political right that contains important elements who view any Democrat, and indeed the government of the United States itself, with implacable hostility. Just listen to talk-radio personalities like Rush Limbaugh, Oliver North, and G. Gordon Liddy and you will see what I mean. The hounding of Bill Clinton has taught the lesson that any chief executive who is subjected to a continuous no-holds-barred personal assault engineered by monied interests and amplified by tabloid journalism can be enfeebled.

Because the American presidency vests the executive branch in a single individual, who is both head of state and head of government, the system itself invites assaults on the mortal being at the center of it all. Four presidents have been assassinated, and several others, including Gerald Ford and Ronald Reagan, have had close calls.

A comparison of American scandals from Watergate to those of the Clinton presidency reveals much about the evolution of American democracy. In an appearance on *Meet the Press* on August 9, 1998, Bob Woodward and Carl Bernstein, the reporters of Watergate fame, put the Nixon and Clinton scandals in perspective. Woodward depicted the facts in Watergate as a president and his close advisers engaging in a criminal conspiracy to use agencies such as the FBI and the CIA to employ illegal wiretaps, break-ins, cover-ups, and other acts to establish what Woodward called "a police state in the United States." By contrast, Clinton had done nothing more than to be caught in a possible perjury involving an alleged consensual sexual relationship. In Clinton's case, no pattern of illegal behavior was established.

The Clinton case was also clearly distinct from the major scandal of the Reagan administration: Iran-Contra. This remarkable criminal conspiracy, which extended all the way to the Oval Office, involved the illegal sale of weapons to the Iranian government, whose proceeds were used to finance the illegal overthrow of the government of Nicaragua. Ronald Reagan and his close advisers cynically sold weapons to the very regime that had condemned the United States as the "great Satan" and had backed the seizing of U.S. diplomatic personnel as hostages. Both the Iranian and Nicaraguan elements of the covert activities were in clear violation of U.S. law and the U.S. Constitution. As Lewis Lapham, the editor of *Harper's* magazine, wrote of the architects of Iran-Contra in his book *Hotel America,* "The scheme obliged them to make a mockery of the Constitution, dishonor their oaths of office and seize for themselves the powers of despotism. . . . The principal conspirators were allowed to depart with no more than a reprimand."

In the Clinton scandals, the Independent Counsel Ken Starr

(an office established post-Watergate to ensure accountability of the chief executive and his officials) was investigating an ancient real estate scheme in Arkansas and various two-bit Clinton administration affairs, "Filegate" and "Travelgate," as well as looking into the suicide of the White House lawyer Vincent Foster in 1993. Starr's costly investigation was going nowhere fast until it encountered Bill Clinton's capacious libido. The president was impaled on the issue of his sex life and nothing more. The lies and the possible cover-up had nothing to do with broader issues of state as was so patently the case with Watergate and Iran-Contra.

Big money, a political culture that legitimizes extreme attacks on political opponents, and low voter turnout form the unsavory trinity that imperils American democracy.

The first president to come to office in the twenty-first century is a man who doesn't pretend to know much about the world. More parochial than his father, George W. Bush is not endlessly curious about the minutiae of government as was his predecessor Bill Clinton. Instead, he exudes good feelings about America and right-wing American values. He is a man of sentiments, not ideas. He is reminiscent of one of the lesser Roman emperors in office during a period when no external power was capable of challenging Rome.

George W. Bush was not exactly elected to office. Al Gore won the popular tally in the presidential election by more than half a million votes. Bush is the first president since 1888 to win the White House while losing the popular vote. In the American system, however, the crucial matter is not who wins the popular vote but who is the winner in the electoral college, the body fashioned by the drafters of the U.S. Constitution in 1787 to stand between the voters and their choice of president.

Winning the popular vote across the United States was vital

in giving Al Gore the standing he needed to challenge the outcome of the vote in Florida. On the morning of November 8, 2000, after six million votes had been counted in Florida, Bush led Gore by 1,725 votes. From there, in a series of heartstopping changes, as judicial struggles proceeded, the Bush lead dropped to 930 votes, then to 537, and, when the Florida Supreme Court ordered the recounting of forty-five thousand "undervotes"—ballots that had been registered by the voting machines as showing no vote for president—to 193.

It is the denouement of the 2000 election that will be remembered far longer than the lackluster campaign itself. The significance of the five-week struggle for power that followed election day will be the subject of controversy for years to come. Many commentators regarded the postelection battle as nothing more than a curious spectacle that grew out of the exceptionally close outcome of the vote. For them it was as if two rather mediocre runners had crossed the finish line of a marathon at virtually the same instant on a foggy night, and the officials, burdened with outdated electronic equipment, couldn't be sure of the winner.

Indeed, there was much self-congratulation in America about how well the fracas following election day was handled. Even under exceptionally trying circumstances, it seemed, American democracy was stable enough to handle an orderly transition of power.

In fact, the struggle for the presidency after election day involved more than a fierce contest between two sides both anxious to win the prize. While the Democrats assembled the best legal team money could buy and pursued their interests with litigious fanaticism, the Republicans were prepared to go to almost any lengths to win the White House. Their spokesmen trashed the courts. Former Secretary of State James Baker called the Florida Supreme Court's decision to allow hand counts of disputed ballots "unacceptable," and Republican

House majority whip Tom DeLay, using military language, stated: "This will not stand." Republican strategists hatched a game plan that extended past the Florida Courts and the Supreme Court of the United States to the Florida State Legislature and, if necessary, to the U.S. Congress. The Republican leadership of the Florida legislature called that body into session to ensure that, if necessary, a Bush slate of electors would be selected. The public rationale for this auda-cious move to substitute the legislature for the voters was to prevent Florida from losing its voice in the electoral college. But since a Bush slate had already been certified by Florida's secretary of state, it was clear that the real Republican motive was quite different. In the event that the Florida recount ended up putting Gore in the lead, the state legislature intended to mount its own slate of pro-Bush electors. If that had happened, Florida could have had two competing slates of electors, with the final choice between them being made by the Republican majority in the United States House of Representatives.

In the end, the Florida State Legislature and the U.S. Congress were not required to act because the U.S. Supreme Court settled the issue in Bush's favor. On December 9, 2000, less than twenty-four hours after the Supreme Court of Florida ordered the recounting of the undervotes, the U.S. Supreme Court issued a stay that stopped the recount while the court considered a Bush bid to have the counting ended once and for all. At the time the recount was stopped, leaks from the count-ing rooms suggested that the Bush lead was now a razor-thin 100 votes. The U.S. Supreme Court had acted just in time to prevent a Gore lead from being announced, a change of lead that could have made a Bush presidency unthinkable.

Late on the evening of December 12, in a seven-to-two ruling, the U.S. Supreme Court disallowed the recount or-dered by the Florida Supreme Court on the grounds that the lack of uniform standards for the counting violated the equal-protection requirements of the U.S. Constitution. The coup de grâce came in a further five-to-four ruling that the counting could not be begun again under new standards because the clock had run out and the electors had to be certified. Catch 22. It was the U.S. Supreme Court itself that stopped the count at the decisive moment and allowed the clock to run out.

Throughout the five-week postelection struggle, the Democrats were desperate to get the votes counted and the Republicans were just as determined to make sure they never were. Almost no one, Democrat or Republican, doubted that if the undervotes were counted Gore would be the winner in Florida. If George W. Bush and his team had thought otherwise, they would have welcomed a manual recount as the one sure way to establish legitimacy for a Bush presidency.

Ten days before the Supreme Court ruling, the *Miami Herald* published an analysis they had commissioned of the vote in the state's 5,885 precincts, which concluded that had the voting been glitch free, Gore would have won Florida by 23,000 votes.[6] Under the state's freedom of information law, a group of news organizations has been granted permission to recount Florida's ballots by hand.

An important legacy of the battle for Florida is that many African Americans believe they were systematically disenfranchised. Stories abound of police barricades set up near polling places to intimidate black voters, of widespread refusal to accept the voter registrations of blacks, and of the disproportionate location of faulty voting machines in their districts. Postelection analyses suggested that the problem of undercounting of black votes was not limited to Florida. In Fulton County, Georgia, for example, which includes much of the Atlanta area, one of every sixteen ballots for president was invalidated. The county, with its large black population, used the notorious punch-card voting machines that caused such havoc in Florida. Meanwhile, in two neighboring counties, which are largely white and lean Republican, and which use more up-to-date equipment, only one ballot in two hundred was invalidated. In heavily black Cook County, Illinois, famous for racking up huge vote totals for the Democrats in election after election, balloting problems, including hard to operate punch-card machines, resulted in the loss of many votes for the Democrats.[7]

In the end, five members of the U.S. Supreme Court showed that they seemingly cared more about stopping Gore from winning the presidency than about upholding the U.S. Constitution. Particularly for the Court's hard-core conservatives—Chief Justice William Rehnquist, Antonin Scalia, and Clarence Thomas, who are usually ardent supporters of states' rights—the decision to interfere with a state high court's interpretation of a state election law was completely out of character. Raising the scent of a partisan bench even higher was the fact that Scalia's son worked for the same law firm that represented Bush before the Supreme Court and Thomas's wife was employed by the Heritage Foundation to review candidates for positions in the Bush administration. Despite these apparent conflicts of interest, neither of these justices chose to recuse himself from the Bush-Gore case.

In a dissent, Justice John Paul Stevens opined: "Although we may never know with complete certainty the identity of the winner of this year's presidential election, the identity of the loser is perfectly clear. It is the nation's confidence in the judge as an impartial guardian of the law."

Actually, the biggest loser may well be the reputation of the United States as the exemplar of democracy in the world. "Our nation is chosen by God and commissioned by history to be a model to the world," intoned Democratic vice presidential candidate Joseph Lieberman a few months before the election. Outside the United States, commentators were scathing in their interpretations of the outcome of the election. For instance, the Washington correspondent of *The Guardian,* the highly influential British newspaper, wrote of the "sheer injustice" of Gore's defeat. Martin Kettle concluded: "Gore defeated Bush by a majority almost exactly the size of Austin, Texas, a city with 541,000 inhabitants. No, this wasn't the closest American election of all time. It was simply the most unfair."[8] Writing in *Liberation,* a widely read French newspaper, columnist Eric Dupin went even further, saying that the 2000 election "devalued" voting in the United States. He charged that the United States had an electoral system that was incapable of assuring a rigorous vote count and a chaotic legal system when it came to overseeing elections. He concluded that the postelection battle displayed an undeniable diminishing of the democratic ideal. In his view, this was a very serious demonstration before the world of the willingness of the sole global superpower to degrade the value of universal suffrage without appearing to suffer any major crisis of conscience.[9]

History's verdict on the 2000 election is likely to read: Election stolen in a temple whose motto is "Equal Justice Under Law."

# ON THE
# HISPANIC FRONTIER

IF THE TWENTIETH CENTURY was born in Vienna with Sigmund Freud as its midwife, it migrated to Berlin for a time and later crossed the Atlantic to New York. But it ended in L.A.

Despite the weight of civilization on its shoulders, L.A. is cloudy on a not very spectacular mid-January afternoon as my plane touches down at LAX. Still, the fact that this is the land of dreams and possibilities is driven home to me when I stop at the rental agency to pick up my car. Having reserved a mid-size vehicle, I am intrigued when the woman behind the desk invites me to upgrade to a Cadillac at no extra cost. I've never driven a Cadillac. Everyone should drive a Cadillac once in his life. What the heck. I say yes, feeling a little flush, and wait outside for what I imagine will be one of those smallish, tasteful, yuppie Cadillacs.

Up comes a full-length, white, garish, fin-tailed Caddie. I need sunglasses just to look at this monster.

Once installed in the driver's seat where I can put my hand on a range of electronic controls that will take me days to master, I feel as if I am the pilot of a B-52. I set the inside temperature at seventy degrees and a gauge tells me the outside temperature is sixty-eight. Another indicator tells me what direction I am going, shifting from east to south as I swing around a corner. I take the big machine onto the freeway and from there out of L.A. and south to Laguna Beach, a bedroom community on the Pacific. The big car doesn't handle too well—it's a little clunky—but it's got power to burn. When you floor it, the Caddie shudders for a second and then takes off like a rocket. I'm hooked.

Laguna Beach is pretty, with hills rolling back from the coast. It's a great escape from winter, I have to admit. As I lounge outside a café, I watch the gray waves and an eclectic mixture of Californians—the wealthy, the rushed, the laid-back, the stylishly aging and the effortlessly young. California is a different world from the rest of America. Maybe it really does represent the future that we are all being tugged toward.

Farther down the coast, where I spend the night, is San Clemente, a town made famous because Richard Nixon maintained a residence here during his presidency. The town is located in wealthy Orange County, a bastion of Republicanism, whose most recent claim to fame is that it went bankrupt in the 1990s as a consequence of reckless investments made on its behalf through the purchase of highly leveraged derivatives. How appropriate that a county that epitomizes wealth should go broke because its administration played with a type of financial instrument most Americans can scarcely understand.

When I go out early in the morning for my run, most of the kids on their way to school are speaking Spanish. Workers cleaning the streets and opening the shops are also mostly Hispanic. Later in the day, the older, wealthy Anglo-American population puts in its appearance. In the early evening, the gray-haired residents of the area flock to seaside bistros and the restaurants on the huge pier, which juts out into the ocean.

En route to San Diego and Tijuana, I drive through depressed Oceanside, a flat coastal town that has seen better days. The most exciting feature of Oceanside is that in its campaign to get drivers to slow down, the police department puts mannequins in police cars at the side of the road. On the town's main coastal thoroughfare, a rather gaudy redheaded mannequin in a police uniform sits behind the wheel of a squad car. She is the only occupant of the vehicle. As soon as I see her, I drive around the block and park. I get out of my car and walk over to take a closer look. She sits there with her garish hair sticking out around the edges of a police officer's cap. Her plastic fingers touch the steering wheel. I stand beside her, staring for a moment and then, growing self-conscious about what could be seen as prurience, I skulk away.

San Diego is closer to paradise than any other city in the continental U.S.A. The city has the warmest American version of the Mediterranean climate. Hot but dry summers and warm but not very wet winters make this an outdoor city where energetic physical activity is almost always possible. San Diegans are reputed to be the fittest residents of any American city and are said to have the most health-conscious dietary regimen. If you want to locate the pot of gold at the end of the American rainbow, you might well decide to position it in San Diego.

I roll down the I-5 through San Diego, heading for Tijuana. South of San Diego is the far side of paradise. Miles of warehouses, factories, and rundown subdivisions lie between the golden city and the Mexican border. I'm running out of American superhighway in my powerful white Caddie. Here's the sign I don't want to miss: "Last U.S. Exit." If I miss this exit, I'm going into Mexico whether I like it or not. When I rented the Caddie, the woman at the rental desk advised me against taking it over to "the other side." I'm reminded that some Americans who have driven past the "Last U.S. Exit" sign at various points along the tense U.S.–Mexican border have ended up spending months in Mexican prisons. That's because it is a criminal offense to enter Mexico with a gun in your vehicle. If you do it and get caught, you'll be immediately incarcerated. Plenty of Americans carry handguns and other firearms in their vehicles, so it's not surprising that some of them have inadvertently missed the last U.S. exit and ended up in a Mexican jail cell.

There is no gun in my Caddie and I don't miss the last U.S. exit. I find a parking lot a couple of hundred yards from the border where I can leave the car for the day. In front of me as I walk toward the border is a high concrete barrier. I can't see what is on the other side. Almost everyone heading for the border on foot is Mexican. Beside us the cars are lined up for hundreds of yards as they near the huge U.S. and Mexican installations ahead. The pedestrians are being funneled toward the border between a chain fence on one side and a concrete wall on the other. Straight ahead is an ugly, heavy turnstile over ten feet high. When you push through it, you are on the other side of the frontier.

Past the turnstile, I walk by five or six Mexican border guards who seem leadenly uninterested in the stream of people walking by them. A hundred yards farther on are hawkers who have placed their leather goods and other trinkets on the pavement. I come upon an open square where several cafés in a state of evident disrepair are located. Vendors are hitting on everyone who looks American, beckoning them in for coffee or fried chicken. I'm trying to fit this scene in with my own experience. For a moment, I fancy that I am somewhere in Italy or Spain. But the squalor here exceeds anything I've seen in southern Europe. The shops I am passing and those farther in the distance have corrugated-metal roofs. The fronts of the shops are all wide open, and shopkeepers stand in the doorways. Every one of them tries to lure you inside with a few words in English, but the come-on is pretty halfhearted. These people are clearly used to having tourists walk past them staring straight ahead.

To get to the center of Tijuana, I have to walk over a huge concrete walkway across a water runoff channel. Children and mothers are sitting in the corners of the staircase leading to the top of the walkway. They reach out to me as I pass, asking for a handout. Urine stains the corners of the staircase. Up on the walkway, I have a more panoramic view of the city. Streets full of shanties with corrugated roofs and the odd small office building recede into the distance. Past the walkway, I am in the city proper, following a dilapidated pedestrian lane that takes me by another row of shops full of shoes, purses, leather bags, toys, jewelry, and other delights. I cross a few main streets, heading toward the city center. There is an air of lethargy here. It is not the real Mexico. It is a border town. After I have wandered around for several hours, refusing dozens of invitations to buy this or eat that, I head back across the walkway to the frontier post.

Approaching the border from the Tijuana side feels very different from going the other way. On the way into Mexico, it did not seem than anyone cared that you were entering the country. The guards were lounging carelessly, taking little interest. It was like walking across the border from Italy to France. You might get questioned in a spot check, but that was not likely. Going into the United States is a different deal. You have to go inside an imposing, fortresslike building to get across the border on foot. On the way inside, signs are posted in Spanish and English warning against illegal attempts to enter the United States and offering rewards to anyone providing information about people using false passes to cross the border on a regular basis. When I get to the guard at the table, he looks quickly at my Canadian passport and nods me through.

The U.S. border with Mexico reminds me of the borders between western and eastern European countries. I remember once driving from Austria into West Germany just east of

Munich in the days soon after the Berlin Wall had opened and
the Communist regimes in the East were tottering. Even though
Austria was not a part of eastern Europe, Germany maintained
a fortresslike border post on the Austrian frontier that was not
unlike the U.S. border post at Tijuana. Its job was to process
the huge number of eastern Europeans who came through
Austria to seek work in Germany. Such border posts mark off
worlds sharply different from each another. It is like the meeting point between high- and low-pressure weather systems.
On one side of these borders is the First World, bursting with
its energy, power, and a high level of development. On the
other side is poverty and despair.

During the years when the Berlin Wall stood, many residents in the East risked their lives to get past the Wall to start
a new life for themselves in the West. These days, Mexicans
risk their lives to make it across the border into the region of
the United States that was once a part of their country. I drive
my Caddie to the northern edge of San Diego, to the museum
that commemorates the city's early beginnings as a Spanish-
speaking settlement. As I tour the large house of a dignitary
who lived here in the first decades of the nineteenth century,
it is driven home to me that this is all conquered territory. The
American Southwest, including the great prize of California,
was wrested from Mexico in the 1846–48 war.

A few days later, I am on the road north of San Diego en route
to Palm Springs.

The sun is almost always shining. Away from the coast and
heading north, I am struck by how much this region resembles
the Côte d'Azur in the south of France. The low mountains
with green vegetation clinging to dry soil could easily be taken
for the terrain a few miles from Cannes. Palm Springs is so
striking because it is a green oasis in the middle of the desert
located in a perfect sun trap. A sun trap exists when a range of

mountains or hills blocks off prevailing, cooling winds. Monaco is a bowl tilted toward the south and the sun and protected from northern winds by a rim of mountains. Palm Springs is snug up against a mountain on its western side. That's why it soaks up the sun and stays warmer than the rest of southern California in winter.

Palm Springs is a mecca for the aging. On Canyon Drive, palm trees reach upward along the wide sidewalks, as paunchy gray-haired tourists wander past restaurants, perusing menus, trying to find the ideal outdoor table. Youngish hostesses do their best to lure the elderly to their establishments, tempting them with the promise of calorie-laden pot stickers. The amplitude of the portions being served stuns me. Huge salads drown in their dressings. Burgers and servings of fries are oversize. But it is the desserts that amaze. These people go the distance. After all that has come before, they have space left for chocolate delights and mountainous sundaes.

It is luxuriantly warm at noon on this mid-January day. The air is dry, comfortable. I am in line at the local Starbucks on Canyon Drive. In front of me a man in Bermuda shorts in his sixties is asking a white-haired woman where she lives. "Santa Monica," she replies. "Santa Monica is a great place," he says, "but they let people sleep in the parks there, don't they?" "Yeah," she says, "I love Santa Monica, but I don't like the politics there." The green oasis of Palm Springs feels a long way from reality.

In southern California, the formula for fabulous wealth is a simple one. Add water to hot desert and you've got it made. But there is trouble in the American paradise that is southern California. In the blooming desert vacation spots, housing subdivisions and giant agricultural tracts spring up like mushrooms. Today's edition of the local newspaper in the Coachella Valley, where Palm Springs is located, reports that the area is fighting it out with San Diego for access to more water. My daily run takes me past several miles of gated communities surrounded by fences, their entrances outfitted with signs issuing dire warnings against trespass. I run past sumptuous golf courses where a copious stream of water is softly sprayed on the perfect grass.

California's huge cities and its gigantic agricultural sector suck in water from wherever they can get it. With twelve hundred dams and immense systems to pump the precious fluid over mountain ranges, the state moves 14 trillion gallons of water a year. Those with the political and financial clout are able to make their corners of the desert bloom. (If you want to understand how this works take a look at the old Jack Nicholson movie *Chinatown,* a flick about L.A.'s water wars.) Green-lawned suburbs are continually spawned. Agribusiness produces water-intensive crops such as rice and alfalfa in a growing region that receives fewer than twenty inches of rainfall a year. For decades, as a consequence of a legal deal giving it an advantageous share of the water of the Colorado River, California has grabbed water from the neighboring states of Arizona, Nevada, Utah, New Mexico, Colorado, and Wyoming. Absurdly, the Colorado River is legally required to provide these states and Mexico with more water than actually flows through it. Deregulation and the creation of a water market in the U.S. West could allow California to grab even more.

By 2020, California is projected to have a population of 50 million people. Long before that, the state's grasping agribusiness and suburban mega-developers will be clawing to parch their thirst with water from much farther afield, including Canada. From the standpoint of California developers, Canada is an enormous reservoir of fresh water, much of which flows "uselessly" into northern seas. As long ago as the mid-1960s, the Frank M. Parsons Company of Los Angeles dreamed up the North American Water and Power Alliance (NAWAPA). NAWAPA was a scheme for trapping the northern-flowing rivers of the Canadian North and Alaska and rerouting them southward. The torrent of rerouted water would flood the Rocky Mountain Trench in B.C., creating an artificial reservoir five hundred miles long (cities, farms, railways, and highways would end up under water). From the reservoir, the water would be pumped to the Sawtooth Reservoir in Montana, and from there it would move south through canals, tunnels, and rivers. Destination California.

California's sprawling growth and the emergence of NAFTA take plans like NAWAPA out of the category of science-fiction lunacy and make them a potential nightmarish reality. Indeed, in 1983 Prime Minister Brian Mulroney, Canada's NAFTA architect, said he supported another massive water export scheme—the so-called GRAND Canal, a plan to feed fresh water flowing into James Bay southward into the Great Lakes for export to the American Midwest. Simon Reisman, appointed by Mulroney to negotiate free trade with the United States, once served as an economic adviser to the GRAND Canal Company. In the mid-1980s, Reisman declared enthusiastically that "the magnitude of the GRAND Canal is some five times the size of the Apollo Moon Project, roughly 100 billion current dollars."

It is not unlikely that one of the great confrontations of the twenty-first century in North America will be the one between California and Canada over water.

Out of Palm Springs in my Caddie, I head north and east, where the full impact of dry land is driven home. A drive of about a hundred miles brings me to the strange town of Twentynine Palms. Little wooden fences surround what would be a lawn in front of a house anywhere else. Inside the fences, there is just hard bone-dry ground. Houses are mostly modest one-story dwellings, a far cry from the ones in sumptuous Palm Springs. The only vegetation in this town are the Joshua trees—so named by Mormon pilgrims in the mid-nineteenth century—the haunting desert shrubs that stand about twenty feet tall, reaching up into the sky with their stubby tuftlike fingers.

Twenty thousand U.S. marines are camped out on the wide desert just next to Twentynine Palms. The town echoes with the booming of their artillery on the huge firing range. There are lots of marines in this town and on the way to and from it. The license on one fire-engine-red pickup reads "Oklahoma OK U.S. Marines." The marines are very young, trim, and fit with a little mat of hair on top of their otherwise shaven heads. They look like the monks I saw at an *integriste* monastery financed by the far right in the south of France. But the marines are not monks. I see a couple of carloads of them with their very young wives and girlfriends at a rest stop on the way to Los Angeles. They are on leave and in a high mood. "I hate it the way my husband drives," one of the young wives drawls cheerily in a Southern accent. The wreckage of some of those young marriages can be seen on the long main drag of Twentynine Palms, where five or six bail bondsmen have signs in front of dumpy little buildings. A lot of young marines leave their wives behind when they move on from here, and there are a lot of young women looking for work in this town.

I am staying on the edge of town at an upmarket, hippielike haven called 29 Palms Inn. It's more expensive to spend a night here than to stay at a chain motel in Palm Springs, but the inn has energy, and people from all over use the inn as their base for seeing the desert. The 29 Palms is not luxurious. It has been put together by savvy owners in eclectic fashion, making use of wood, cement blocks, odd chairs and tables, and a string of self-contained little cabins with tiny yards beside them that display not a single blade of grass. A swimming pool lies between the main building and the dining room, which is really the heart of the operation. "We discourage misery and welcome alternatives" proclaims the notice in front of the main building. The menu is first-rate: good vegetables and a wide range of entrées. The inn is a counterpoint to the town and the marines. It focuses your thinking on the desert not as a demon to be overcome—what we can call the Palm Springs model—but as a fascinating realm to be experienced and understood.

I set out for Joshua Tree National Park, which covers 870 square miles of granite mountain ranges rising out of valleys. The park is only a few miles from Twentynine Palms. The floor of the desert is about three thousand feet above sea level, and the mountains soar to about six thousand feet. The bone-dry air sharpens the perception of the ridges and the weird rock formations that erupt from the desolate floor. Spiked plants and flowers stand like aliens from outer space in ghostly gardens by the side of the road.

A few miles inside the park, the desert falls away into an enormous valley that stretches off to the southeast. Millennia ago, a tribe of indigenous people lived on what was then a lush terrain alive with a bountiful supply of game. Slowly the climate changed, and as the valley dried, the sources of life ebbed away. Remains indicate that the members of the tribe perished on the land that had once so amply sustained them.

Miles farther on, I come upon an astonishing lookout. From here, I can see an immense distance across the rocky, reddish, dry landscape as it drops toward the south. A hundred miles in the distance, Palm Springs shimmers like smashed bits of a Coke bottle. Taking in the splendid view are a middle-aged woman and man from Seattle. They are on a lengthy motorcycle tour of the Pacific states. In their black riding garb, they look like overweight birds, their hair swept back by the wind into angry feathers. Somehow the man and I get into a discussion about the mountains in Washington State. He tells me that though he had been a hundred miles away when it happened, he actually heard the explosion of Mount St. Helens in 1980. The woman, who is ebullient, points across the vast prospect and tells me that down there is a fault line that runs across California. "You mean, on the other side of that line is the part of California that will someday be blasted out into the Pacific Ocean?" I ask. She loves that thought and quips that we could all buy some real estate on this side of the fault line since it will be the new oceanfront land of the future.

In the end, in California, it all comes down to water.

Dry California, America's most populous state, is where I have most often been told to go if I want to encounter the future. One way this is indisputably true is that California is on the leading edge of a vast demographic transformation in America whose center is the swift rise of the Hispanic population.

The tale of American demography weaves a wondrous tapestry. When we look at the human dimensions of America, going back two centuries to the year 1800 and projecting ahead fifty years to 2050, we see how the tapestry unfolds over the span of a quarter of a millennium. Among the great countries of the world, America's demographic record is unique, both in its rise from a small population base to a huge population and in its weaving of a fabric of such diverse ethnic strands over a similar time frame.

Four snapshots illustrate this transformation.

The first snapshot captures America's population in 1800, when the young republic still clung to the Atlantic seaboard. At the dawn of the nineteenth century, the United States had a population of 5.3 million. With the exception of a relatively small number of natives, this number was made up of two components—4.3 million whites and 1.0 million blacks.[1] These were, of course, two populations whose diametrically different conditions were at the root of what has always been the most important chasm in American life, the divide between whites and blacks. The overwhelming majority of the 18.9 per cent of inhabitants of the United States who were blacks were slaves.

Although their presence was noted in important ways in the Constitution of the United States, they and the small number of free blacks in the country had absolutely no say in framing the American political order. Tension over the slavery question did come close to wrecking the 1787 Constitutional Convention at times, just as it was to plunge the union into civil war three-quarters of a century later. But those who had more at stake in that great debate than anyone else—the slaves themselves—had no voice in it. Also disfranchised at the time were indentured servants, men who did not have sufficient property to enjoy the right to vote, and, of course, the largest group of all among the disfranchised—women.

A century later, we take our second snapshot. By 1900 the population of the United States had soared to 76 million. The dominant groups, as a century earlier, were whites and blacks. Over the course of the nineteenth century, the white proportion of the population had increased while that of blacks had decreased. In America in 1900, there were 66.8 million whites and 8.8 million blacks; only 351,000 residents were classified as belonging to other groups, most of these Native Americans.

As the twentieth century began, the ethnicity of those who made up the white population underwent a huge transformation. The first ten years of the twentieth century turned out to be the decade when the highest number of immigrants ever were admitted to the United States. Most of the immigrants were Europeans, but there was a pronounced shift away from immigration from the British Isles to newcomers from continental Europe. This was the era when Ellis Island, just off New York, was the point of entry for millions of Italians, Jews, Germans, Poles, Scandinavians, and others seeking a new start in the New World.

The addition of millions of people from nontraditional immigration sources changed the character of white America, adding a whole range of new identities to it. Newcomers from very different backgrounds could join white America in a way that would have been much more difficult in European countries like Britain or France. When I lived in France, my neighbors regularly referred to a man in the area as "the Italian," because his ethnic background was Italian, even though he was born in France himself and spoke French with an accent that was indistinguishable from that of the people in the region. It was not that newcomers to America forgot where they came from, or that their neighbors did not have prejudices about them. What was significant, and very different from what I saw in France, was that the skin of white America could be stretched to accommodate the newcomers and provide their descendants with an identity as white Americans. The American melting pot had come into being. With the indispensable assistance of the public school system, the sons and daughters of millions of non–English speaking immigrants grew up as Americans.

That newcomers became part of white America did not mean similar assimilation for African Americans. Despite their generations-old pedigree on American soil, blacks have remained on the other side of a racial divide that has had a determining effect on the conditions under which they live. Indeed, the hard-edged nature of the racial divide actually had the effect of placing a very high premium on skin color as a way of distinguishing between those who "belonged" and those who did not. Whiteness itself was a valued attribute in America, much the way the proper blood has been prized in Germany, where German citizenship was offered to those with German ancestry, even if they spoke no German, in preference to German speakers of Turkish ancestry who were born in Germany.

We take our third snapshot just before the end of the twentieth century, in 1997, when the U.S. population reached 267.9 million people. This time, the dramatic change taking place was the swift rise in the Hispanic population in the United

States, which reached 29.3 million in 1997. The Hispanic population in America has been increasing much faster than the black population, which in 1997 stood at 33.9 million. In addition, the population of Asian Americans was also growing much more rapidly than the black population. Between 1980 and 1997, the number of Asians in the United States increased from 3.7 million to 10.0 million. Meanwhile, the white population of the United States increased from 194.7 million to 221.0 million between 1980 and 1997.[2]

Our final snapshot takes us into the twenty-first century and an imminent revolution in the racial, ethnic, and cultural character of America. The U.S. Bureau of the Census has produced three levels of projections of the growth of the American population over the next half century: a lowest series, a middle series, and a highest series. According to the middle projection, by 2010 the Hispanic population, at 41.1 million, will exceed the black population, projected to be 40.1 million. Hispanics will soon constitute the second-largest ethnic-cultural force in America (the word *race* is not appropriate, since Hispanics can be of any racial origin). This will by no means end the crucial importance of the black-white divide, which will remain a central fact in American life. What it is bound to do, however, is to shift the dialogue in American society away from an overwhelming focus on the black-white polarity toward a dialogue in which culture and language play a much bigger part.

Driving the demand of Hispanics for linguistic and educational rights will be the sheer rise of their numbers in the country as a whole, and even more significantly, in crucial regions including the great crescent of territory from Texas to California. The Bureau of the Census projects that by 2050, there will be 96.5 million Hispanics in the United States, which would give them just over a 24 percent share of the American population, projected then to be 393.9 million.[3]

Long before one-quarter of the U.S. population is Hispanic, Hispanics will form the majority of the population in key regions, even states. In New Mexico and, more significantly, in Texas, California, and probably Florida, it will be very difficult to deny collective rights to Spanish speakers. In cities, states, and important regions of states with Hispanic majorities, the Anglo-American near-monopoly of political power is sure to be broken. And the breaking of that monopoly is likely to legitimize the emergence of new political paradigms, outlooks on society and the state that are quite different from those favored in Anglo America. This vast set of changes, many of which will be seen long before the middle of the century, promises to be among the most profound in the whole of the American experience. Moreover, the rise of the Hispanic population is only the most dramatic of the projections made by the Bureau of the Census. By 2050 the black population of the United States is projected to reach 60.6 million. Blacks would then constitute 15.4 percent of the American population, a proportion of the population not matched since 1850, two hundred years earlier.[4]

Between them, by 2050, if these projections are correct, Hispanics and blacks will make up about 40 percent of the American population. To fully appreciate the demographic revolution that is under way, we need to add in the projections for Asians and Native Americans. Of the five major groups identified in the projections of the Bureau of the Census, the fastest growing is Asians and Pacific Islanders, whose numbers are expected to increase from 10.0 million in 1997 to 34.4 million in 2050. Native Americans are projected to increase in numbers from 2.3 million in 1997 to 4.4 million in 2050.[5]

By 2050 non-Hispanic whites, who have dominated American life since the early seventeenth century, will constitute only 50 percent of the American population.

If God created paradise, He or She would surely color it aqua, splash it with flowers, and lavish sunshine and shady trees on it.

In 1996 I finally gave in to decades of my friends' urging me to go south for a winter vacation. My destination—Key West, Florida—was hyped as superior to other parts of Florida, which all too often look like suburban strip malls up against a beach. The southernmost bit of land in the continental U.S.A., Key West is a tangle of clapboard houses, palm and banyan trees, and tropical flowers circled by soft blue seas. After twenty-four hours in a superb, and very old, hotel, I thought I had truly found paradise in America—a town populated by writers, artists, and other seekers after escape and pleasure.

I seemed to be fitting in pretty well in paradise. The first morning, as I was completing my daily run, the tour train—Conch Train, as it is called—was rounding the corner. "The guy on the left is the southernmost jogger in the continental U.S.A.," the tour guide called out to her riders.

That afternoon, at a funky outdoor bar on the main drag, I was reading the *Miami Herald*, whose front-page headline was "Lost, Then Murdered." The story recounted the horrific fate of a Dutch woman, who was shot to death in her car outside a Miami convenience store while her husband was inside seeking directions. When I tore off the front page of the paper, the bartender, who looked like Harrison Ford, asked, "Now why'd you have to go and do that?" He was annoyed that I was paying so much attention to the story of the Dutch woman. He shrugged and said that she and her husband had just gone to the wrong part of town. I had arrived in Miami the same morning as the Dutch couple. How were any of us to know the right from the wrong part of town?

The car rental people had put us on our guard, issuing a "Traveler's Safety Alert," which warned "criminals have used a number of ploys . . . to distract motorists or get them to stop." These include "yelling, honking, or pointing at your car as if something is wrong with your vehicle; and bumping your vehicle from behind." As for stopping by the side of the road in response to the call of nature—just forget it!

By the next morning, I had put the incident behind me. Over cappuccino, I thought I could face *The Miami Herald*'s new front-page headline, which turned out to be "MiGs Shoot Down Cuban Exile Planes." What now? Key West is the closest bit of America to Cuba, a mere ninety miles from Havana. I rushed to the TV in my hotel room to find the local stations going live on the story. A young reporter was reassuring the public that the United States had assembled plenty of military power in the region since the end of the Cold War. Key West is outfitted with a nuclear submarine and all kinds of other navy and air force hardware.

When I had set out for paradise, I had completely forgotten that the Caribbean was the locale for numerous American invasions—the Dominican Republic, Panama, Grenada, Mexico, and Cuba itself. Oh God, I'm going to be in a war, I thought. Certainly a lot of people on local TV seemed to be spoiling for one. It's tragic that the bully boys in Cuba's air force shot down two small unarmed planes, flown by anti-Castro Cubans. I wondered, though, how many times the United States would allow foreign planes to fly into American airspace and buzz Miami before the U.S. Air Force started shooting.

The next day on local TV, the plight of the Dutch tourist and the downing of the planes had been replaced by yet another scare. There they were, steel-gray marauders with lifeless black eyes—sharks, thousands of them, swimming close to shore in the waters of south Florida. I yawned. It's like that in paradise. Murder, war, and natural predators. Ernest Hemingway, who certainly saw life that way, lived in Key West, with the second of his four wives, when he wrote *To Have and Have Not*. Hemingway defined courage as "grace under pressure." Paradise is where God tests illusion against reality.

Since 1798 the United States has conducted eighty-six military expeditions in Latin America and the Caribbean.[6] Policing the hemisphere to prevent developments seen as inimical to American interests and to keep other great powers out has been the most consistent long-term external policy of the United States. Even during periods when the United States was isolationist vis-à-vis Europe, it was never isolationist vis-à-vis Latin America and the Caribbean. During the 1920s and 1930s, the golden age of so-called isolationism, there were six U.S. military interventions in the Western Hemisphere.[7] The American record of military expeditions in the Western Hemisphere is that of an imperial power consistently fighting and using its muscle to maintain and implant regimes both friendly and subservient to the United States.

The American saga on the Hispanic frontier has not simply involved domination of other countries in the hemisphere; it has, of course, involved the conquest of territories from Spain and Mexico that now make up a considerable portion of the United States. After battles between the Americans and the Spaniards over Florida, the United States purchased that territory from Spain in 1819. Then came the struggle first for Texas and, after that, for the golden lands west of Texas in the great crescent that included California. In Texas, American colonists were inspired to seize territory from Mexico, not least to protect the institution of slavery from potential abolition by the government in Mexico City. Slavery again was the critical question that the admission of Texas to the United States turned on. Anti-slavery Northerners were opposed to the admission of Texas because it would add to the number of slave states. Later, when it appeared that the independent Republic of Texas, under pressure from Britain, might abolish slavery, Southerners pushed for and ultimately achieved the admission of the new state in 1845.

The U.S. war against Mexico, fought from 1846 to 1848,

had as its primary goal the seizure of California from Mexico. While large parts of the American West were taken from native peoples, the Mexican war was America's greatest war of conquest against a foreign state. It brought much new territory into the union, with the effect of unhinging the balance between North and South in the great struggle over slavery. Without the war of 1846–48, there might never have been a civil war in the United States, certainly not the one that erupted in 1861.

Today, 60 million Americans live in territory seized from Mexico (including Texas and California). It is particularly in this region of the West and Southwest that the Hispanic population is currently undergoing a dramatic increase. Of California's 31.4 million residents in 1994, 8.9 million were Hispanics. By 2010 an official U.S. government projection predicts that the population of California will be 37.6 million, and that of these residents 14.2 million will be Hispanics. Thus, over this sixteen-year period, California's Hispanics are projected to rise from 28.3 percent of the population to 37.7 percent.[8] In 1994 the population of Texas was 18.3 million, of whom 5.0 million, 27.3 percent, were Hispanics. By 2010 the projection is that Texas will have a population of 22.8 million, of whom 7.4 million, 32.5 percent, will be Hispanics.[9]

For two centuries, the great Southwest and West have been borderlands between two competing civilizations, the Anglo one of the United States and the Latino one of Mexico and the rest of Spanish-speaking America. In the nineteenth century, it was the Anglo civilization of the United States that was on the march, armed with superior weapons and technology and reinforced by a rapidly expanding population that included many Europeans of non-Anglo origin who were being assimilated into the new American norm. The annexation of Texas, California, and the rest of the Southwest were the fruits of that expansionism.

But collisions between civilizations are not simple one-time events. The seizure of the borderlands by the United States did not end the matter. During the First World War, Imperial Germany foolishly reopened the question, much to its detriment, when it was exposed as having considered offering a military alliance to Mexico against the United States. At the successful conclusion of a war with the United States in alliance with Germany, Mexico was to recover the territories lost in the war of 1846–48. The exposure of this boneheaded scheme played an important part in converting the administration of Woodrow Wilson to the view that the United States had to enter the war against Germany on the side of Britain, France, and Russia.

This comic-opera historical chapter involving Germany aside, we are now living in an era when the Hispanic impact on the Southwest and West is rapidly increasing, with potentially revolutionary consequences. In the not too distant future, non-Hispanic whites will constitute a minority of the population in California, Texas, and New Mexico. The impact of this demographic transformation on the politics of this huge and critical region of the United States is certain to be profound.

Historically, the great social impetus in American life has been that of groups on the margin to join the mainstream. And in America, despite the talk about multiculturalism in recent years, the overriding assumption has been that there is a mainstream, a single society for people to join. The rise of the "Hispanic fact" in America cannot help but introduce notions of another cultural schism into the life of the United States. While the drive of Hispanics to learn English and to find their place within the American way of life will remain powerful, even dominant, the demand for linguistic, educational, and cultural rights for Spanish speakers in the United States is certain to intensify. On the political right in the United States, fears about the rise of the Hispanic fact have already inspired a movement that favors the establishment of English as the official language, and, as a corollary, severe restrictions on the public role of any other language.

How Americans will adapt to the challenges that will flow from their unprecedented diversity will be one of the greatest hurdles facing them in this century. At issue will be no less than a redefinition of the American system of government and the way Americans conceive of the nature of the state and its relationship to society. The domination of American politics by an Anglo-centered political class will be challenged. Even the American republic as conceived and established by its eighteenth-century Anglo political forefathers is likely to be questioned and major alterations almost certain to be proposed. Who knows how far the demand for Spanish-speaking rights will ultimately extend in the American republic?

# AMERICA IN THE WORLD

IT IS RARE THAT GREAT GLOBAL changes conveniently coincide with the shift from one century to the next. That's why historians habitually date the nineteenth century as running from 1815, the battle of Waterloo, to 1914, the outbreak of the First World War. This modified nineteenth century corresponds with the age of the Pax Britannica, the century when Britain was the dominant international power. Similarly, historians have taken to shortening the twentieth century so that it runs from 1914 to 1991, from the beginning of the First World War to the collapse of the U.S.S.R. That way the twentieth becomes the century of the world wars and the failed challenges to the West from fascist and Communist regimes.

By that reckoning, the first big crisis of the twenty-first century was the 1991 Gulf War. That action was a harbinger of what the world would be like in the post–Cold War era and how the United States, the world's only superpower, would behave in the new century.

The Gulf War was sold to the public as a new kind of conflict, one that featured smart weapons directed at their targets by

high-powered computers. In daily briefings, U.S. Gen. Norman
Schwarzkopf told a worldwide audience about strikes that were
surgical to the point of being like laser incisions made in an
operating room. Here was warfare raised to a new level—
immaculate warfare. Warriors were no longer brutal killers;
they were surgeons deploying the most advanced products of
science to cut a tumor out of the body politic. For the first time,
live reports on CNN from downtown Baghdad brought war to
the living rooms of the world from the heart of the country
under attack. Although these telecasts transmitted dismaying
evidence that the bombs striking Iraq were not entirely smart
after all and that civilians were indeed dying, they conveyed
the impression that everything was under control despite the
fact that a war was on. They reassured the people of an
American-centered world. And even if Saddam Hussein, as
the principal malignancy, had not been excised, the spread of
the cancer to other parts of the Middle East had been halted.

Since the United States pulled its armed forces out of
Vietnam in the 1970s, the watchword of American military
policy has been that it is fine to fight wars, but there must be
virtually no American casualties. Techno-wars are now the
Pentagon's stock-in-trade.

Despite its high-tech billing, the Gulf War was, in reality,
one of the oldest kinds of conflict. It was fought between con-
testants at very different levels of military development. During
the U.S.-led ground assault on Iraqi forces after many weeks
of bombing, thousands of putrefied bodies littered the roads
of southern Iraq. Saddam Hussein's hapless forces were caught
on the unforgiving desert, where they were pounded to ham-
burger from the air and the ground. U.S. tanks pulled plows
behind them. As the tanks motored past Iraqi trenches, firing
into them at point-blank range, the plows covered the trenches
and the Iraqi soldiers with huge mounds of sand, burying them
dead, wounded, or alive.[1]

There is well-documented evidence that the Americans in uniform who conducted the slaughter were revved to a high pitch of excitement as they laid waste to their helpless foes. A report from the British newspaper *The Independent,* a paper that supported the war, told the story of gleeful American pilots who were thrilled as they massacred Iraqis retreating from Kuwait in a long convoy. Loudspeakers on the U.S. carrier *Ranger* blared the *William Tell* overture as pilots took off to drop the bombs. The pilots returned cheering "we toasted him". . ."we hit the jackpot". . ."a turkey shoot". . ."shooting fish in a barrel". . ."it's the biggest Fourth of July show you've ever seen, and to see those tanks just 'boom,' and more stuff just keeps spewing out of them . . . they just become white hot. It's wonderful."[2]

While tens of thousands of Iraqi soldiers perished, the Iraqi military was almost wholly unable to strike back and to inflict casualties on its opponents, a coalition of forces led and dominated by the Americans. George Bush's war in the gulf would have been very familiar to nineteenth-century Europeans. It was a war in which an imperial power laid down the law to a lesser power. The nineteenth century was replete with such conflicts, and indeed, well into the twentieth century, the British fought battles that ranked somewhere between policing actions and small wars to keep the subjects of their far-flung empire in line.

The effect on the American people of the high-tech low-cost victory in the gulf was electric, if short-lived. A couple of weeks after the end of the conflict, I spent a week and a half driving two thousand miles up and down the eastern U.S. seaboard in a ten-day period to assess the mood. General Schwarzkopf was at the height of his fame. Everywhere I went, patriotic fervor was in the air. On flat southbound Interstate 95, where billboards provide most of the scenery, motorists were subjected to extravagant praise for the U.S. military.

American flags and yellow ribbons were everywhere. At one service station southeast of Washington, D.C., where military personnel were offered a discount on their gasoline, soft-drink cases were piled up so that their colors fashioned a U.S. flag.

All along the route, towns and cities were cheering the return of units from the gulf. Cars and pickups sported flags and yellow ribbons and hand-lettered signs supporting U.S. forces. At truck stops, I sometimes saw men wearing desert-style military fatigues. If the yellow ribbons created the impression of a cult group, a brotherhood of sorts, it was easy to identify the headquarters of the cult. Over the front door of the White House in Washington was a giant yellow wreath—the yellow ribbon to end all yellow ribbons. Most impressive to me was the astonishing outpouring of senti-ment in the grimy, depressing industrial cities of eastern Pennsylvania, about an hour's drive from Philadelphia. No fewer than 40 percent of the tattered frame houses in a sec-tion of one city, heavily hit by plant shutdowns, had flags draped inside their front windows.

Not once among all the symbols, ribbons, flags, and slogans did I see a reference to Kuwait, the emirate for which the war was ostensibly fought, to the United Nations, which ostensi-bly had authorized the use of military force, or to the allies who ostensibly were fashioning the New World Order along-side the United States. All the emotion was directed inward. Americans were speaking to other Americans and to no one else. America was exorcising the ghosts of Vietnam. This was triumphalism unalloyed.

But the Gulf War euphoria was extremely short-lived, as George Bush discovered when he lost the presidential elec-tion of November 1992 to Bill Clinton. At the time I drove along the Eastern Seaboard just after the war, Bush was bask-ing in record-high approval ratings. But a sluggish American economy quickly took the sheen off his presidency.

If the Gulf War unveiled a new kind of post-Vietnam military mode through which America could exercise its hegemony, the battle for Kosovo in the spring of 1999 honed it to perfection. As in the case of the Gulf War, the strategic goal of the United States in the Balkans was stability. The Clinton administration aimed to prevent further spreading of ethnic antagonisms that could lead to a major conflict and a serious threat to American interests in the eastern Mediterranean. In the war over Kosovo, the United States and its NATO allies undertook something never before achieved in the history of warfare—the imposition of military will through air power alone. During the eleven-week bombing campaign designed to force the Yugoslav president, Slobodan Milosevic, to capitulate and allow NATO troops to occupy Kosovo, predictions that the United States would fail were offered on all sides. Militarists argued that Clinton was an incompetent, constrained by weak-kneed NATO allies, and that unless he mounted a ground invasion he was bound to fail. From the other side of the political spectrum, anti-war activists pleaded for a halt in NATO's bombing, insisting that NATO's air war against Yugoslavia was provoking a heightened campaign of ethnic cleansing by Serbs against ethnic Albanians, that in the name of saving the Kosovars, NATO was destroying them.

The result surprised critics from both sides. Without suffering a single combat casualty during the air war, NATO forced Milosevic to capitulate and to withdraw his forces from Kosovo. From the viewpoint of an American empire seeking stability within its strategic realm, the successful use of air power alone mattered.

But in another important way, the war over Kosovo complicated the position of the U.S. military in Europe. For the first time since 1945, Germany participated in a shooting war in Europe. As the largest country in the European Union and its economic titan, Germany has long held the key to Europe's playing a much larger role in its own defense. As long as Germany, still coping with the historical record of Hitler's Third Reich, refused to act militarily outside its borders, Europe had little choice but to lean on the United States to deal with European crises such as those in Bosnia and Kosovo. Germany's willingness to act in Kosovo made the long-running European discussions about creating a more effective European defense structure considerably more momentous.

Much is revealed by American reactions to the prospect of Europeans shouldering the burden of their own defense. For decades it has been common for editorialists and politicians to berate Europeans for doing too little to defend themselves, thus forcing the United States to do most of the heavy lifting. This sentiment has often been linked to outpourings of resentment about the price American decision makers have to pay to achieve consensus in an alliance whose members aren't worth much when it comes to playing a part in military actions. On the other hand, Americans are deeply ambivalent in response to any signs that Europeans actually intend to do something to relieve the United States of the need to defend Europe. An editorial in *The Washington Post* at the end of the war over Kosovo illustrated the ambivalence. The *Post* began by commenting sarcastically on an initiative through which Europe would set up its own defense structure: "What? Europe defending itself? After all these years of relying on Uncle Sam?" Next came a little paternalism: "The Europeans are always torn . . . between their pride at asserting their own 'defense identity' and their doubt that they can afford it." Then an assertion of American superiority: ". . . some separation of American and European military planning may occur on its own, as the ever-higher-tech Americans leave Europeans farther and farther behind." In conclusion, hope: "A strong tie to the United States will surely remain the foundation of Europe's defense."[3]

How else would an empire behave? Much in evidence was annoyance at having to bear the burden of defending lesser allies and even at having to listen to them. And this was mixed with anxiety at the prospect that they might actually defend themselves. Par for the course.

If one generalization is safe about empires, it is that those who create them are very efficient killers. In his study *A History of Warfare,* the military historian John Keegan wrote, "What most distinguished the warfare of the Romans from that of their contemporaries and neighbors was not its motivation . . . but its ferocity."[4]

Absolutely central to the rise of the American empire is that Americans have made themselves the most proficient killers in the history of the world. That may seem an unkind thing to say about a country that has always prided itself on fighting wars abroad to liberate people, not to enslave them. But the statement is a simple fact, and, as I will illustrate, maintaining America's status as the world's most effective killer is a policy that has the overwhelming support of American elites and the American people. Indeed, no other activity of the U.S. federal government has a higher priority.

Not only does the United States spend vastly more on the means of compulsion—its armed forces—than any other country, but also its military intervened in far more countries throughout the course of the twentieth century than did any other country's. Certainly, the armed forces of Germany, Japan, the Soviet Union, Britain, and France engaged in combat in many countries during the twentieth century, but the military interventions of the United States have far exceeded those of any of the countries on this list.

Some might object that this is an unjust comparison, that countries like Germany, Japan, and the Soviet Union invaded other nations, subjugating them to occupation against their will. They might further make the case that America played

the role of global liberator during the twentieth century and
that its interventions abroad were in aid of freedom, not oppression. The case I am making here has nothing to do with whether
America has been a liberator or oppressor when compared
with other powerful countries, only with the sheer number of
military actions in other countries. Even in the period since
the end of the American involvement in Vietnam—generally
thought to be an era of peace for the United States—American
armed forces have engaged in hostilities in Grenada, Libya,
Panama, Somalia, Iraq, Sudan, Afghanistan, and Yugoslavia.

What do these recent forays have in common? In all these
cases, the United States has deployed its arsenal to secure the
stability of the American-centered international order. In
Grenada, Libya, Panama, Sudan, and Afghanistan, U.S. armed
forces undertook punitive actions that led to the overthrow
of rogue governments in Grenada and Panama and that struck
at terrorists who had allegedly targeted the United States. In
the cases of Iraq and Yugoslavia, more substantial threats to the
American-centered international system were countered in
much larger military campaigns. Ironically, three of the leaders targeted in these U.S. military campaigns—Panama's
Manuel Noriega, Iraq's Saddam Hussein, and Afghan terrorist Osama Bin Laden—were former American protégés.

The emphasis on stability in recent American military
interventions establishes the United States as "a status quo
power." Throughout the past century, great powers have habitually adopted the antithetical postures of status quo powers,
those largely committed to the preservation of the present
international order, and revisionist powers, those intent on
altering the international order to their advantage. In the two
world wars, Germany and Japan—opponents in the First
World War and allies in the Second—were classic revisionist powers. Germany's aim in the First World War was to
achieve hegemony in a new European order. In World

War II, Hitler's goals grew from a desire to reestablish German dominance in central Europe to a lust for a Europe-wide or even global German empire. Similarly, Japan was a revisionist power, fighting to expand its sphere of influence at the expense of European powers in the First World War and, on a much greater scale, to win a huge Asian empire for itself in the Second. On the other hand, Britain and France were classic status quo powers in both conflicts. Britain fought to avoid German hegemony in Europe and to maintain the integrity of its threatened global empire. France also fought to stave off German dominance in Europe and to sustain its increasingly marginal position as a great power.

The two powers that emerged as the key victors in 1945, the U.S.S.R. and the United States, are more complicated cases. In the First World War, Russia fought to prevent Austro-German encroachment into its desired sphere of influence in eastern Europe. Following the Bolshevik revolution of November 1917, the new Soviet Union was forced to sign a highly disadvantageous peace treaty with Germany. In the Second World War, Stalin's U.S.S.R. fought for stark survival in the face of Hitler's all-out assault against the country in June 1941. But once the tide turned by the beginning of 1943, Stalin's goal became the creation of a huge sphere of influence for his country in central and eastern Europe. The Soviet Union had gone from being a desperate status quo power to a revisionist power with a large appetite.

In both world wars, the United States was drawn into conflict when it concluded that its vital interests were threatened. In World War I, German threats to neutral shipping on the high seas and the German initiative to fashion an anti-American alliance with Mexico drew the United States into the conflict. American entry into that war ultimately doomed the Central Powers, Germany and Austria-Hungary, and led to the decisive victory of the Allies on the Western Front in

November 1918. The United States greatly expanded its influence in Europe, although temporarily, as it turned out, and therefore qualified as the most successful of the revisionist powers following that engagement. Again in World War II, the United States was a reluctant participant, forced into hostilities by the Japanese attack on Pearl Harbor on December 7, 1941. As the war progressed, the United States swiftly emerged as the world's leading superpower. During the last year of the conflict, the United States, with its allies, was busily planning the construction of the postwar economic and political order. At Bretton Woods, New Hampshire, in the summer of 1944, the United States dominated a conference of nations that drew up a blueprint for the postwar international economic order. Bretton Woods decided that the American dollar was to be the reserve currency of the world and established free trade and free flows of capital, both in the interests of the United States, as the key goals. The United States had won the jackpot. At the conclusion of three decades of ceaseless struggle among the great powers—the 1914–18 and 1939–45 conflicts were the "thirty years' war" of the twentieth century—the United States emerged to occupy a position unique since the rise of capitalism five centuries earlier. Over the course of the era of the two world wars, the United States became the ultimate revisionist power, drawn much against its wishes into the struggle, only to succeed in reordering the entire international system.

Faced with the military threat of the Axis powers in World War II, the United States played the central role in developing and building the atomic bomb and then made the fateful decision to use it twice on human beings in the bombing of Hiroshima and Nagasaki. Since its air force dropped the most terrible bombs ever used in anger, the highest military priority of the United States has been to protect its nuclear supremacy and to prevent other nations from acquiring and deploying nuclear weapons.

In 1953 Julius and Ethel Rosenberg died in the electric chair for supplying a Soviet agent with classified information that the prosecution said could aid the Russians in building an atom bomb. In the late 1990s, the charge that U.S. government officials and private corporations had failed to prevent China from acquiring American know-how that could improve its nuclear arsenal became a salient issue in American politics. In addition to placing a very high value on preventing American nuclear secrets from reaching others, the United States has fought to prevent nuclear proliferation, the spread of nuclear weapons to nonnuclear states. The American position has nakedly revealed that the key goal is to maintain U.S. supremacy. While the United States has used economic sanctions, the withdrawal of aid, and threats of military action to prevent proliferation, it is unwilling to consider meaningful nuclear disarmament for itself.

Nuclear supremacy was far from being enough to satisfy American strategic planners at the beginning of the new millennium. The Pentagon's working doctrine was that the United States should be in a position simultaneously to fight and win two major wars in widely separated parts of the world. Not since Rome has a single power enjoyed such military sway over its potential adversaries.

The strategy is very deliberate and rests on a long-term perception of America's global position. The Pentagon's Planning Guidance for the fiscal years 1994–99 laid out the strategy this way: "Our first objective is to prevent the reemergence of a new rival, either on the territory of the former Soviet Union or elsewhere, that poses a threat on the order of that posed formerly by the Soviet Union. . . . We must account sufficiently for the interests of the advanced industrial nations to discourage them from challenging our leadership or seeking to overturn the established political and economic order. . . . We must maintain the mechanisms for deterring potential competitors from even aspiring to a larger regional or global role."[5] This is nothing less than a strategic road map, a design for the future of the American empire. At the core of this design is the huge defense budget of the United States: in 1995, the United States spent $354 billion. The combined expenditures on defense of the next eight powers in 1995 were $345 billion: Russia, $76 billion; China, $64 billion; Japan, $50 billion; France, $48 billion; Germany, $41 billion; Britain, $33 billion; Italy, $19 billion; South Korea, $14 billion.[6]

That the American people believe in the right of their country to possess and, if necessary, to use weapons of mass destruction is clear enough. In Los Alamos, New Mexico, where the atomic bomb was first developed during the Second World War, there is a visitors' center with replicas of "Little Boy" and "Fat Man," the bombs that devastated Hiroshima and Nagasaki. The visitors' book at the center provides testimony about the attitude of later generations of Americans to the killing of tens of thousands of Japanese with nuclear weapons in 1945. In general, American comments are highly positive about the destruction of Hiroshima and Nagasaki with atomic bombs. There is every reason to believe that most Americans would favor the use of weapons of mass destruction in the future if this was seen as the only way to preserve America's vital interests against external foes.

In 1989–91, as the Communist regimes in eastern Europe were crashing, the fashionable hypothesis was the "End of History"—the idea that liberal capitalism, having triumphed over Marxism, would dominate the world into the distant future. According to this view, the West's defeat of Marxism had settled all the great issues of the past century.

By the early 1990s the Gulf War, the war in Bosnia, and other conflicts inspired quite different analyses, which shifted the emphasis away from the economic competition, which was central to the "End of History." One new theory that arose in the early post–Cold War years was called the "Clash of Civilizations." In the summer 1993 issue of the prestigious U.S. periodical *Foreign Affairs,* the lead article by Samuel P. Huntington developed it.

The idea was simple enough—it was that in the future, the critical global conflicts would not be between nation-states or ideological opponents but would be between the world's civilizations. Huntington, the director of the John M. Olin Institute for Strategic Studies at Harvard, listed the following civilizations as the principals in this new era of conflict: Western, Confucian, Japanese, Islamic, Hindu, Slavic-Orthodox, Latin American, and African. According to Huntington, the fault lines that divide civilizations are centuries old, running much deeper than political differences. Although a person could be converted from a Communist to a capitalist, he contended that the division between Muslims and Christians went much deeper. Huntington concluded that "the efforts of the West to promote democracy and liberalism as universal values, to maintain its military predominance and to advance its economic interests engendered countering responses from other civilizations. Decreasingly able to mobilize support and form coalitions on the basis of ideology, governments and groups would increasingly attempt to mobilize support by appealing to common religion and civilization identity." While the "End of History" celebrated the victory of the West, the "Clash of Civilizations" attempted to prepare the West for a host of new opponents.

As an analysis, it had plenty of drawbacks. It treated civilizations as absolutes, setting them up against one another in a simplistic fashion, which took insufficient account of neocolonialism and social class and of other great economic, environmental, and technological issues. Worst of all, it made conflict between civilizations appear natural, almost inevitable. Far from being a scholarly and disinterested analysis, it was an

incendiary account of the state of the world with all too obvious political implications. Although Huntington's analysis,
developed in the aftermath of the Gulf War, warned the West
that the great struggle of the future would be against Islam, he
believed that Islam would enjoy the backing of Confucian civilization (for Confucian, read China). The importance of his
analysis was the promotion of the idea that "the next world
war, if there is one, will be a war between civilizations." Since
Huntington developed his thesis, the relationship between the
United States and China has followed a rocky path. The idea
of a war with Islam has receded somewhat, but the notion of
a showdown with China has gained ascendancy.

America's posture vis-à-vis China is shaped by a number of
interests and considerations. Crucially important is the appetite
of American corporations for wider access to the immense
and rapidly expanding Chinese market. American corporations are determined not to be outflanked by European and
Asian economic interests in the drive to expand production
and sales in China. Such corporations are much more interested in broadening their opportunities in China than they are
in helping prevent the acquisition of strategically sensitive
technology by the Chinese. If the main pressure of corporate
America is for access to the Chinese market, there is a powerful segment of American business that does have a contrary
interest. It serves U.S. defense contractors well to side with
those who are making the case that China poses a long-term
military threat to the United States, one that needs to be countered by increased military spending.

Two domestic American scandals have served to increase
the American public's suspicions about China. The first involved
the allegation that the Chinese government funneled campaign
contributions to support the Clinton-Gore ticket in the 1996
presidential election. The second involved the allegation that
China systematically stole American strategic technology in

the 1980s and 1990s, during the presidential terms of Ronald Reagan, George Bush, and Bill Clinton.

This second allegation created an incendiary mix: genuine fear of China's behavior, and calculated malice borne of perceived partisan political opportunity. The right wing of the Republican Party began a deliberate campaign to whip up jingoistic American antagonism against China. The effort bore an uncanny resemblance to the campaign waged by Republicans after the Communist victory in the Chinese Civil War in 1949, whose purpose was to brand the Democrats as the dupes who had "lost" China. That campaign played no small role in generating the frenzy of McCarthyism and in deepening the intensity of the Cold War with both the Soviet Union and China.

In the fight for the Republican presidential nomination for 2000, both Gary Bauer and Pat Buchanan stoked the fires of anti-China sentiment. Bauer's scorn was evident during his speech at the Boone County Fair in July 1999, when he referred to Chinese imports as "junk." Pat Buchanan spoke at Ames, Iowa, on the occasion of the Iowa Republican presidential straw poll there in August 1999. He similarly snarled contemptuously about China, referring to their exports as "chopsticks." Bauer and Buchanan were deliberately fomenting anti-Chinese hysteria. (Shortly after the meeting at Ames, Buchanan left the Republican Party to seek the presidential nomination of the Reform Party.) Their comments and sneering tone had a racist edge. During the long and tense years of the U.S. standoff against the Soviets, I had never felt the physical loathing that came through in these remarks. The yellow peril, that scourge of American thinking in the late nineteenth and early twentieth centuries, was being relegitimized.

At the Pentagon, military planners have been going over to the assumption that the next great war is likely to be fought against China. The rhetoric and mentality of containment, developed to such a high pitch during the decades of the Cold War with the Soviet Union, are being deployed against the potential new foe. It was as though during the Cold War, the American public and their strategic planners had cultivated a mind-set in which a principal foe was essential as an "other" against which to define themselves.

China has characteristics that lend it ideally to becoming America's "next" adversary. It has had a very long history of cultural separateness from the rest of the world. Moreover, China's leaders have developed a deep resentment against what they see as a drive to contain their country to block it from taking its rightful place in the world as a great power. The aging, authoritarian leadership of China is strongly averse to notions of pluralism or functional autonomy for regions and minorities. Their instinctual response to the autonomist movement in Tibet, or to the growing tendency of the government of Taiwan to claim independence from China, is to threaten force to stamp out challenges to Beijing's authority. Behind these challenges, the Chinese leadership has been all too willing to see malevolent foreign actors playing a key role.

The stage is being set—an anxious China determined to avoid containment and a wary America bent on preventing challenges to its world order—for the great showdown of the new century. But before the recent rise of anti-Chinese sentiment in the United States, most American analysts saw the Islamic world, particularly Islamic countries in the Middle East, as the likeliest source of future conflict. Indeed, combustible materials remain in place for the generation of future conflicts between the United States and the Islamic countries, particularly in the Middle East.

Three complex intersecting factors are at work that could set off dangerous new conflicts in the Middle East. First, anti-Western Islamic movements remain potent in many countries in the region. Should these movements come to power in one or a number of countries, the strategic balance could be tilted against Israel and the United States. Second, the relationship between the Palestinians and Israel could be imperiled by a change of regime in the Palestinian Authority, which in turn could be affected by a long-term worsening of the socio-economic conditions endured by the Palestinians. Third, a factor not thought of much until the early months of 2000, a new oil-supply crisis of the type experienced in the 1970s could develop. Since the early 1980s, there has been a glut of oil on world markets, which has made it virtually impossible for the oil-producing countries that are members of the Organization of Petroleum Exporting Countries (OPEC) to collude to drive up prices by limiting their output. For the past two decades, OPEC has been a paper tiger, hardly the ravenous beast that fostered anxiety in the industrialized nations in the seventies. In the closing months of 1999, however, OPEC began to reassert itself as a cartel. The organization introduced new petroleum production quotas that reduced world output. Even more surprising, OPEC's members stuck, more or less, to the quotas. As a result, the global price of crude oil shot up to $30 a barrel by February 2000, from about $11 a barrel in December 1989.

The prolonged oil glut was a major contributor to the great American boom of the 1990s. Though there has not been much critical thinking on the subject in recent years, the industrial world basically still runs on oil. That's why low oil prices have underwritten the other sectors of the economy. Petroleum and other fossil fuels are finite resources whose producible time horizon is very far from infinite. Low prices have enfeebled the drive to discover new deposits of petroleum, in either conventional or nonconventional forms (oil sands and oil shales). There is a strong possibility of a prolonged petroleum-supply crunch that would lead to sustained high oil prices. Such a development would inexorably heighten all the other tensions that exist in the Middle East, which is still the world's most important oil-producing region.

The great American economic boom of the past decade has pushed worries about serious competition with Japan and Europe onto the back burner. This happy state of affairs, from the American point of view, is not likely to persist over the long term.

A decade ago, Americans were highly conscious of the rise of the Japanese economy and the competitive thrust of Japanese corporations in key sectors, particularly the automotive, micro-electronics, and financial-services sectors. For several decades, Japan's rate of economic growth outpaced that of the United States, and in key sectors Japanese productivity and industrial techniques had surpassed those of American producers. And while Japan was on the rise, U.S. industries were losing their markets, and the United States was being pushed from the status of a net creditor nation to a net debtor nation. In 1986, for the first time since 1919, Americans owed more money to foreigners than foreigners owed to Americans. Japan had replaced the United States as the world's leading creditor nation. The United States was borrowing money from foreigners on a gigantic scale. Soon the U.S. net debt to foreigners would total $1 trillion. America had become the country with the highest net foreign debt.

In the early 1990s, however, the Japanese miracle makers stumbled. Japan slid into a stubborn recession, by far the most severe since the Second World War. The economic downturn coincided with a full-scale crisis of the Japanese political regime. A principal factor in making the recession so serious was the crash in real estate prices at the end of the 1980s. During the 1980s Japan led the world in a frenetic bidding up of real estate prices, so that by the end of the decade, on paper at least, the islands that constituted Japan were worth more than the United States. The value of small bits of prime land in downtown Tokyo had reached astronomical levels.

When the real estate implosion occurred—it hit the United States and Europe as well—land prices in Japan plunged to about one-quarter of their former superinflated levels. The immediate effect of the real estate crash was to wipe out much of the paper assets of Japanese banks, leaving many of them virtually bankrupt, a fact that the Japanese banks and government were extremely loath to acknowledge. The banking breakdown played a big part in triggering a full-scale crisis in the relations between the Japanese state and Japanese business. Being flushed out into the open were the details of a web of cronyism in which kickbacks, favoritism, and transactions that were not transparent were revealed as an integral part of the Japanese system.

The Japanese economic crisis has driven the notion of Japan as a threat to American economic supremacy off radar screens for the time being. Japan's woes are not likely to continue indefinitely, however. A Japanese economic recovery would once again put on full display the economic strengths that caused Americans to grow anxious during the 1980s. These include a labor force whose technological literacy is greater than that of the United States; mastery of computer-driven flexible production systems that give Japanese industry the edge over American industry in key sectors; and Japan's advantage in relation to the United States because it remains the country with the greatest pool of capital for export, while the United States continues to run up its net indebtedness to foreigners. Today, Japan's per capita income exceeds that of the United States, and the gap between Japanese and American per capita incomes is likely to grow in Japan's favor.

Japan's economy is actually the third largest in the world, behind that of the United States, the world's second-largest economy. The European Union, with its fifteen member countries, now has the world's largest single economy, with a Gross Domestic Product for the EU as a whole that is greater than that of the United States. Americans were never as worried

about the rise of Europe as they were about the more spectacular rise of Japan. Under the sheen of the economic boom,
Americans have also turned away from the perception that the
United States has to be concerned with economic competition with Europe.

For a time prior to the completion of the single European
market at the end of 1992, American analysts and policy makers paid attention to the implications for the United States
of an economically united Europe. But relatively slow growth
in Europe in the 1990s, accompanied by long-term widespread unemployment, meant that when the U.S. economy
took off in the mid-1990s, Americans largely forgot about
any potential threat from Europe.

The only major development that kept American eyes focused
on Europe was the launch of the euro, the European single currency, on January 1, 1999. For most of the decade prior to the
creation of the euro, the received wisdom in the English-speaking world, mostly promulgated from Britain, with its anti-EU
bias, was that the single currency would never become a reality. Indeed, many British analysts had previously written off the
single market as something that would never be realized. The
British position, in both cases, was that European national
rivalries and antagonisms were simply too strong for these
developments to come to pass. Underestimating the strength
and durability of the Franco-German axis in the EU, British
analysts, who had a very large impact on how Americans viewed
Europe, never saw clearly what was happening.

The launch of the euro, and the run-up to the launch in the
last few months of 1998, did receive widespread attention in
the United States. But the swift depreciation of the euro against
the dollar in 1999 caused Americans to stop thinking of the
new currency as any kind of threat to the global position of
the dollar.

The American reaction was understandable, if shortsighted.
In the first decades of the twenty-first century, the United

States will likely have to grapple with the power of the new Europe in a variety of ways. The most visible challenge will come from the euro, which more than any other currency has the weight to challenge the dollar as a global reserve currency. Because the United States runs a large current-account deficit every year, other countries end up paying a price for using the dollar as a reserve currency. The EU runs a current-account surplus every year, an attractive long-term basis for a reserve currency. It is not unlikely that the pricing of commodities, perhaps oil, may shift from the dollar to the euro.

In the present era, European rivalries and hesitations about how far the process of integration should go make it convenient for the EU and its member states to lean on the United States as a provider of global order and security. Even in this realm, though, changes are taking place. The participation of German aircraft in the NATO assault on Serbia in 1999 was an epochal event. As long as Germany, as a consequence of its history, was unwilling to participate in military operations aimed at ensuring European security, there was no real alternative to the United States acting as the final arbiter of military matters in Europe. The Germans and the French had taken preliminary steps toward the creation of a European military force, which would be made up of personnel from EU member countries. But while that initiative had raised eyebrows at the Pentagon and in Britain, without a German willingness to commit forces to combat it meant little. As the EU continues to grow more coherent, the United States could face the day when it will become a military, as well as an economic, competitor.

A further major challenge that is bound to confront the United States as a global power in the twenty-first century does not arise out of the power of other states. Environmental change and degradation are bound to generate domestic and global threats to the United States and its sociopolitical order.

One report after another, from respected international agencies, predicts that as the global climate warms as a consequence of the pollution generated by human activities, so too will the frequency of global climatic catastrophes. In 1999, for instance, the Intergovernmental Panel on Climate Change (IPCC) released a special report pointing out the alarming contribution of aircraft-engine emissions to the generation of greenhouse gases, such as carbon dioxide and water vapor, and consequently to the process of global warming. With air travel projected to grow by about 5 percent a year in coming years, unless new technologies and operational methods are developed there will be a large increase in fuel consumption by the world's airlines—from 130 million tons of fuel a year in 1992 to a projected 450 million tons annually by 2050.[7] This dramatic and highly alarming prediction can be reproduced in many other industrial sectors. Reports warn of the potential for more numerous hurricanes, the expansion of deserts in some regions, rising sea levels and flooding in other regions. This far-from-benign prospect poses a serious challenge to the prevailing American outlook, which is that technological advances driven by economic demand and opportunities generated in the marketplace are the best ways to deal with altered conditions. Overwhelmingly, American business and the political leadership in the United States have a strong ideological preference for relying on the market rather than on public-sector planning to deal with such problems as the onset of climatic changes. Indeed, on the political right in the United States it remains fashionable to deny that anything important really is happening at all on the climatic front. Right-wing commentators regularly make the case that predictions of global warming and other climatic consequences of human activities are the unsubstantiated product of eco-extremists, whose real goal is to undermine the American way of life.

The global warming challenge is a particularly difficult one for America, precisely because it calls into question two ideological axioms held dear by the American political class, indeed by the American people. The first, referred to above, is that resorting to public planning to achieve major objectives, with the exception of national defense, is a highly suspect notion. To accept that the earth's limitations are such that humans may have to place systematic and large-scale limitations on the market is very difficult for Americans to swallow. The second axiom is that the United States should not cede sovereignty in any meaningful way to international bodies or covenants. The American political class is deeply intent on maintaining American sovereignty, on the idea that no law must ever be permitted to override the U.S. Constitution, the fount of law and order in the American mind.

What makes the challenge of climatic change so inherently difficult is that, by its very nature, it remains subject to skepticism and denial long after changes can be observed and measured, certainly long after the point when the processes leading to the changes can be reversed without enormous effort. In his right-wing populist way, Rush Limbaugh, the conservative talk-radio star, has long understood how to lambaste those who have warned about impending environmental catastrophes. He once labeled concern about the ozone layer "balderdash. Poppycock." According to Limbaugh, the people who worry about it are "environmental wackos," "dunderhead alarmists and prophets of doom."[8]

A society that is deeply committed to the quest for short-term fulfilment is not well positioned to cope with a long-term, gradually increasing, major threat of the kind posed by the environment. American hubris toward the natural world may prove the undoing of the American empire the way external human threats have proved the undoing of earlier empires.

# EPILOGUE:
# AMERICAN CENTURY

*"My name is Ozymandias, king of kings:*
*Look on my works, ye Mighty, and despair!"*
*Nothing beside remains. Round the decay*
*Of that colossal wreck, boundless and bare*
*The lone and level sands stretch far away.*
—Percy Bysshe Shelley

IN THE FAMOUS INTRODUCTORY CHAPTER of his book on America, published in 1835, Alexis de Tocqueville remarked that in American society, "the equality of conditions is the fundamental fact from which all others seem to be derived."[1] In Tocqueville's time, Americans were fashioning a democratic republic whose foundation—in striking contrast to the prevailing inequality in Europe—was social and political equality. In our time, at the dawn of the new millennium, Tocqueville's proposition needs to be stood on its head. Despite the fact that Americans have always scorned the idea of an empire, the United States now presides over the greatest empire in the history of the world. And despite the attachment of Americans to the idea of equality, the United States is now more marked by social inequality than any other country in the industrialized world. My conclusion, therefore, is the reverse of Tocqueville's: *in the United States today, the inequality of conditions is the fundamental fact from which all others seem to be derived.*

The rulers of tribes, city-states, and nations that eventually construct great empires do not start out with visions of empire in their minds. When Huey Long, the most talented populist

politician in American history, ran for the governorship of
Louisiana in 1927, his slogan was "Every Man a King, But No
One Wears a Crown." Long was later nicknamed the "Kingfish,"
a mocking reference to monarchy befitting a man who was
in the process of making himself a people's king. The name
Kingfish was borrowed from a speech by William Jennings
Bryan, himself a populist who ran for the presidency as a
Democrat in 1896.[2] Long's ironic moniker went to the heart
of what was American and what distinguished America from
Europe. The Declaration of Independence stated that "all men
are created equal" and accused Britain's monarch, George III,
of setting out to establish "an absolute Tyranny over these States."

The American Revolution proclaimed the right of a people to dissolve its ties to another people when they suffered
abuses as a consequence of that political link. A people had
the right to oust its distant monarch and to erect a government of its own making. If the American people have the right
to self-determination, as asserted in the Declaration, then
surely it follows that all other nations have the same right.
Indeed, the famous opening passage of the Declaration is cast
in terms of the general right of nations to self-determination:
"When in the course of human events, it becomes necessary
for one people to dissolve the political bonds which have connected them with another, and to assume among the powers
of the earth, the separate and equal station to which the Laws
of Nature and of Nature's God entitle them . . ."

The enduring historical tradition in America that links the
founding and independence of the nation to the will of the
people has placed an immense barrier in the path of the creation of a formal empire. How can a nation, created through
the self-determining will of its people, subject other nations
to the kind of rule that is rejected in the Declaration of
Independence? By contrast, the British had no such ideological problem with empire. Their proudest boast at the end of

the nineteenth century was that "the sun never sets on the British Empire." They loved to make maps of the world, coloring red the territories over which the Union Jack flew. Queen Victoria was seldom as fulfilled as when her prime minister, Benjamin Disraeli, invented for her the position of Empress of India.

Americans could never bask in such overt imperialism. Of necessity, in constructing what was to become the greatest empire ever, Americans were forced to camouflage what they were doing, to wrap it in an ideological bunting that makes it appear different from all the empires that came before. Because Americans are so little inclined to compare their country to others, they have a very difficult time understanding that the United States has traveled far down the road from a republic to an empire.

Americans prefer the term *superpower* to the old-fashioned word *empire* when they describe the global role of the United States. The word *superpower* sounds up-to-date, even forward-looking; the baggage of the word *empire* is avoided. But Americans today are in such denial about what they have created that they can't squarely reveal the nature of their empire to themselves even in their midnight dreams.

It was not exactly novel when President Bill Clinton delivered a speech in the spring of 1998 in which he expressed the hope that the twenty-first century, like the twentieth, would be "an American century."[3] One canny observer of the world scene who can hardly be regarded as anti-American is Mikhail Gorbachev. In his Moscow office, on a day when NATO bombs were falling on Yugoslavia, the former Soviet leader commented on Clinton's hope for another American century. "Then where should Russia go?" he asked. "To Mars? Or where? What about China? If you translate this goal into policy, it becomes obvious at once that it's a dangerous policy." Gorbachev compared the American outlook to the policies of the leaders of the former Soviet Union. The concept of a world dominated by the United States "would be a repetition of our Communist utopia, when we tried, through a global Communist revolution, to make everybody happy—with consequences familiar to us all."[4]

If the term *superpower* sheds little light on the nature of the American relationship with the rest of the world, the notion of an "American century" points us in a more useful direction. At the root of the idea is that the United States is the leader of the world, setting the agenda for humanity in fundamental ways. Certainly, there is a material side to this—that the United States is the pacesetter when it comes to technological development and the production of goods and services. This aspect of the concept of an American century is closely linked to the entire project of progress, which has been the central preoccupation of Western civilization for several centuries. When Clinton says he hopes that the twenty-first century will be an American century as the last century was, he is projecting the hope for American material supremacy into the future.

But the notion of an American century extends far beyond material production. At its core is the idea that the United States is the potent source of values and culture that have been taken up by much of the world and that those who resist the norms of American civilization will do so in vain. Regimes hostile to Washington are called "rogue states," an epithet that does not even concede to them the possibility that they represent some alternative worldview to that of Washington. How could there even be another point of view? Today's global dissenters, the rogue states, are no better than bandits, and they deserve no more than the respect due to bandits. The concept of rogue states exists only in opposition to the monolithic character of the American-centered global order.

The phrase *American century* encapsulates the idea of an American global civilizing mission. It asserts that the United

States represents the future, that if we inform ourselves about the leading trends in American society, we are simultaneously glimpsing the future of the world as well. Americans visiting Toronto have often told me that if I want to understand what problems my city will face—urban decay, youth violence, whatever—I should make a journey to the future, which is already on display in America. And if I want to glimpse potential solutions to these problems, they're also there for me to see—in the United States.

While the term *American century* sounds positive, there is a clear element of compulsion in it. The dark side of the idea is encountered when we consider the fate of the foes of America. Those who believe that their country is engaged in a civilizing mission think not only that they have positive things to teach the world but that they have a right, even a duty, to neutralize or eliminate those whose views run counter to the mission. To get a visceral feel for what the phrase *American century* connotes, try applying the phrase to the names of other nations. How would you feel about a German century, a Russian century, or a Chinese century? If those sound more malevolent than American century, it's probably because the American version of the idea has become so sanitized as to appear benign.

It was the nascent Cold War that forced the American leadership to give definition to their unacknowledged empire for the first time. Even before the Second World War was over, it became clear to Washington that the struggle for global power would not end with the defeat of the Axis nations. When the Truman administration dispatched the bombers to eviscerate Hiroshima and Nagasaki in August 1945, their goal was certainly to bring a swift end to the war with Japan, but they also had an eye on Moscow. The use of the most terrible weapon in the history of the human race delivered the message that America's global position rested on a new order of power.

Deciding what frontiers are defensible at a cost that is not prohibitive has always been a primary concern of the rulers of empires. The Romans and the British were vexed by this problem long before Americans had to worry about it. It was this classic problem of empire builders that prompted Washington to introduce an element of coherence into the construction of their global sphere.

During their Cold War struggle against the Soviet Union, American policy makers had to decide what territories had to be held if the empire was to endure and to prosper. The Americans and their allies referred to non-Communist countries as "the free world." American strategists labeled the global realm they decided had to be held as "the Grand Area." Including the Western Hemisphere, western Europe, and Japan, the Grand Area was the inner redoubt, the essential terrain that could not be conceded to the enemy. If the empire's minimum was thus defined, its maximum was always a much vaguer matter. Consequently, it was subject to debate, danger, and miscalculation.

In 1947, when the British announced their intention to pull their forces out of the eastern Mediterranean, Washington came to the relief of waning Britannia. In his message to Congress asking for funds to arm Greece and Turkey against the Communist threat, President Harry Truman enunciated this general principle: "It must be the policy of the United States to support free peoples who are resisting attempted subjugation by armed minorities or by outside pressures."[5] This so-called Truman Doctrine was the foundation on which U.S. administrations erected their initiatives for the next forty years. It would be the justification for the American showdown with Moscow during the Berlin airlift of 1948 and the rationale for American interventions in Korea and in Vietnam.

Since Vietnam, America's leaders have had to accept the fact that wars could be fought only if casualties were kept to a strict minimum. In the past, imperial powers have always relied on the willingness of their own people to fight, albeit with increasing use of foreign mercenaries in cases such as that of Rome. The unwillingness of the American people to accept large numbers of body bags shipped home during a war has forced the Pentagon to turn to high-tech weaponry as an alternative.

As it sails on the seas of the twenty-first century, America is caught between its anti-imperialist republican origins and the pressures that arise as a consequence of the unprecedented global power it wields. The transition from republic to empire is not a smooth one, and the wild, independent ways of America's past are standing in the way, if sometimes in farcical fashion. Neo-isolationism, expressed by the most xenophobic elements in American politics, presents itself in the garb of George Washington's two-century-old warning: "'Tis our true policy to steer clear of permanent alliances, with any portion of the foreign world."[6]

An ideal example of this came in the autumn of 1999 during the Senate debate over whether the United States should ratify the Comprehensive Test Ban Treaty, the international agreement to prohibit the testing of nuclear weapons by the world's states. In the debate, the two sides of the American imperial dilemma are graphically captured. In the Senate, which has to ratify international treaties by a two-thirds majority, Democratic Senator Daniel Patrick Moynihan of New York warned that the spread of nuclear technology would be "ineluctable" should the United States fail to ratify the test ban treaty. Moynihan drew an ominous historical parallel: "We must not reject this treaty. The word will be that we said, 'No,' just as in 1919 we said 'No' to the treaty of Versailles."[7] (The failure to ratify the post–First World War Treaty of Versailles opened an isolationist chapter in American history.) Moynihan's logic was that of the rational supporter of American hegemony. Proceeding from the premise that the

United States is a status quo power and that it has an interest in locking in the current global order through international agreements, he warned Americans against the error of failing to participate in an arrangement beneficial to the United States.

Republican senators made the case against the treaty in a way that made clear their rejection of the very notion that the United States ought to be required to play by rules that bind other states. Jon Kyl, Republican senator from Arizona, argued in unusually blunt terms: "The world community, which does not want the United States to develop a ballistic missile defense, which doesn't want the United States to do anything that would require an amendment to the ABM [Anti-Ballistic Missile] Treaty, and some of which is very much in favor of total nuclear disarmament and has agreed to participate in this treaty only after leaders promised them that this Comprehensive Test Ban Treaty would be one of several key steps toward nuclear disarmament—all of these people in the world, I submit, are not people we want to make United States national defense policy. Their goals are not the same as our goals." Kyl continued, making his rejection of the views of the world community very clear: "We have an obligation, as the leader of the free world, to ensure that our nuclear deterrent is safe and reliable. They don't. So I frankly don't care much if people around the world who don't want us to defend ourselves against ballistic missile attack are going to criticize us for rejecting a flawed unverifiable, ineffective Comprehensive Test Ban Treaty."[8]

Americans have the right, indeed the duty, Kyl was saying, to preserve their capacity to destroy the rest of the human race, and to remain free to enhance that capacity, subject to no limitations whatsoever.

The test ban treaty debate exposed an American political elite caught between the independent republican past and an imperial present and future. The clear goal of the treaty was to safeguard and strengthen a global strategic order in which the United States is the only superpower. For a hegemonic power like the United States, there is a definitive interest in preventing other states from developing weapons of mass destruction that can imperil America itself and can threaten to upset an international order in which the United States is paramount. Since the United States has the world's largest and most sophisticated nuclear weapons arsenal, it stands to benefit most from an international agreement whose effect is to substantially slow the development of nuclear weapons by other states. This includes both the declared nuclear powers and those countries known to be, or suspected of, developing nuclear weapons. But while the hegemonic instincts of the United States incline its leaders to want to ratify a deal confirming their country's superiority, the isolationist and xenophobic instincts in America incline it to turn down the treaty. Why should the United States have to play by the rules it wants others to respect? It comes down to the old question, Where does the largest gorilla sleep? The answer—anywhere it likes. Far from wanting to do what George Washington aspired to—that is, to use geographic distance to enforce isolation—American xenophobes believe in the aggressive pursuit of America's national interests anywhere on the globe. In that sense the terms *isolation* or *neo-isolationist* are misnomers for them. What they truly want to isolate America from is commitments to join in international covenants that subject the United States to the same rules that bind other nations.

Since the administration of George W. Bush was sworn into office, the crucial strategic debate has been about whether the United States should deploy a large-scale antimissile defense system. During the 2000 election campaign, Bush made it clear that building an antimissile shield would be a cornerstone of his defense policy. Bush's choice of Donald Rumsfeld as secretary of defense reinforced his determination to proceed with the highly controversial project. In 1998 Rumsfeld oversaw a commission on America's national security that concluded that "rogue" nations could threaten the United States with ballistic missiles in the near future. Both Rumsfeld and Secretary of State Colin Powell have gone on record in favor of a missile defense system.

The deployment of missiles that can shoot down attacking missiles has been a Republican dream since Ronald Reagan envisioned a Star Wars defense in the 1980s. The trouble with the idea is that to date most experiments with missiles that intercept missiles have ended in failure; the Russians and the Chinese are hostile to the concept; and America's major European allies are wary of the idea as well. Russian president Vladimir Putin contends that a U.S. decision to deploy a major anti-missile shield would violate the U.S.–Soviet Anti-Ballistic Missile Treaty of 1972. He has undertaken a worldwide diplomatic offensive in opposition to American deployment. There are already signs that the issue is driving the Russian and Chinese governments toward a closer strategic relationship. In addition, western Europeans and other U.S. allies are highly alarmed at the prospect that missile defense will provoke a new global arms race and renew tension between the West and Russia and China. Disagreement over missile defense is likely to encourage European Union members to push ahead with the establishment of a rapid deployment force that operates outside the structure of NATO. Far from assuring America splendid isolation guaranteed by military supremacy, anti-missile defense could actually weaken the strategic position of the United States in the world.

Like Caesar, Americans have crossed the Rubicon in the creation of their empire. And like Augustus, they remain in denial about it, which is sure to make matters worse since self-delusion is never a good idea where important matters are concerned. The republican tradition still carries enormous weight in the sentiment of Americans, particularly among those on the political right. But America's elites, with little resistance from the people at large, have grown used to living in a country that exercises power across the world, and they are thoroughly committed to maintaining this posture into the indefinite future.

The imperial mind-set is on display when leaders talk of an American century. In more banal fashion, it is on display when a politician like George W. Bush proclaims that his goal is to lead "the greatest nation of all the nations of the earth." This is the phrase he used, to rousing applause, in a speech in Georgia during the contest for primary votes in that state in March 2000.[9] Such ideas, which are so universally espoused in the United States as to be completely uncontroversial, form the basis for an American outlook toward other countries that is deeply antithetical to respect for the sovereignty of others. It is the norm for Americans and their leaders to believe that the United States should interfere with or negate the sovereignty of other countries when American interests are perceived to be at stake. The justification for that outlook, so deeply held as to be virtually instinctual, is that the United States is such a special creation of man, under the guidance of God, that it has a moral obligation to protect its interests, no matter what the costs are to others. In short, it is a conviction among Americans at every level of the society that the United States should never share sovereignty with other countries.

In the advanced industrialized countries today, that is a unique outlook and one that is highly dangerous. In the rest of the advanced, democratic world, the tendency is to move in the opposite direction. In Europe, the world's greatest experiment in the voluntary pooling of sovereignty has been under way for nearly half a century. While Europeans certainly remain strongly attached to their own countries and cultures, the attitude toward other Europeans has undergone a profound shift. The egotistical nationalism at the heart of Europe's twentieth-century tragedy has receded in favor of a much more nuanced view of one's own country and the countries of neighbors. America shows no signs of heading down a postnationalist road.

We would do well to heed the warning, the fruit of the best of the Western tradition, that the quest for the universal, homogeneous state, whether or not it is ever achieved, is the road to tyranny.

Unchallenged empires are empty affairs. In the end, an empire's legitimacy—the extent to which it is tolerated—rests on its capacity to do two things: deliver the goods to its ruling social classes; and provide political, military, and social stability throughout its wider realm. Such goals, by definition, strike at the capacity of such a system to aspire to more bracing principles, among them a widened and effective democracy that gives the mass of the people of the empire a real say. The American republic was born in the struggle for liberty, and for much of its history the United States provided a refuge for those in pursuit of liberty the world over. The American *empire* extends the power of the United States over other peoples, whether they like it or not, and in doing so constitutes a barrier to the very liberty it purports to hold so dear.

# *notes*

## Introduction

1. *International Herald Tribune,* 12 March 1990.

## Chapter 3: The High-Risk Life of the Marlboro Man

1. Bureau of the Census, *Statistical Abstract of the United States, 1998* (Washington, D.C., 1998), 110.
2. Ibid., 108.
3. Information on slave revolts is from Howard Zinn, *A People's History of the United States, 1492–Present* (New York: Harper Perennial, 1995).
4. Samuel Eliot Morison and Henry Steel Commager, *The Growth of the American Republic* (New York: Oxford University Press, 1962), Vol. 2, appendix.
5. *Time,* 6 July 1998.
6. *Star-Telegram* (Fort Worth), 23 November 1998.
7. *International Herald Tribune,* 18, 19 March 2000.
8. *Statistical Abstract of the United States, 1998,* 109.
9. Ibid., 213.
10. Ibid., 110.
11. Ibid.
12. Ibid., 108.
13. Ibid.
14. Ibid.
15. Ibid.
16. Bureau of the Census, *State and Metropolitan Area Data Book, 1997–1998* (Washington, D.C.: 1998), 10.
17. *Washington Post,* 17 November 1996.
18. *Statistical Abstract of the United States, 1999,* 153.
19. Associated Press, 9 October 1998.
20. *Statistical Abstract of the United States, 1999,* 153.
21. Robert Dreyfuss, "George W. Bush: Calling for Philip Morris," *The Nation,* 8 November 1999.
22. *Time,* 7 December 1998.
23. *Statistical Abstract of the United States, 1999,* 639.
24. *Detroit Free Press,* 8 January 2001.
25. Ibid.

## Chapter 4: American Carnival

1. Mark Goldman, *High Hopes: The Rise and Decline of Buffalo, New York* (Albany: State University of New York Press, 1983), 273–75.
2. Bureau of the Census, *State and Metropolitan Area Data Book, 1997–98* (Washington, D.C., 1998), 60.

## Chapter 5: Choice and Its Foes

1. *New York Times,* 13 January 1998; CNN Interactive, 2 February 1999.

2. National Abortion Federation, 1999.

3. Associated Press, 17 September 1999.

4. Ibid.

5. "Why Do Women Have Abortions," *Family Planning Perspectives,* July/ August 1988.

6. CNN Interactive, 26 October 1998.

**Chapter 6: Death and God in Texas**

1. *Statistical Abstract of the United States, 1997,* 223.

2. *International Herald Tribune,* 2 January 1998.

3. *Newsweek,* 21 April 1997.

4. *Harper's,* February 2000: 39.

5. *International Herald Tribune,* 15 December 1999.

6. Mark Costanzo, *Just Revenge: Costs and Consequences of the Death Penalty* (New York: St. Martin's Press, 1997), 95–111.

7. *Statistical Abstract of the United States, 1997,* 223.

8. Zinn, *A People's History of the United States, 1492–Present,* 561.

9. CNN Morning News, 16 July 1998.

**Chapter 7: Old and New West**

1. Alexis de Tocqueville, *Democracy in America* (New York: Schocken Books, 1970), Vol. 2, 161.

2. Morison and Commager, *The Growth of the American Republic,* Vol. 2, 619.

3. Ibid., 357.

4. Nathaniel Burt, *Wyoming* (New York: Compass American Guides, Inc., 1991), 22, 23.

5. *Time,* 3 May 1999.

6. *Denver Rocky Mountain News,* 25 July 1999.

7. Ibid.

8. Svi Shapiro, "The Littleton Tragedy," *Tikkun,* July/August 1999.

9. *National Post* (Toronto), 18 August 1999.

**Chapter 8: Corporate Gurus and Revealed Truth**

1. Howard Schultz and Dori Jones Yang, *Pour Your Heart into It: How Starbucks Built a Company One Cup at a Time* (New York: Hyperion, 1997).

2. Bill Gates, *The Road Ahead* (New York: Viking, 1995), 15, 17.

3. *Time,* 27 December 1999.

**Chapter 9: Greed, Gluttony, God, and the American Dream**

1. Greg Critser, "Let Them Eat Fat," *Harper's,* March 2000: 42, 43.

2. Ibid.

3. *Time,* 7 December 1998.

4. Jamie Buckingham, *Power for Living* (Commissioned by the Arthur S. DeMoss Foundation, rev. ed., April 1999), 41–47.

**Chapter 10: Beautiful Losers**

1. Altina L. Waller, *Feud: Hatfields, McCoys, and Social Change in Appalachia, 1860–1900* (Chapel Hill: University of North Carolina Press, Chapel Hill, 1988), 2–5.

2. Ibid., 249.

3. For a history of this little-known chapter of American history, see Lon Savage, *Thunder in the Mountains: The West Virginia Mine War, 1920–21* (Pittsburgh: University of Pittsburgh Press, 1990).

### Chapter 11: American Pyramid

1. *Forbes,* 13 October 1997 and 11 October 1999.

2. The figures come from two sources. For the assets of the superrich, I am using the Forbes 400 rich list, *Forbes,* 13 October 1997 and 11 October 1999. For the assets of American households, I am using the U.S. Bureau of the Census figures for 1993, the most recent comprehensive figures for the whole of the American population. From U.S. data since 1993, it is clear that there have been no basic changes to the patterns discussed here. For example, on 23 February 2000, in testimony before a Congressional Committee in Washington, Federal Reserve Board Chairman Alan Greenspan stated that up until the middle of the 1990s, income distribution in the United States continued to be further skewed in favor of upper-income earners. Since then, he said, the relative distribution of income has not changed: lower-income groups have not improved their position vis-à-vis upper-income earners, nor has their position worsened.

3. Gates, *The Road Ahead,* 183.

4. Zinn, *A People's History of the United States, 1492–Present,* 265, 266.

5. Ibid., 367.

6. *International Herald Tribune,* 23 November 1999.

### Chapter 12: Government of the People

1. *Statistical Abstract of the United States, 1997,* 33.

2. Ibid.

3. *Statistical Abstract of the United States, 1998,* 33.

4. Ibid.

5. Robert Shogan, *None of the Above* (Mentor, 1982), 13.

6. *Miami Herald,* 2 December 2000.

7. *International Herald Tribune,* 28 December 2000.

8. *The Guardian,* 22 December 2000.

9. *Liberation,* 19 December 2000.

### Chapter 13: On the Hispanic Frontier

1. *Statistical Abstract of the United States, 1998,* 8, 14.

2. Ibid.

3. Ibid.

4. Ibid.

5. Ibid.

6. William Blum, *Killing Hope: U.S. Military and CIA Interventions Since World War II* (Montreal: Black Rose Books, 1998), 444–452, and table of contents.

7. Ibid., 451, 452.

8. *Statistical Abstract of the United States, 1997,* 34, 35, 38.

9. Ibid.

## Chapter 14: America in the World

1. *Los Angeles Times,* 12 September 1991, cited in Blum, *Killing Hope,* 334.

2. *Washington Post,* 27 February 1991; *Los Angeles Times,* 27 February 1991; Ellen Ray, "The Killing Deserts," *Lies of Our Times* (New York) April 1991: 3, 4 (cites *The Independent*), cited in Blum, *Killing Hope,* 336.

3. *International Herald Tribune,* 14 June 1999.

4. John Keegan, *A History of Warfare,* (Toronto: Key Porter Books, 1993), 265.

5. *New York Times,* 8 March 1992, cited in Blum, *Killing Hope,* 2.

6. *Statistical Abstract of the United States, 1998,* 858.

7. Intergovernmental Panel on Climate Change, IPCC-No. 99/01, Geneva, Friday, 4 June 1999.

8. *X-tra!,* July–August 1994.

## Epilogue: American Century

1. Tocqueville, *Democracy in America,* Vol. 1, xvii.

2. T. Harry Williams, *Huey Long* (New York: Vintage Books, 1981), 262.

3. *International Herald Tribune,* 22–23 May 1999.

4. Ibid.

5. Morison and Commager, *The Growth of the American Republic,* Vol. 2, 905.

6. Ibid., Vol. 1, 356.

7. *New York Times,* 9 October 1999.

8. Ibid.

9. CNN, 1 March 2000.

# acknowledgments

I WISH TO EXPRESS MY GRATITUDE to the many people, on both sides of the border, who helped me in researching and writing *Discovering America*.

Researching this book involved a large number of journeys and adventures over a period of years. I want to thank those who accompanied me on one or more of these adventures: my great spouse Sandy, my children Emily, Jonathan, and Michael, Mike Price, Gerry Caplan, John Henry, and Sten Kjellberg.

I am indebted to those who helped me organize my journeys and who made suggestions regarding the manuscript and my approach to the book: my old friend Jim Littleton, Gerry Caplan as always, Norm Simon, Paul Brannigan, Michael Kainer, Catherine Yolles, Ethan Poskanzer, Naomi Duguid, Jeff Alford, Linda McQuaig, Barbara DiFerrante, Henry Popkin, Sue McKay, Dennis Deeb, Mary Jo Gardner, Wilf Gardner, Scott Sellers, Patsy Aldana, and Matt Cohen, who I miss so much.

Cynthia Good and everyone else at Penguin Canada have been supportive. Alison Reid once again did a terrific job copy editing this book. Jackie Kaiser, now my literary agent, was the most wonderful editor who has ever worked on any of my books. She believed in this project and was indefatigable in pushing it along. Without her critical input at every stage, this book would never have been possible. Thank you, Jackie.

At The New Press, Diane Wachtell has done a careful and thoughtful edit of the U.S. edition. I am grateful as well to Lucas Smith.

To Sandy, Emily, and Jonathan, I owe a debt of gratitude for putting up with my America obsession over the past several years.

# index

WITHDRAWN